POSITIVE PREACHING
AND THE
MODERN MIND

Authors in the Biblical and Theological Classics Library:

POSITIVE PREACHING
AND THE
MODERN MIND

By
P. T. Forsyth, M.A., D.D.

paternoster
press

Copyright © 1907 P.T. Forsyth
First published in 1907 by Independent Press Ltd., London
Printed by the Stanhope Press Ltd., Rochester, Kent
Second Edition 1909
Third Edition 1949

Reprinted in 1998 by Paternoster Publishing
as part of the Biblical and Theological Classics Library series

04 03 02 01 00 99 98   7 6 5 4 3 2 1

Paternoster Publishing is an imprint of Paternoster Publishing,
P.O. Box 300, Carlisle, Cumbria, CA3 0QS, U.K.
http://www.paternoster-publishing.com

British Library Cataloguing in Publication Data
A catalogue record for this book is available from the British Library.

ISBN 0-85364-876-X

Cover design by Mainstream, Lancaster
Typeset by WestKey Ltd, Falmouth, Cornwall
Printed in Great Britain by
Caledonian Book Manufacturing Ltd., Glasgow

τω ἀγαπήσαντί με καὶ παραδόντι ἑαυτν
ὑπὲρ ἐμοῦ

Preface

May I remind those who honour me by looking into this book that it consists of lectures, and that I have been somewhat careful not to change that form in print. Also, as the audience consisted chiefly of men preparing for the Ministry, it was inevitable that I should speak chiefly ad clerum. I trust this may help to excuse a shade of intimacy that might not befit address to a wider public, possibly something of a pulpit style at times, and a few repetitions. I need hardly add that the lectures were abbreviated in delivery.

I should also like to mention that as the lectures were given to a post-graduate audience I have taken more for granted in places than if I had been speaking to a more general assembly. While I am grateful for any who will listen to me, I confess I have kept in view rather students than mere readers – those who do not resent an unfamiliar word, who are attracted rather than impatient towards a dark saying, who find the hard texts the mighty ones, and who do not grudge stopping the carriage to examine a mysterious cave or to consider a great prospect.

It has cost the writer much to find his way so far. And he has yet a long way to go. But he believes he has found the true and magnetic North. And a voice is in his ears, καὶ σὺ ποτε ἐπιστρὲψας στήρισον τοὺς ἀδεχφούς σου. This voice he would obey – humbly to it, respectfully to his brethren. How grateful he is to the great university of Yale for giving him such an opportunity of service, and providing him with a world-pulpit in such an apostolic succession as his predecessors make.

I have to thank my colleague, Rev. Prof Bennett, D.D., Litt. D., for valuable assistance with proofs, and my pupil, Mr. Sydney Cave, M.A., B.D.,[1] for the table of contents.

---

[1] The Rev. Principal Sydney Cave, D.D., New College, London.

Contents

The final authority in Christianity that of a Redeemer;
so the authority of the pulpit is evangelical – It is God
in His supreme saving act in Christ's Cross – Christ so
to be preached as to be the Creator of faith, the
absolute Redeemer.

III

THE PREACHER AND HIS CHURCH; OR, PREACHING AS WORSHIP

The modern neglect of the idea of the Church – The
Church as the great preacher in history – The
preacher's place in the Church not sacerdotal but
sacramental – A sermon as an act involving the real
presence of Christ – A preacher's first business is with
the Church – His work interpretive, not creative, of
Revelation – The preacher as the Church's means of
self-expression, and as the mandatory of the great
Church for the individual Church and for the world –
The corresponding responsibility of the preacher and
his need for sober knowledge – Some consequences in
regard to (1) the preacher's private views, (2) questions
of Biblical Criticism, (3) the demand for short sermons.

IV

THE PREACHER AND THE AGE

The relation of the preacher's message to the mental
vernacular of his time – Two observations thereon: (1)
In its greatest ages the Church marked by an attitude
to the world of detachment; the example of Gnosticism; (2) our creed to be minimal and our faith maximal, belief to be reduced and emphasis redistributed –
The need of forcing a crisis of the will – The old
Theologies to be interpreted completely and with sympathy – Reduction not Repristination necessary – The
casualness of the Public – The value of pessimism as a

IX

Foreword

Peter Taylor Forsyth: An Appreciation

Peter Taylor Forsyth was born in 1848 in Aberdeen, the son of a postman. He studied classical literature at Aberdeen University and graduated in 1869 with outstanding honours. He was invited to be assistant to the university professor of Latin, a post which he held for one academic session and which could doubtless have led him directly into a glittering academic career in the subject. But it was to ordination within the Congregational tradition that Forsyth found himself called, receiving his theological training in Göttingen and London, and embarking in 1876 upon a quarter of a century as minister to churches in Bradford, London, Manchester, Leicester, and Cambridge. His brilliance as a preacher, speaker and writer (on art, culture, politics and current affairs as well as theology) quickly established him as a bright star in the Congregationalist firmament, and he was duly called (in 1901) to be Principal of Hackney College, London, a post which he held until his death in 1921.

Forsyth's reputation as a churchman and theologian in his own day was considerable. His total written output amounted to some twenty four books and hundreds of articles, striking even in an age admittedly more generous to the printed word than our own. Yet it is for the quality, erudition, range and force of his writings (rather than their number) that Forsyth was acknowledged; and for the range of his reading and thought, engaging, as he did, with key figures in the worlds of painting (Holman Hunt, Rossetti), music (Wagner), literature (Flaubert, Hardy, Wordsworth), drama (Ibsen), psychology (William James) and philosophy (Hegel, Nietzsche, Schopenhauer), filtering their contribution through the mesh of his own distinctly evangelical Christian vision. The result is a rich vein of theological reflection which takes the reader straight to the heart of Christian doctrine without ever leaving behind the shared experiences and concerns of life as creatures in God's world.

Forsyth wrote significantly about all the key Christian doctrines: the person of Christ; the revealed character of God; the nature of salvation and human need of it; the church, its ministry and sacraments; the last things; prayer and other aspects of Christian living. All these and more besides fall beneath his penetrating gaze and are duly illuminated for us. There is, though, a common theme woven through all his writings, and it is that of the Cross and its relation to the moral order of creation. Whatever his temporary focus, Forsyth's eye is constantly drawn to this theological point of reference, and his subject treated *sub specie crucis*. The most notable manifestation of this cross-centred approach is Forsyth's deliberate reclaiming of the language of God's holiness. The God of the gospel, he insists, is not 'love' in some abstract sense but very particularly *holy* love, and his attitude towards us is one of forgiving grace rooted and expressed in an atonement designed to bring us also into a condition of holiness.

Forsyth's style is not often easy, but patient reading is always rewarded by depth of insight, and is made easier by the presence of passages of great passion and power, as well as his inimitable and eminently quotable aphorisms. God's gracious self-giving to humans in revelation and redemption 'does not come to grout the gaps in nature'. Well meaning but misguided talk about the Church having a restraining influence on the First World War was 'meeting the Atlantic with a mop'. 'The pulpit has lost authority because it has lost intimacy with the Cross, immersion in the Cross. It has robbed Christ of Paul.' 'So much of our religious teaching betrays no sign that the speaker has descended into hell, been near the everlasting burnings, or been plucked from the awful pit. He has risen with Christ . . . but it is out of a shallow grave, with no deepness of earth, with no huge millstone to roll away.' And so on.

Forsyth was a prophet as much as a theologian, and his writings bear many of the best and the worst marks of prophetic personality. Brilliance of insight combined with passionate rhetoric. An unsystematic and uneven approach to theology which yet betrays a profoundly integrative and comprehensive vision. Focus on very particular social and political situations fused with a grasp of the universal which spans the years separating his day from ours. For all these reasons Forsyth's writings bear a careful re-reading in our own day. The republication of this volume is very welcome indeed. It is to be hoped that it may serve to draw renewed attention to one of the few truly great minds of the British theological tradition.

Trevor Hart
Professor of Divinity
St Mary's College
University of St Andrews

One

The Preacher and his Charter

The fundamental importance of preaching for Christianity – God's chief gift not the Church and the Sacraments but the Word – The Bible as the world's greatest sermon – Its unity that of the history of redemption – To what extent is the Bible a *record* of God's word? – The nature of its inspiration and infallibility – Its final criticism not the higher rationalism but the highest grace – The Holy Spirit and the historic Christ – The need of contextual preaching – The true context of the Bible is the race's consciousness of sin – The difficulty due to the general disuse of the Bible – The Bible as the preacher's Enchiridion.

It is, perhaps, an overbold beginning, but I will venture to say that with its preaching Christianity stands or falls. This is surely so, at least in those sections of Christendom which rest less upon the Church than upon the Bible. Wherever the Bible has the primacy which is given it in Protestantism, there preaching is the most distinctive feature of worship.

But, preaching a feature of worship! I will ask leave to use that phrase provisionally, till, at a later stage, I can justify the place of preaching as a part of the cultus, and not a mere appendix.

Preaching (I have said), is the most distinctive institution in Christianity. It is quite different from oratory. The pulpit is another place, and another kind of place, from the platform. Many succeed in the one, and yet are failures on the other. The Christian preacher is not the successor of the Greek orator, but of the Hebrew prophet. The orator comes with but an inspiration, the prophet comes with a revelation. In so far as the preacher and prophet had an analogue in Greece it was the dramatist, with his urgent sense of life's guilty tragedy, its inevitable ethic, its unseen moral powers, and their atoning purifying note. Moreover, where you have the passion for oratory you are not unlikely to have an impaired style and standard of preaching. Where your object is to secure your audience, rather than your Gospel, preaching is sure to suffer. I will not speak of the oratory which is but rhetoric, tickling the audience. I will take both at their best. It is one thing to have to rouse or persuade people to do something, to put themselves into something; it is another to have to induce them to trust somebody and renounce themselves for him. The one is the political region of work, the other is the religious region of faith. And wherever a people is swallowed up in politics, the preacher is apt to be neglected; unless he imperil his preaching by adjusting himself to political or social methods of address. The orator, speaking generally, has for his business to make real and urgent the present world and its crises, the preacher a world unseen, and the whole crisis of the two worlds. The present world of the orator may be the world of action, or of art. He may speak of affairs, of nature, or of imagination. In the pulpit he may be what is called a practical preacher, or a poet-preacher. But the only business of the apostolic preacher is to make men practically realize a world unseen and spiritual; he has to rouse them not against a common enemy but against their common selves; not against natural obstacles but against spiritual foes; and he has to call out not natural resources but supernatural aids. Indeed, he has to tell men that their natural resources are so inadequate for the last purposes of life and its worst foes that they need from the supernatural much more than aid. They need deliverance, not a helper merely but a Saviour. The note of the preacher is the Gospel of a Saviour. The orator stirs men to rally, *the preacher invites them to be redeemed*. Demosthenes fires his audience to attack Philip straightway; Paul stirs them to die and rise with Christ. The orator, at most, may urge men to love their brother, the preacher beseeches them first to be reconciled to their Father. With preaching Christianity stands or falls because it is the declaration of a Gospel. Nay more – far more – it is the Gospel prolonging and declaring itself.

*

I am going on the assumption that the gift to men in Christianity is the Gospel deed of God's grace in the shape of forgiveness, redemption, regeneration. *Im Anfang war die That*. But I should perhaps define terms.

By grace is not here meant either God's general benignity, or His particular kindness to our failure or pity for our pain. I mean His undeserved and unbought pardon and redemption of us in the face of our sin, in the face of the world-sin, under such moral conditions as are prescribed by His revelation of His holy love in Jesus Christ and Him crucified.

And by the Gospel of this grace I would especially urge that there is meant not a statement, nor a doctrine, nor a scheme, on man's side; nor an offer, a promise, or a book, on God's side. It is an act and a power: it is God's *act* of redemption before it is man's message of it. It is an eternal, perennial act of God in Christ, repeating itself within each declaration of it. Only as a Gospel one by God is it a Gospel spoken by man. It is a revelation only because it was first of all a reconciliaion. It was a work that redeemed us into the power of understanding its own word. It is an objective power, a historic act and perennial energy of the holy love of God in Christ; decisive for humanity in time and eternity; and altering for ever the whole relation of the soul to God, as it may be rejected or believed. The gift of God's grace was, and is, His work of Gospel. And it is this act that is prolonged in the word of the preacher, and not merely proclaimed. The great, the fundamental, sacrament is the Sacrament of the Word.

What I say will not hold good if the chief gift to the world is the Church and its sacraments, instead of the work and its word. Wherever you have the ritual sacraments to the front the preacher is to the rear, if he is there at all. In Catholicism worship is complete without a sermon; and the education of the minister suffers accordingly. So, conversely, if the preacher is belittled the priest is enhanced. If you put back the pulpit, by the same act you put forward the altar. The whole of Christian history is a struggle between the apostle, i.e. the preacher, and the priest. The first Apostles were neither priests nor bishops. They were preachers, missionaries, heralds of the Cross, and agents of the Gospel. The apostolic succession is the evangelical. It is with the preachers of the Word, and not with the priestly operators of the work, or with its episcopal organisers. Our churches are stone pulpits rather than shrines. The sacrament which gives value to all other sacraments is the Sacrament of the living Word.

I note that the Catholic revival of last century is coincident with complaints elsewhere of the decay of preaching. And if this decay is not in the preaching itself, there is no doubt of the fact in regard to the pulpit's estimate and influence with the public. Even if the churches are no less full than before, the people who are there are much less amenable to the preached Word, and more fatally urgent for its brevity.

This coincides with the Catholic revival on the one hand, as I say, and with something to which I have not yet referred, on the other – I mean the decay among our churches of the personal use of the Bible. Preaching can only flourish where there is more than a formal respect for the Bible as distinct from the Church, namely, an active respect, an assiduous personal use of it, especially by the preacher. But to this point I shall have to recur.

The Bible is still the preacher's starting-point, even if it were not his living source. It is still the usual custom for him to take a text. If he but preach some happy thoughts, fancies, or philosophies of his own, he takes a text for a motto. It was not always so; but since it became so it is a custom that is fixed. And this from no mere conservatism. The custom received ready, nay inevitable, confirmation from the Reformers. It corresponded to the place they gave the Bible over the Church, on the one hand, and the individual on the other. It is the outward sign of the objectivity of our religion, its positivity, its quality as something given to our hand. Even when we need less protection against the Church, we still need it against the individual, and often against the preacher. We need to be defended from his subjectivity, his excursions, his monotony, his limitations. We need, moreover, to protect him from the peril of preaching himself, or his age. We must all preach *to* our age, but woe to us if it is our age we preach, and only hold up the mirror to the time.

And not only so, not only do we adhere to texts, but there is a growing desire for expository preaching – for a long text, and the elucidation of a passage. The public soon grow weary of topical preaching alone, or newspaper preaching, in which the week's events supply the text and the Bible only an opening quotation. And the new scholarship is making the Bible a new book, a new pulpit for the old Word, a new golden candlestick for the old light. Preachers are inspired by the historic freshness of it, as the public are interested by its new realism. It is a great recent discovery that the New Testament was written in the actual business and collo- quial Greek of the day. And less than ever is the textual style of preaching like to die, or the Bible to cease to be the capital of the pulpit. Preaching has a connexion with the Bible which it has with no other book. For the Bible is the book of that Christian commu- nity whose organ the preacher is. Like the preacher, it has a living connexion with the community. Other books he uses, but on this he lives his corporate life. It is what integrates him into the Church of all ages. Preachers may, for the sake of change, devote their expositions on occasion to Tennyson, Browning, or Shakespeare. They may extract Christianity from modern art, or from social phenomena. They may do so in order to lay themselves alongside the modern mind. But they will be obliged to come back to the Bible for their charter, if they remain evangelical at all. If they cease to be that, of course, they may be driven anywhere and tossed.

*

But the great reason why the preacher must return continually to the Bible is that the Bible is the greatest sermon in the world. Above every other function of it the Bible is a sermon, a σήρυγμα, a preachment. It is the preacher's book because it is the preaching book. It is still a book with an organic unity of idea and purpose. I admit all the truth intended when the Bible is called a library, and part of it a national library. It was quite needful that that fact should be strongly urged on us. But when we have recognized the Bible as the literature of a nation, and subject to its literary and historical conditions, we soon recognize that that nation had a providential function. It was the people of the Word. It arose at God's hands to be the preacher among the nations – with the preacher's perishableness, but also the preacher's immortality, with the fugitiveness of the preacher, but with the perpetuity of his message. And this message is one, definite, and positive. It runs through the whole literature of that nation (with one or two exceptions, like Esther or the Canticles, which do not destroy the general fact). The library is a unity in virtue of this historic message and purpose. It is not nationalist. It is not a history of Israel, but it is a history of redemption. It is not the history of an idea, but of a long divine act. Its unity is a dramatic unity of action, rather than an aesthetic unity of structure. It is a living evolving unity, in a great historic crescendo. It does not exist like a library in detached departments. It has an organic and waxing continuity. It is after all a book. It is a library, but it is still more a canon. You may regard it from some points as the crown of literature, for it contains both the question and the answer on which all great literature turns. It is the book, as Christ is the person, where the seeking God meets and saves the seeking man.

The crown of literature is thus a collection of sermons. It is one vast sermon. It is so much more than literature, because it is not merely powerful; it is power. It is action, history; it is not mere narrative, comment, embellishment or dilution. It makes history more than it is made by history. There is no product of history which has done so much to produce history as the Bible. Surely that which had in it so much of the future had also in it more than the mere past. It had the Creator.

It is akin to the press on one side, as to the pulpit on the other. Its value is in its news more than in its style. It is news to the world from foreign parts – but, remember, from foreign parts unseen, which ought not to have been so foreign to us as they are. And it is akin to the world of action more than the world of sentiment. It deals more with men's wills than with their taste, with conscience more than with imagination. It is the greater literature because it never aimed at being literature, but at preaching something, doing something, or getting something done. It is so precious for the preacher because it is so practical. It is a '*That-predigt.*' It is history preaching.

*

How far is the Bible a record? It has been common of late to speak of the Bible, not as God's Word, but as the *record* of God's Word. The Word, it is said, is the living Word, Christ. There is much truth in this view also. It is another symptom of the great historical movement which has passed over religion, the great restoration of the person of Christ to its place in Christianity. It is one side of the movement which sends us back to the historical study of the Bible, as the Reformers went back to its grammar. But it is only a partial truth after all. It is only in a modified sense that we can speak of the books of the Bible as historical records. They are not records in the strict historian's sense of archives. They are not documents of the first value for scientific history. There is hardly a book of the Bible that is a document in that severe sense. And certainly the object of the Bible was not scientific history, as we know that science. Why is it that we find it hard, if not impossible, to write a biography of Christ? Because the object of the New Testament writers was not to provide biographical material but evangelical testimony. The New Testament (the Gospels even), is a direct transcript, not of Christ, but of the preaching about Christ, of the effect produced by Christ on the first generation, a transcript of the faith that worshipped Him. It is a direct record not of Christ's biography but of Christ's Gospel, that is to say of Christ neither as delineated, nor as reconstructed, nor as analysed, but *as preached*. The inmost life of Christ we can never reach. We cannot reconstruct the nights of prayer.

Well, is this not to say that the first value of the Bible is not to historical science but to evangelical faith, not to the historian but to the gospeller? The Bible is, in the first instance, not a voucher but a preacher. It is not a piece of evidence. The Gospels are not like articles in the dictionary of National Biography, whose first object is accuracy, verified at every point. They are pamphlets, in the service of the Church, and in the interest of the Word. They are engrossed with Christ, not as a fascinating character, but as the Sacrament, the Gospel, to us of the active grace of God. The only historical Christ they let us see is not a great figure Boswellised, but a risen eternal Christ preached, a human God declared by His worshippers. They are homiletical biography, not psychological; they are compiled on evangelical rather than critical principles. The stories told are but a trifling selection, not chosen to cast light on the motives of a deep and complex character, but selected entirely from a single point of view – that of the crucified, risen, exalted, preached Saviour.[1] There is not an idyllic feature in them that is not imbedded in the great doom, and sobered by the supreme tragedy whose conquest made the Church. It is the Saviour born to die that is the burthen of the New Testament; it is the Redeemer, not the Messiah, not the champion of humanity, not the spiritual hero, not the greatest of the prophets, not the exquisite saint. The history is history with a purpose, history unto salvation, history unto edification, history made preacher, history whose object is to create not an opinion on our part but a determination. The story is on a theme. It is there for the Gospel. It is inferior as art, but it is mighty as action. It is a crisis of spiritual action. It is preaching, I repeat. The object is not proof, but life. The appeal is not to intelligence but to will. These things 'are written that ye might believe that Jesus is Messiah and Son of God, and that believing ye might have life in His name.' They spoke from faith to faith. They were not proofs to convince the world. Neither the miracles nor the Gospels were advertisements. They were not evidences. They were there to feed rather than to fascinate, to edify more than defend, and to confirm more than to convince. They were material to build up the Church. They spoke to believers. They appeal not to an estimate of evidence but to a fault of will, to our need of a Saviour and our experience of grace. They belong to the literature of power, not of knowledge. The news they bring is of an impressive creative act, and not a cold cause, or a still

---

'The first Church troubled about "the real Jesus" only in so far as suited the Jesus living for their faith. . . . Had Mark attempted or achieved such a model biography of Jesus as historical science demands his work would have been useless for religion.' – Jaülicher, *Neue Linien*, p. 71.

fact. Their inspiration is not in regard to mere truth, but to the truth as it is in Jesus, to Jesus as the Truth, to truth as a personality, and a personality gathered up in a universal redeeming act.

It is inspiration, therefore, which does not guarantee every statement or view, even of an apostle. The inspiration is not infallible in the sense that every event is certain or every statement final. You may agree with *what* I say without agreeing with *all* I say. The Bible's inspiration, and its infallibility, are such as pertain to redemption and not theology, to salvation and not mere history. It is as infallible as a Gospel requires, not as a system. Remember that Christ did not come to bring a Bible but to bring a Gospel. The Bible arose afterwards from the Gospel to serve the Gospel. We do not treat the Bible aright, we do not treat it with the respect it asks for itself, when we treat it as a theologian, but only when we treat it as an apostle, as a preacher, as the preacher in the perpetual pulpit of the Church. It is saturated with dogma, but its writers were not dogmatists; and it concerns a Church, but they were not ecclesiastics. The Bible, the preacher, and the Church are all made by the same thing – the Gospel. The Gospel was there before the Bible, and it created the Bible, as it creates the true preacher and the true sermon everywhere. And it is for the sake and service of the Gospel that both Bible and preacher exist. We are bound to use both, at any cost to tradition, in the way that gives freest course to the Gospel in which they arose.

The Bible, therefore, is there as the medium of the Gospel. It was created by faith in the Gospel. And in turn it creates faith among men. It is at once the expression of faith and its source. It is a nation's sermon to the race. It is the wonder-working relic of a saint-nation which was the living organ of living revelation. What made the inspiration of the book? It was the prior inspiration of the people and of the men by the revelation. Revelation does not consist of communications about God. It never did. If it had it might have come by an inspired book dictated to one in a dream. But revelation is the self-bestowal of the living God, His self-limitation in the interest of grace. It is the living God in the act of imparting Himself to living souls. It is God Himself drawing ever more near and arrived at last. And a living God can only come to men by living men. Inspiration is the state of a soul, not of a book – of a book only in so far as the book is a transcript of a soul inspired. It was by men that God gave Himself to men, till, in the fullness of time, He came, for good and all, in the God-man Christ, the living Word; in whom God was present, reconciling the world unto Himself, not merely acting through Him but present in Him, reconciling and not speaking of reconciliation, or merely offering it to us. He acted not only through Christ but in Christ. He who came was God the Son, and not a sinless saint dowered and guided by the Spirit. In Christ we have God Himself, and no mere messenger from God. That truth was the substantial victory gained by Athanasian theology for the Church once for all.

*

Now if this be so, that the Bible exists for the Gospel which created it, then this Gospel is the standard of all that the Bible contains. If the Bible is the great discourse, and may even be called a preacher above all else, then it is to be interpreted as a sermon is interpreted, and not as a dogmatic, nor as a protocol.

We do not treat a preacher fairly when we judge him by statements, logic, anecdotes, or phrases. We must judge him by his positive and effective message. The preacher claims to be thus understood. He protests bitterly against the mindless isolation of his *obiter dicta*, and the throwing up into large type of chance phrases. He asks that we will give much more attention to his message than to And if his methods eclipse his message he feels, or ought to feel, that he has failed. He has preached himself. His idiosyncrasy has stepped in front of his Gospel.

Well, what the preacher claims from the public in this way the Bible claims from the preacher. Measure it by its message, not its phrase, its style, its incidents, episodes, views, or faults.

The Bible is the preacher for preachers. It speaks to them above all, and with a word and not a creed. It makes believers into preachers or agents in proportion as it lays hold of them. Its first congenial appeal is not to the scientific theologian. It handles his ideas, but it does not speak his methodic language. St. Paul, for instance, was no dogmatician in the sense of Aquinas or Melanch-thon. He was comparatively careless about the correct form of his belief, what could now be called its orthodoxy (indeed he was the great heretic of his day); and he was lost in the experimental reality of it. He was the first of Christian theologians only because he was the greatest of Christian experimentalists. To express a reality so unspeakable he strained language and tortured ideas, which he enlisted from any quarter where he could lay hands on them. No, it is not to the scientific theologian, far less to the correct theologian, the orthodoxist, that the Bible first speaks. It is a preacher to preachers. And as the preacher's first concern is not dogma but Gospel, not creed but grace, so it is with the Bible. Every part of it is to be valued in the perspective of grace, in the proportion of faith in grace. It is all to be measured by its contribution to God's redeeming grace, by its effect as an agent of grace The final criticism of the Bible is not the 'higher criticism' but the highest, the criticism whose principle is God's supreme object in Bible, Church, or even Christ – the object of reconciling grace. The final criticism of it is neither literary nor scientific but evangelical, as the preacher must be. If the Bible is a preacher its first object is not to carry home divine truth but divine mercy. It is not formal but dynamic, not scientific but sacramental. The theologian has charge of the Gospel as truth, the preacher has it in his charge as grace. The very iteration of the word grace in my style only reflects the continuity, the dominance of the thing in our faith. The Bible, like its preacher, is not the organ of God to the scientific intelligence, but the sacrament of God to the soul, of the living God to living men, of the gracious God to lost men.

If we ask what is modern Christian theology, it is the Gospel taking the age seriously, with a real, sympathetic and informed effort to understand it, in the interest of no confession, but always keeping a historic and positive salvation in the front, and refusing everything in any age that is incompatible with it. It takes its stand neither on the spirit of the age, nor on the Christian consciousness, nor on the Christian principle, but on the historic and whole New Testament Christ.

*

May I illustrate what I mean when I say that the final criticism of the Bible, as a preacher, is not the higher rationalism but the highest grace. The question of the Virgin Birth is one that already exercises many and is shortly bound to exercise many more. How is that question to be settled? It is generally admitted that if it were not for the opening chapters of Matthew and Luke no other parts or the Bible would leave it tenable, by direct evidence at least. Now the higher criticism claims the right to dismiss these early chapters, and to say whether they are integral with the rest of the Gospels in which they are incorporated; or, if so, whether they represent the earliest truth, or a later tradition used by the evangelist. But supposing it came to be generally held that the story is integral to the literary whole of the book in which it occurs, that does not settle the question of fact. Such could only be the case if we agree beforehand that everything stated integrally in the Bible is historically true. Nor would the question be settled if we held that the story was believed by the Church at a stage earlier than the Gospels. That would settle it only if we agreed in advance that whatever was held by the Church of the first decades was true – including the explanation of epilepsy by demons. Or if, on the other hand, critics came to agree that the narrative was quite detachable from the rest of Matthew or Luke, that would not settle the question against its historicity. It could do so only if we agree in advance that nothing is historically true but what proceeded from the pen of a particular apostolic writer or writers. That is to say, the matter is not really to be settled by any decision of the literary critics acting simply as critics. So also it might be shown not to be at the mercy of historical criticism either. The real settlement of the question lies farther within theological territory. It is really a theological question and not a critical, as I hope later to show. The Virgin birth is not a necessity created by the integrity and infallibility of the Bible; it is a necessity created (if at all) by the solidarity of the Gospel, and by the requirements of grace. Was such a mode of entry into the world indispensable for Christ's work of redemption? If it was otiose to that work then we can leave it to the methods of the critics. But if it was essential to that work we must refuse them the last word. If it was essential to the perfect holiness of Christ's redeeming obedience, what is unhappily called His sinlessness, then it must stand, whatever the critics say. I am not here called on to decide that question. I only quote it as an illustration of method, to show what is meant by saying that there is a dogmatic criticism of the Bible higher than what is called the higher. And it consists in judging the parts of the Bible by its whole message and action, in bringing every detail to this test – how does it serve the one divine purpose which makes the library a book and the book the Word – the purpose of preaching saving grace?

This is actually Luther's test – does this or that passage 'ply Christ, preach Christ'? Is it in solidary connexion, direct or indirect, with Him? But the way I have ventured to put it, by saying the Gospel instead of Christ, makes the issue a little more distinct, perhaps, and the test more pointed. As I said, we cannot have a biography of Christ. We cannot easily tell what is or is not congruous with a character of whose psychology we know so little as the Gospels tell us. But we do know above all other knowledge the scope, object, and act of Christ's person. We do know the Christ of our faith better than any Christ of our constructive imagination, for all its precious results from modern methods. He was gathered up for us, as for God, in the consummation of the Cross. And the Cross is there as the agent of God's grace in redemption. Christ was born to die. To preach Christ really means to preach the Cross where His person took effect as the incarnation and the agent of the atoning grace of God. For this, therefore, I say that Christ Himself existed – not to present us with the supreme spiritual spectacle of history, but to achieve the critical thing in history. The Gospel is an act of God, gathered in a point but thrilling through history, and it calls for an act, and inspires it. Its preaching must therefore be an act, a 'function' of the great act. A true sermon is a real deed. It puts the preacher's personality into an act. That is his chief form of Christian life and practice. And one of his great difficulties is that he has to multiply words about what is essentially a deed. If you remember what men of affairs think about the people who make set speeches in committee you will realize how the preacher loses power whose sermons are felt to be productions, or lessons, or speeches, rather than real acts of will, struggles with other wills, and exercises of effective power. The Gospel means something done and not simply declared. For this work Christ existed on earth. And to give this work effect Bible and Church alike exist; We treat the Church as plastic to that work and its fulfilment, do we not? That is the true Church, and the true form of Church, which gives best effect to the Gospel. So also we must treat the Bible with much flexibility. The test and the trial of all is the grace of God in Jesus Christ, and in Him as crucified. Everything is imperishable which is inseparable from that.

*

The Bible, I have said, is the preacher to the preacher. But I shall be met perhaps by the observation that the preacher to the preacher is the Holy Spirit. It is an observation quite just. But it does not impair the force of what I have said. What is the principle of the Spirit's action on men? The Spirit is so much the spirit of Christ that we find in Paul's mouth the expression, 'the Lord the Spirit' – the Lord is the Spirit. I will not discuss the hard question thus raised as to the relation between the kingly Christ in Heaven and the Holy Spirit. For my purpose I may speak of the Spirit's action as the action of Christ in that heavenly kingship of His, which is the completion of His work as prophet and priest. The same Christ as on earth was both prophet and priest is in Heaven king also, by His finality and perfection in both. He does not sit on a height apart, retired, and simply watch, with a parental eye, the progress of the great kingdom He set on its feet, the great concern He founded and left to run. He still continues his prophetic and priestly work in a supreme and kingly way. But how, precisely? Is it merely by the emission of waves of spiritual force, supplementary and propulsive to the fundamental work of His earthly life? It is sometimes so viewed, as if the Spirit were a new and even a superior dispensation. We find the tendency both among the dogmatic pietists and among the undogmatic Christians who renounce theology in the interest of the Christian spirit or temper. In the history of the Church men and movements arise under a strong religious impulse which is either vague or extravagant. It is vague as being undefined by the positive principles of faith; or it is extravagant as being uncontrolled by the authority of a historic revelation. Certain mystic movements have their vogue by their independence of the Bible. They gratify our modernity, our subjectivity, our spurious spirituality, our impressionism. Some Christianized forms of natural piety manage to combine much human grace and religious sympathy with little personal use of Scripture. And other movements in the direction of a superior sanctity seem, at least at times, to associate sanctification much less directly with justification than the Bible does. But the action of the glorified Christ is always represented in the New Testament not as making new departures, or issuing fresh waves, but as giving fresh effect to His own historic work, keeping it a personal act, and preventing it from being a mere spiritual process. One of the greatest actions of the Spirit in modern thought is to preserve Christ's influence from being detached from His act and turned into a moral process. His spirit brings the act to remembrance; or takes of the work of Christ and shows it to the Church. He leads the Church into all truth, but it is the truth as it is in the whole Jesus. And nothing is more shallow and pretentious than the attempt to reform Church or creed by giving the Bible the go-by, or pooh-poohing its theology in the interest of an aesthetic or an idealist construction of religion.

This return to history is especially shown at the great crises of the Church's career, whether you take Luther, Wesley, or Schleiermacher. The Lord from Heaven forces the soul of the Church into a closer contact with His historic person and work, and gives a deeper penetration of it. It is the only condition of real revival. It is the inspiration of evangelical preaching in the great sense of the word. It was particularly the case with Paul, from whom these other great names have their apostolic succession. He fastened on the Cross, if I might venture so to say, and pressed the whole divine life out of it for our healing. And the history is our great protection now against both an idealism and an extravagance which readily run down into aloofness, feebleness, and futility. It keeps faith from the sentimentalism which to-day so easily besets it, by keeping it in the closest contact with the focus of the world's moral realism in the Cross. Our aim must be an ever fresh immersion in the Bible, an immersion both scholarly and experimental. We see deeper into it than our deep fathers did, though on other lines; for the new age has new eyes. It has new needs, and need makes wit. Through the ever-deepening need of man Christ is pressing His one personal, fundamental, and final work into our souls. He unfolds and freshens its searching meaning and eternal power. New men and new occasions do but elicit from it fresh wealth of resource. But it all comes from the Bible Christ, from the Christ of the Cross. The more He changes the more He is the same. Stability is not stiffness. Jesus, the same yesterday, to-day, and for ever, is not a dead identity, a monument that we leave behind, but a persistent personality that never ceases to open upon us. All permanent work in the kingdom is His work, of His initiative and not only in His succession. It is because He acts on us from the other world that that world is not a mist, a riddle, or a desert for us, and we are not aliens there. But from there He acts on us through what He was and did in history once for all. Our real and destined eternity goes round by Nazareth to reach us. What abides in history is not the impression He made, nor a Church's report. But it is His historic self, prophetic and priestly still in the kingly way of eternity. He is born again in each soul that is born anew. And those who preach are the channels and agents of the preaching, praying Christ, working from His spiritual world, but working still through Jerusalem, through the Bible. If it is not so our Protestant doctrine of Scripture, its constant use, free function, and first necessity for every soul, is a mistake and an unreality.

*

But if the Bible is the supreme preacher to the preacher, if it is through the Bible and its gospel above all that the Holy Ghost works upon him, how is the preacher to preach the Bible? Is his relation to it suggestive or expository? Is he to read in, or read out? Is he to preach whatever it may strike from his mind, or what his faith truly finds in it? Is he to treat it as a jewelled mass of facets of trembling lights, or as the living source of a positive revelation? Is it a huge brilliant, finely cut, afire with all kinds of rich and mystic hues, or is it a sun which issues the energy of the new world more even than its light? Is the preacher's work to lead the people into a larger modern world of suggestion which the Bible, without creating, has yet the power to stir, or shall he lead them into the Bible's own great renewing heart? There is no doubt the modern man inhabits a world larger in some ways than the Bible view of the cosmos or of man, a world of conception not due to the Bible but rather to art, science, exploration, industry and the like. And the Bible does possess on its part, in many words and phrases, that feature of inspiration which we might call glancing lights, as distinct from penetrative power, the flash rather than the force of the Spirit's sword. The book of Job, for instance, apart from its place in the history of moral revelation, has an extraordinary modernity both in theme and phrase. It is full of angles of reflection of the modern mind. All that is true. But our whole view or the relation of the Bible to the Gospel must be changed if we hold that that *suggestive* power is the main feature of the Bible, or its main function, that the Bible is there like a work of art, *nimium lubricus adspici*, offering, like a bird's neck, a play of fleeting hues for every man to seize what he has affinity to find. The Bible does not appeal to our affinities so much as to our needs, nor to our ingenuity so much as to our penetration, nor to our spiritual fancy so much as to our faith. To treat the Bible chiefly in that casual way is to return by another route to the old textual, atomistic, individualist fashion of dealing with it, the old, unhistoric, and often fantastic Biblicism. Whereas one of the great tasks of the preacher is to rescue the Bible from the textual idea in the mind of the public, from the Biblicist, atomist idea which reduces it to a religious scrap book, and uses it only in verses or phrases. There is a true place for such a use, but it has monopolized the Bible with the general public; and that is not right. The Bible is much more than a collection of spiritual apophthegms, or the gnomic *reliquiae* of moral sages. And a great part of the preacher's work is to rescue the Bible from this treatment, which is largely due to textual preaching, and is part of the price we pay for it. He must cultivate more the free, large, and organic treatment of the Bible, where each part is most valuable for its contribution to a living, evangelical whole, and where that whole is articulated into the great course of human history. This is one of the benefits we learn from the study of comparative religion, and particularly from the work of the new religious-historic school, when rightly used. But at first it will be less popular than the more fanciful treatment in which the public loves to roam and pick up the stray gifts that belong to whoever can find. Their right is not here denied if it be kept in its due place, which is the second, not the first. Who can deny the Bible's fragmentary and suggestive power? Who should refuse it in private meditation? Who would forbid textual preaching? But for the public purposes of Church and ministry there is another and higher point of view. The Bible is primarily there for a single and public purpose, for a historic, social, and collective purpose, for a purpose of the race. It is there not as a fountain of stray suggestion but as a channel of positive revelation and a source of spiritual authority. Bible preaching means leading people into the Bible and its powers. It is not leading them out of the Bible into subjectivities, fancies, quips, or queries. The Bible has a world and a context of its own. It has an ethos, if not a cosmos, of its own. It cannot simply be assigned a leading place among the literatures of the world, or given the hegemony of those fine forces of the human spirit 'bound to get to God.' It has a place far beyond what it takes in the history of religion, if we think of religion only as the Godward projection of man. It has also a supreme, a solitary, place of its own in the action of revelation, thinking of revelation 'as the manward movement of God.' It not only stirs our opinion as another religion might do: it demands our decision, our selves. The ethos of the Bible is beyond our cosmos, however largely you construe that cosmos, though you extend it to all modern dimensions. And not only so, but it represents the God of the cosmos. If it is to be integrated with the cosmos at all, it is as the final purpose always controls the evolving process, and the drift the context.

When I speak of Biblical context I am not thinking on the mere textual scale. I mean the context of the whole spiritual order in which the Bible is imbedded. It is necessary, of course, for any preacher who would deal seriously with the verse of his text to

study and handle it in its context. But what is true of a text from
the Bible is truer still of the whole Bible as a text. It can be truly
and fruitfully studied only in its moral context of history. And
by that again I do not merely mean either the context of each
passage in the history of Israel, or the whole book's context in
the history of religion, in its relation to other religions, other
contemporary or previous systems amid which it arose. Great is
the light that comes from that source, and it entails some change
in divers of our interpretations. But there is such a thing as the
Bible's evangelical context, its organic moral relevancy to the
conscience of Humanity, and I mean that. I mean its function in
the actual moral condition of the total perennial human soul, in
the great tissue and issue of human destiny. I mean the whole
moral situation which Christianity reveals in man as truly as it
reveals the holy grace of God. I speak of the moral context of the
Bible as a whole in the race's conscience – the human sin which
the holy Saviour casts into the deeper shade, the lostness revealed
by the Gospel that finds. In respect of the cosmos, whether of
nature, the soul or society, the Bible may be very suggestive; and
it may give rise to many theologoumena, some speculative, some
merely fantastic, as most amateur theologoumena are. The Bible
is like the United States (will you pardon this glancing light?),
the richest ground in the world for every variety of 'crank.' But
in respect of the ethos, in relation to the fundamental moral
condition of the race, the Bible is much more positive for conscience than suggestive for fancy. It has a definite message and a
central task. It has something imperative, which overrules all the
suggestions of fantasy or ingenuity; and something crucial which
transcends the mere play of thought, or the mere practice of
poetry. It compels an attitude, a choice, a line to be taken. Its
reality appeals to our reality in will. It has at its core something
which demands to be met actively, and crucially if need be,
something that closes with history in moral conflict. It has a
Gospel, nay *the* Gospel, for the worst condition of the whole
energetic race. It has mankind's inevitable word and its eternal
destiny.

*

It is that word that the preacher must bring to the people. It is in that word he must himself live; especially with historic study, avoiding the artificial paradigms and surface 'railways' that disfigure its meaning to the untaught. The Dutch gardeners do the Bible as much harm as the people who but pick the flowers. Let the preacher's suggestion teem by all means, as it will teem, in the quickened vitality given to his personal resources by the Word of Life. Let the gift of his fancy be stirred up, as well as all his other gifts, by this life beyond all gifts. But let every suggestion keep its true place in the economy and proportion of faith. Let it wear the clear livery of the Gospel, and conspire to lighten and magnify that. For instance if, as the preacher reads the words 'He shall show you an upper room furnished,' it strikes him with a flash that Christ's Gospel not only lights up the ideal world over him but stocks it with a content of positive truth for our spiritual dwelling and use, by all means let him preach a sermon to that effect from the text. But let it be clear that he is using some sacred fancy in so doing. And let him realize that such a treatment of the Bible is on a very different footing from that which he employs if he preach on central words like these: 'Being justified by faith we have peace with God through our Lord Jesus Christ.' It is into the Bible world of the eternal redemption that the preacher must bring his people. This eternal world from which Christ came is contemporary with every age. To every age it is equally near, and it is equally authoritative for every age, however modern. It is never antiquated in its final principles and powers. The only preaching which is up to date for every time is the preaching of this eternity, which is opened to us in the Bible alone – the eternal of holy love, grace and redemption, the eternal and immutable morality of saving grace for our indelible sin.

It is not the preacher's prime duty then to find happy texts for the exposition of modern thought. Nor must he sink the Gospel to a revelation which puts people in a good humour with themselves by declaring to them that the great divine message is the irrepressible spirituality of human nature. It is an inversion of his work if he begin with Christ and enlarge into Goethe. Let him begin with Goethe, if he will, so that he go on to enlarge into

Christ. Let him learn from the first part of Faust; he has nothing
to learn from the second. Let him state the problem as powerfully
as Shakespeare left it, but let him answer it with the final answer
Christ left. No genius has or can have it but from Christ. For He
is the answer that they but crave. And they but state, as only genius
can, the human tragedy which it is Christ's to retrieve.

*

But the preacher who tries to follow this advice will find himself
in one great difficulty. The Bible may be his text book, but it has
ceased to be the text book of his audience. The Bible is not read
by the Christian, or even by the churchgoing public, as a means
of grace greater even than churchgoing. Our people, as a rule, do
not read the Bible, in any sense which makes its language more
familiar and dear to them than the language of the novel or the
press. And I will go so far as to confess that one of the chief
miscalculations I have made in the course of my own ministerial
career has been to speak to congregations as if they did know and
use the Bible. I was bred where it was well known and loved, and
I have spent my ministerial life where it is less so. And it has taken
me so long to realize the fact that I still find it difficult to adjust
myself to it. I am long accustomed to being called obscure by many
whose mental habits and interests are only literary, who have felt
but a languid interest in the final questions of the soul as the New
Testament stirs them, who treat sin as but lapse, God's grace as
if it were but love, and His love as if it were but paternal kindness.
At first I believed I was obscure, and I took pains to be short in
the sentence and unadorned in style. But I found my critics still
puzzled. And I have come to think the obscurity is at least in some
degree due to the fact that while I am attracted by such matters
beyond all else, I am often dealing with people to whom they are
not only strange but irritating. They have applied to religion what
William Morris applied to life, 'Love is enough.' They have given
a Christian varnish to what in him was mainly pagan, but they
have not really stepped out of his natural world. They have risen
to locate the affections in God; but they have not realized faith as
the inroad, the uprise in us of a totally new world, Christianity as
a new creation, and the new life as a new birth. Grace for them

is only love exercised on the divine scale, not in the divine style, not under the conditions of holiness and sin. They read in the heart more than in the Bible.

The old Protestant principle, therefore, no longer rules the relation of preacher and people. They are not spoken to from their Bible as they are from their preacher. Consequently they do not easily find the thing they like in the preacher who lives in his Bible. And, on the other hand, they are unable to exercise on the preacher the check of personal experience of the Bible and first-hand knowledge of it, as they did in the days of the great classic preachers. But that is the habit in the people which makes great preachers in the pulpit. And it is that principle that is the basis of the people's place, the place of the laity in a Protestant Church. Anything else is in principle Catholic. It is a Catholic treatment of the Bible to leave it in the hands of the minister alone. And, unless there be a change, it is to that that Protestantism is coming. Outside an evangelical Protestantism, amply construed, there is nothing for us but Catholicism. For general Atheism is permanently impossible. I trust you will not here think me extravagant. The final action of a principle, to those disaccustomed to principles, is sure to seem fanciful. And I am only stating the action of one of those deeper principles which in the end form the logic of history, and override all the tactics of the hour. And the principle is that where Protestantism falls into the Catholic treatment of the Bible, namely its disuse by the laity, we are rapidly getting ready for the Catholic idea of the Church, and the Catholic construction of the priest. To restore to the people an intelligent and affectionate use of the Bible is a service to Protestantism far more needed than those violent and ill-informed denunciations of the priest which are so easy and so cheap.

*

Bible preaching then means that we adjust our preaching to the people's disuse of the Bible. We have to regain their interest in it. It is, therefore, not the preaching of doctrine with proof passages. It is not preaching which does the Bible the lip homage of taking a text. Nor is it simply preaching historic facts on the one hand, or personal experience on the other. But it is the preaching of those facts and gifts of grace which are experimentally verifiable and creative of experience. It is only on points so verifiable that the Bible can be doctrinally used by the laity. A fact like the Virgin Birth is not at all on the same footing as the Resurrection of Christ, who is met as the risen Lord by His disciples to this day. Christianity is not the religion of a book, though it is a book religion. Nor is it the religion of a Church, though it is a Church religion. But it is the religion of a Gospel and a grace. These are the facts that make the Church. Doctrine as doctrine is a precious and indispensable possession of the Church, but it was not such doctrine that made the Church. Neither ideas nor truths could do that, but only persons and powers. Nor does such doctrine make the great changes of the Church. The Reformation was not a reformation of theology, but of faith. It is remarkable how little of the theology it changed in its first stage. It was the renewed action, not of truth, but of grace. It was the greatest of evangelical revivals. That is why it re-discovered the Bible. It was not the Bible that lighted up grace for Luther, but grace to his needy soul lighted up the Bible. Biblical preaching preaches the Gospel and uses the Bible, it does not preach the Bible and use the Gospel.

For the Gospel the Bible must be used. The minister must so live in it that he wears it easily. One reason why people are repelled from it is that the preachers cannot carry it with easy mastery. They are in Goliath's armour. Now the ideal ministry must be a Bibliocracy. It must know its Bible better than any other book. Most Christians hardly know their Bible at first hand at all. They treat it with respect, no doubt. They keep a great Bible in the house; but it is on a little table, not very steady, in the parlour window, and it has stiff clasps. It is in the room least used; it carries a vase of once pretty flowers; and it gets in the way of the rich lace curtains. Which is all an allegory. Some preachers know it only in the way of business, as a sermon quarry. But the true ministry must live on it. We must speak to the Church not from experience alone, but still more from the Word. We must speak from within the silent sanctuary of Scripture. We do not realize always how eager people are to hear preaching which makes the Bible wonderful by speaking from its very interior, as men do who live in it and wonder themselves. I do not believe in verbal inspiration. I am with the critics, in principle. But the true minister ought to find the words and phrases of the Bible so full of spiritual food and felicity that he has some difficulty in not believing in verbal inspiration. The Bible is the one enchiridion of the preacher still, the one manual of eternal life, the one page that glows as all life grows dark, and the one book whose wealth rebukes us more the older we grow because we knew and loved it so late.

Two

The Authority of the Preacher

The urgent modern need of an Authority – The authority of the Pulpit due to the divine Person it proclaims – Our authority must be objective *and* inward – This inward authority not the natural conscience, whether crude or refined – Our supreme need of redemption – The final authority in Christianity that of a Redeemer; so the authority of the pulpit is evangelical – It is God in His supreme saving act in Christ's Cross – Christ so to be preached as to be the Creator of faith, the absolute Redeemer.

I venture here to state at once what I will go on to explain, that the preacher is the organ of the only real and final authority for mankind. He is its organ, and even its steward; but he is not its vicar, except at Rome.

The question of the ultimate authority for mankind is the greatest of all the questions which meet the West, since the Catholic Church lost its place in the sixteenth century, and since criticism no longer allows the Bible to occupy that place. Yet the gospel of the future must come with the note of authority. Every challenge of authority but develops the need of it. And that note must sound in whatever is the supreme utterance of the church, in polity, pulpit, or creed. It seems clear, indeed, unless the whole modern movement is to be simply undone, that the Church must draw in the range of its authority, and even Catholicism must be modified if it is to survive. But the Church can never part with the tone of authority, nor with the claim that, however it may be

defined, the authority of its message is supreme. That is the very
genius of an evangelical religion; for it declares that that which
saves the world shall also judge the world, and it preaches the
absolute right over us of the Christ who bought us – the active
supremacy in conscience of our moral redemption. It is the
absence of the note of authority that is the central weakness of so
many of the churches; and it is the source of their failure to impress
Society with their message for the practical ends of the Kingdom
of God. It is useless to preach the Kingdom when we do not carry
into the centre of life the control of a King. The first duty of every
soul is to find not its freedom but its Master. And the first charge
of every Church is to offer, nay to mediate, Him.

*

The authority of the preacher was once supreme. He bearded
kings, and bent senates to his word. He determined policies, ruled
fashions, and prescribed thought. And yet he has proved unable
to maintain the position he was so able to take. He could not
insure against the reaction which has now set in as severely as his
authority once did. That reaction has long been in force; and
to-day, however great may be his vogue as a personality, his
opinion has so little authority that it is not only ignored but
ridiculed. In that respect the pulpit resembles the press, whose
circulation may be enormous, while elections, and such like
events, show that the influence of its opinions is almost nil.

But between the press and the pulpit there is this mighty
difference. The pulpit has a Word, the press has none. The pulpit
has a common message and, on the strength of it, a claim, while
the press has no claim to anything but eternal freedom of opinion
and expression. The one has a Gospel which is the source of its
liberty, the other has no Gospel but liberty, which in itself is no
Gospel at all. Liberty is only opportunity for a Gospel. The true
Gospels not only claim it, they create it. But, in itself, it is either
the product of a Gospel, or a means thereto; it is not an end. It is
no more an end than evolution is, which is only the process of
working out an end that the mere process itself does not give.
Liberty in itself is not an end; and it has only the worth of its end.
The chief object of the liberty of the press is facts. It must be free

to publish facts. But the pulpit has not merely a fact but a Word. The press is there for information, or for suggestion at most, it is not there for authority; but the pulpit is there with authority; and the news it brings is brought for the sake of the authority. The press may offer an opinion as to how the public should act, but the pulpit is there with a message as to whom the acting public must obey and trust. The press is an adviser, but the pulpit is a prophet; the press may have a thought, the pulpit must have a Gospel, nay a command. If I may use press language, the pulpit's news is there for the sake of the leader, the leader is not a mere opinion about the news. The Gospels are there for the sake of the Epistles, for the sake of the Gospel.

Therefore, the pulpit has an authority. If it have not, it is but a chair and not a pulpit. It may discourse, but it does not preach. But preach it must. It speaks with authority. Yet the authority is not that of the preacher's person; it is not mere authoritativeness. For us that goes without saying. What does not go unsaid, what needs saying is, that the preacher's authority is not the authority even of his truth. In the region of mere truth there is no authority. Mere truth is intellectual, and authority is a moral idea bearing not upon belief but upon will and faith, decision and committal. (See Lect. VIII.) It is not statements that the preacher calls on us to believe. It is no scheme of statements. It is not views. It is not a creed or a theology. It is a religion, it is a Gospel, it is an urgent God. In the region of mere theology we may be bold to say there is no authority; the authority is all in the region of religion. The creed of the Church Catholic should have great prestige, but not authority in the proper sense. Belief, in the region of theology, is a matter of truth or truths; it is science, simple or complex. And science knows no authority. But in the region of religion belief is faith. It is a personal relation. It is belief in a person by a person. It is self-committal to him. With the heart man believeth unto salvation. It is a personal act towards a person. It is trust in that person, and response to the power of his act. It is soul answering soul, and act act, and choice choice. In science, knowledge is the relation of a person to a fact or law – to something inferior to a person, and therefore not his authority. But in faith knowledge

(I shall show later that faith is an organ of knowledge) is the relation of a person to a person who is like us yet over us. It is a moral relation of obedience and authority.

The authority of the pulpit is thus a personal authority. Yet it is not the authority of the preacher's person, or even of his office. His office may demand much more respect than the fanatics of freedom allow, but it cannot claim authority in the strict sense. The personal authority of the pulpit is the authority of the divine person who is its burthen. It is an external authority, but it is the authority of an inward objective, living, saving God, before whose visitation the prophet fades like an ebbing voice, and the soul of the martyr cries invisible from under the altar of the Cross.

*

I know well the feelings which arise in many at the very mention of words like 'authority' and 'external.' They are feelings of recalcitrance and resentment – often very blind. We are put upon the defence of our independence. It seems forgotten that the supreme thing in life must be uppermost, not merely in place but in dignity, not merely in position but in right, not as a stratum might be, but as a throne. It is not the soul's top storey but the soul's suzerain power. For the soul, and conscience, the words higher or lower mean authority or they mean nothing. Even in the celestial time when the soul shall be in complete harmony with God the relation must always be worship, and therefore authority and obedience. The supreme thing is not a weight that lies on us but a crown that governs us and lifts us up for ever. Unless we frankly adopt the positivist position, where humanity is to itself not only a law but an object of worship, there must be an authority both for man and men. And as for the externality of it – surely if there be an authority it must be external. It must come to us, and not rise out of us. It must come down on man and not proceed from him. It is a word to our race, not from it. The content of our conscience descends on us, it is no projection of ours. It were less than conscience if it were; for the law that we made we could unmake and the order we issued we could recall. Treat the autonomy of conscience as you will, but do not remove the accent from the *nomos* to the *autos*. If it be a *nomos* it is a product of more than ourselves, more than man – it is of God. Otherwise it would be but a self-imposed condition, from which at any time we might be self-released. And it could bind none, even while it remained binding, but him who had imposed it on himself. And then it would not be conscience but earnest whim.

But then, it is asked, is it not one of the greatest and surest results of modern progress that, if there be an authority, it must be inward, it must be in the soul, it must be by consent? Yes, indeed, that is one of the greatest and best blessings of the modern time. But do you realize what that means? Surely the more inward it is the more is it external. The more we retire to our inner castle the more we feel the pressure of the not-ourselves, and the presence of our Overlord. The more spiritual we are the more we are under law to another. To internalize the authority is to subtilize it, and therefore to emphasize it; for it is the subtler realities that bear upon us with the most persistent, ubiquitous, and effective pressure. The more inward we go the more external the authority becomes, just because it becomes more of an authority, and more unmistakably, irresistibly so.

If we were not so Philistine that the most accurate words seem pedantic, the proper word would be not external but objective. Because external has come, for the man in the street, to mean outside his own body, or his own family, or his own self-will, his own individuality; while what we are really concerned with is outside our own soul, our own personality. What we are suffering from is not mere externality but unconquered inwardness, subjectivism, individualism, ending in egotism. It is our subjectivism which gives externals their enslaving power over us. If within us we find nothing over us we succumb to what is around us. It is a cure for our subjectivism that we need, a cure for our egotism. And that is to be found in nothing physically external, nothing institutionally so, but only in an objective, moral and spiritual, congenial yet antithetic, in an objective to the ego, yea to the race, which objective alone gives morality any meaning. Our suzerain must indeed sit in the court of the soul, but he must be objective there. What he is he must indeed be for the soul – the soul's *vis-à-vis*, which must be also soul. Soul is relative only to soul, will to will. But while he is not anything else than soul, he is other than *my* soul. He is not *an* other, but he is *my* other. He is my objective. But objective he must be, no less than he must be mine. He is my authority, but it is not a heteronomy, it is no foreign rule. Any autonomy of mine is due to his congenial power, to the homonomy of his authority, to its kinship with my soul.

By all means then the divine authority must be inward – if we are sure what we mean, if we do not come to mean that we are our own authority – which I am afraid is the popular version with which the preacher has to contend. The authority must be inward, it is true. The modern preacher must accept that principle, and correct all its risks of perversion and debasement. His message must be more and more inward. But it must be *searchingly* inward. That is to say, it must be inward with the right of search, as an authority; and not simply as a servant, a suppliant, an influence, an impression, a sensibility. It must be above all else a moral authority, having right and not mere influence or prestige, demanding action, obedience and sacrifice, and not merely echo, appreciation, stirrings, and thrills.[1]

---

[1]   It must be a moral authority. The *grand être*, the oversoul, the totality supreme being, call it what you will, which teaches us our place and conducts us to it, and so to our blessedness, must be moral in its nature. The law of being is a moral law. The nature of reality is not only experience, as the modern drift of thought teaches, but it is moral experience. It is a will's action. It is decision. Now religion is no exception to the universe of reality. That is not what is meant by its autonomy. Rather is it the key to that universe. It opens reality. It contains it. Religion is part of our consciousness. And consciousness is primary; it is not deduced from any prior reality of another nature. It is part of reality. Reality has therefore the nature of consciousness. And consciousness is moral. For it is of the will in its nature. We are conscious of ourselves as will-powers; The great reality is thus a supreme will. And our recognition of it is an act of moral submission. That is, it is a relation of authority and obedience. And the preacher's word of grace to faith is thus all of a piece with the word of the universe to the Soul, with

> Der ewige Gesang,
> Der unser ganzes Lebenlang
> Uns heisser jede Stunde klingt.

Thus when we move the authority from an external church or book to the forum of the conscience, when in the face of humanity or society we claim to call our soul our own, we have not ended the strife; we have but begun one more serious on another plane. And, in many cases, we have but opened the gates of confusion, and let loose the floods of inner tumult. The recognition of the inwardness, in many cases, seems to destroy the authority. Perhaps it does so in most cases at first. We are too full of ourselves to desire another to rule over us. And even when we desire it there are few who are so familiar with their inner selves as to be able to distinguish with any certainty the shepherd's voice, amid the gusts or sighings of their own fitful selves.

*

The questions that arise are such as these:

1. What is the inward authority, to which the claims of a Gospel, or its preacher, must be brought? Is it the natural conscience, uneducated, and therefore (it is said) unsophisticated? Is it the stalwart *Natur-kind* from the far West, whose pockets bulge with Walt Whitman? Is it the amateur private judgment, so dear to the sturdy moralist of the street? Is it a moral mother-wit, sitting with a hair-trigger at the centre of an individualism whose self-confidence is impregnable, and passing its prompt verdict upon everything done or devised? There is no doubt about the popularity of this order of rationalism, especially among the more independent races, and their more unschooled strata. It is a claim, too, which a democratic Christianity does much to encourage. The pushing tradesman of a small town enters a theological discussion to say that he always wants a straight answer to a straight question; and he is not going to be cowed by the people who understand it, or bent to a theological popery. But that the supernatural eternal Gospel should be staked on an appeal to the healthy and untutored natural conscience is a view so far outgrown that perhaps it need not occupy us longer. Sociology teaches us that even the most self-sufficient man is not a self-made man, but he is made by centuries of heredity and ages of solidarity. And if Christianity meant healthy-mindedness, that itself would surely mean something more than the light of nature or the verdict

of the decent pagan man. We may, moreover, take it that the authority of a holy Gospel cannot be proved to the natural man. The offence of the Cross has not ceased. It must first capture him and make him a supernatural man.

*

2.   Then, is the adjudicating faculty which chooses our authority the natural conscience educated, when it has in some serious fashion gone to school? Is it the natural conscience refined? Is it the natural conscience stimulated by contact with historic and imaginative ideals, and thus developed to a nicer tact of judging the higher claims? Well, no doubt, a moral teacher and hero like Socrates has a rich and rare power of rousing the conscience, and educating it to approve ideas it once ignored or condemned. He wins our admiration and trust. He elicits our personality. He stirs in us a mind as constant as his own. He quickens also our moral intelligence, and trains our moral discernment. And he does so by sympathy and not antagonism, by an imperative which is congenial and not merely imperious, dialectic and not only dogmatic. He may rouse bitter hostility but he also rouses heroic friendship, insight, imitation, or obedience. Or, if he does not actually raise ourself to his own height, at least he stirs in us the sense that we ought so to rise, and to become such a soul in our place and way. A moral nature is born, or he leaves us morally more than he found us.

It is here recognized, you note, that the appraising self must be educated in some due school; it is not ready to our hand. The preacher would be then principally a formative pastor, tutor, teacher. He is educative rather than evangelical. His method is dialectic and maieutic rather than regenerative. He analyses our truth, and brings our best self to light, rather than creates a new man. But is his result, in this conception of him, always a success? Does he lay more problems than he stirs? Does he give us power to deal with final questions and command final answers? Does he plant us on the rock of finality, where the problems range about a base which they cannot eat away? Does he not rather stir new questions more urgent than the old? Thus: 'I ought to rise to that height. But how shall I? I know I should, I do not know how I can. In this region I feel an impotence I feel nowhere else. I can master problems, but how am I to rise to tasks, and keep at their level? I am a sinful man. My new ideal does as much to oppress me as to exalt me, and often much more. The more it teaches me to see, the less I am able to do. The more it smiles on me as my ideal, the less it seems as if it could ever become mine. "It is lovely, but it has no arms." It does not grasp, it does not save. O, wretched man! How shall my ideal become my destiny, and my vision my goal? How can my sinful self become my true free moral self? I want a power to give me not vision, nor truth, nor conviction alone, but myself. Yea, I want relief from myself. I must be redeemed from myself into the moral freedom I have now learned to crave.

> O for a man to arise in me
> That the man I am may cease to be.'

It is not with our moral freedom, you may mark, as it is with our ordinary mental vision. Intellectual progress takes what it finds already to hand, and builds on it. Thus each generation adds to the great reef which is growing under the waves of time to a new mental world. We take up science, discovery, or invention, where our fathers left them. But it is otherwise with our moral selves, and especially with our spiritual selves. We have to start from the beginning, or very much nearer it than the intellect does. There is little historic progress in the region of the elemental humanities. Love, hate, jealousy, valour, loyalty, awe, pity, or beauty, are substantially the same for us as they were for Homer and his age. Man is very permanent in what most makes him man. In the case of our central moral man, for all the latent furniture of heredity, and all the long bias of evil, we can say of each soul –

> He is the first that ever burst
> Into that silent sea.

What we have with each soul is rather a fresh case than a new development. And so when God comes to us He brings more than a mere extension of our previous horizon, a supplement to nature, or a development of it. It is not a mere enrichment of our previous mentality. His is not the touch which unfolds the latent germ. It is not merely a case of slitting our husk, or of eliciting the vitality. It is not education. It is revelation. It is not giving effect to our native power, and enlarging us to the destined fullness of our hidden resource. It is not the opulent expansion of our individuality. That is all too romantic. It is a fresh spontaneity of His, a new creation, a free gift. It is a pure gift to our weakness, our need, our helplessness. It is an absolute salvation, not an aid to our self-salvation. Our receptivity is room rather than faculty. We receive a new life rather than gain a new facility. There is not an evolution so much as a new creation.

Between man and man it is otherwise. What man does for man is on a basis of parity. He tries to elicit what is latent in a common humanity. It is give and take on both sides. The teacher may even gain more than the taught from acting upon him. But it is not so when one of the parties is God. It is then a relation of disparity. The Christian God at least is man's God in being his Saviour, i.e., in virtue of His difference from man rather than His identity. Christ always stood with God over against man. The object of God with man is not to elicit slumbering divinity, and kiss the sleeping beauty into life. Nor does He gain from us as the teacher does from the taught. God needs none of us as we all need Him. It is not give and take; it is all giving on His part. In receiving anything from man He receives but what He gives, and in His life we live. Our synergist pride is quelled as we realize that. Our self-satisfaction has its saving rebuff. We are no partners with God, fellow-workers as we may be. Our best faith with all its works is purely the gift of God, because it is roused by His one gift, Christ. He receives man in no such sense as man receives Him. His work with us is much more than educative, more than maieutic. It is paternal, creative. The conscience before Him is in a state where education will not serve it. Merely develop sinful man, and in spite of all the good in him, you only have a greater sinner. The disparity of God and man is not gradual, it is not a matter of degree. And what God has to deal with is not our relative imperfection. He does not simply stoop to us as we keep doing our poor best to reach Him. He does not simply wait for us, and cheer us on with a tender remembrance of the time when He was at our stage and felt the need of a sympathetic father or even brother. The gulf between us is much more, even than the gulf between the creature and the Creator. Great as that distance might be it does not exclude communion. What ails us is not limitation but transgression, not poverty but alienation. It is the breach of communion that is the trouble – the separation, the hostility. We are not His counterparts but His antagonists. There is not only the distance between Creator and creature, father and child in the natural sense; but there is a vast and serious disturbance of even that relation. There is a huge dislocation. There is that in us and in our sin which is in its very essence intractable to all the processes of a reconciling idea; something which, to the end, by its very nature, refuses to be taken up as a factor into the largest and most comprehensive procession of divine action; something which can never be utilized, but can only be destroyed in a mortal moral war; something which, if God cannot kill it, must be the death of God. And as a race we are not even stray sheep, or wandering prodigals merely; we are rebels taken with weapons in our hands.

Our supreme need from God, therefore, is not the education of our conscience, nor the absorption of our sin, nor even our reconcilement alone, but our redemption. It is not cheer that we need but salvation; not help but rescue; not a stimulus but a change; not tonics but life. Our one need of God is a moral need in the strictest holiest sense. The best of nature can never meet it. It involves a new nature, a new world, a new creation. It is the moral need, not to be transfigured but to be saved. And the inner authority is the power which does that. It not merely aids us, nor enlightens us, nor kindles us, nor presents us with an ideal, or a contagion, or a sympathy; but it redeems us by the destruction of our guilt, the neutralizing of the evil we have done, and the hallowing against us of His own holy name. It is the authority of a Redeemer, of one who is the organ to us of a new world. It is a new world in total contrast with the old, yet interpenetrating it; underlying it, yet not imbedded in it like a germ, but haunting it and urgent at every point, and at one point leaping to light and final effect.

*

3. This authority of the Redeemer is the final authority in Christianity. And, observe, I do not say the authority of Christ, but the authority of Christ as Redeemer, as our new Creator, the authority of Christ's person as wholly gathered up and completely expressed in the Cross, its work, and its Gospel. He is our peace not in His person alone, for that were too quiescent, exemplary, and aesthetic – but in the mediation which is the energy, act, and effect of His person for ever. I certainly do not mean the authority of Christ's teaching, supreme as that is over all other teaching on spiritual things. Nor do I mean the authority connected with the magnetism, the impressiveness of His personality – the authoritativeness of it. Still less do I mean the authority of such of His beliefs as were solid with the naïve religious consciousness of His land and age – as for instance, His references to the Davidic authorship of a Psalm. I mean His authority in the true region where the word authority has its ultimate meaning, in the region of personal interaction, in the moral, the religious region alone, the region where grace acts and faith answers, the evangelical region and not the theological. In the theological region I have said there is, properly speaking, no authority – authority being predicable not of a truth in theology, but of a theological person whose action on my person makes my religion. This is the authority realized by the most classic types of the Christian experience – the authority, not of the conscience, however enlightened, but of Christ in the conscience; and in the conscience, not as its oracle simply, or its needle, but as its redeemer, regenerator, and new creator. The seat of authority is not the enlightened conscience but the redeemed and regenerate.

Thus alone do we do justice to moral realism. It is a moral authority that concerns us, I have said. That means, it is the authority for men not in some abstract and conceivable position, nor in some primeval perfection which never was real, but for historic man in his actual moral state; which is a state not of imperfection only but of impotence for holiness, and not of impotence alone but of collective guilt. The more we realize the solidarity of man the more his moral condition becomes a collectivism of guilt. That is to say, the moral authority must be in relation to guilt, and to the guilt of the race; it must be more than ethical, it must be a religious authority, a saving one, an evangelical one. It is an authority acting not merely on our moral perception but on our moral perdition – at least on our moral crisis – and acting by way of redemption, and not merely by way of injunction, nor by way of impression, nor by way of prestige. And the redemption thus demanded by our actual case is not merely eschatological, at the far consummate end of things. Nor is it merely ethical, in the way of promoting our moral development and improvement. The chief criterion of Christianity is not its ethical results and amendments. These are but the consequences of it, the fruits of its reconciliation. It is evangelical in this way – that it begins with reconciliation. It is the destruction by God in Christ of sin's guilt and sin's distrust, and sin's blocking of the sky. Such is our central case and need. Whatever, therefore, meets that is the final and sole authority of our race, from which all that claims authority must deduce. Set that right in every man by what sets right also the race, and right views and right relations will follow as the night the day. The great creed and the great millennium must be alike confessions of the living faith which is our contact with Him who sits on the throne and makes all things new and true.

*

But this is to say that the final authority in human affairs is, after all, the preacher's authority. It is on this authority alone that the preacher must rely; and the preacher's is the only function that must rely on this authority alone. He, of all men, is most dependent on his message. He is dependent on his personality only as his Gospel makes it, and as it shows forth the Gospel. You hear it said, with a great air of religious common sense, that it is the man that the modern age demands in the pulpit, and not his doctrine. It is the man that counts, and not his creed. But this is one of those shallow and plausible half-truths which have the success that always follows when the easy, obvious underpart is blandly offered for the arduous whole. No man has any right in the pulpit in virtue of his personality or manhood in itself, but only in virtue of the sacramental value of his personality for his message. We have no business to worship the elements, which means, in this case, to idolise the preacher. (Fitly enough in Rome the deification[2] of the priest continues the transubstantiation of the elements.) To be ready to accept any kind of message from a magnetic man is to lose the Gospel in mere impressionism. It is to sacrifice the moral in religion to the aesthetic. And it is fatal to the authority either of the pulpit or the Gospel. The Church does not live by its preachers, but by its Word.

*

The last authority, then, is the evangelical. For what is our authority but that to which we are not our own? And that is what we find absolutely in our evangelical faith. Its appeal is not to the natural conscience, individual, amateur, and self-sufficient. Nor is it to the enlightened conscience of civilization, cultivated by all the moral thought and discipline of history, society, or imagination. But it is to the *actual* conscience of the race, to the conscience taken as we find it, to the conscience as sinful and redeemed, the conscience struck into self-despair, horrified with the world's moral tragedy, and plucked into salvation by God's and man's last moral crisis in the Cross, where the greatest tragedy turns the greatest triumph of all. The appeal is to a conscience in such a state that it must be saved, and re-empowered; and saved by no mere contact with God, but only by a moral act of God at least as energetic as the universe, as real, historic, and tragic as the sin, i.e. by God's holy reaction of grace, of invading, mastering, regenerating grace. The inmost authority being moral is the most objective thing we know; speaking to and through the conscience, and to a conscience made capable by grace of appraising and appropriating in a way impossible to the natural self. It emerges and wells up under psychological conditions, but it is not a psychological product. It may be subliminal rather than supernal, but it is not ourselves, it is objective. And nothing is so objective, so authoritative as that which at our inmost moral centre saves us from ourselves. The thing most immanent in us is a transcendent

---

[2] 'Eritis sicut dii.' Cp. Gen. iii. 5 with the *Catechism of Trent*, II. 7.2: *Sacerdotes non solum angeli sed dii appellantur.*

thing, nay, a descendant thing. The more immanent the forum, the more objective and invasive do we feel the redemption. But we must be redeemed, ere we realize this. To the natural man it is foolishness. He finds all salvation to be but the great recuperative effort of man's inalienable divinity, his indefectible essential identity with God, which is the only true eternal life. And the act of saving grace is nothing but our own act of faith in our profound and innate selves. Against all which I would say, in a word, we have to be redeemed into the power of appreciating redemption, and appropriating the greatest moral act man knows – the Cross.

Thus we can never settle the question of a final moral authority (which is the last authority of all) except in the region where will meets will and faith takes home God's act of grace. It is quite insoluble in the region where cosmic process takes the place of moral action, or in the region where conscience responds but to an ideal, or reason accepts truth. It is not with truth we have to do but reality. And reality is a moral thing, a matter of a person, and his will, and his act. Life in its reality is a great act and choice, and not a long process. And therefore the authority is not a standard, as a truth, or an architecture of truths, might be. It is a living law. And a living law, not in the sense of a historic institution, acting as the custodian of truth, and the trustee of its development. It is a living, holy, historic God and Saviour witnessed, preached, and truly conveyed, by the whole Church, but dispensed by none. It is a living and holy God in much more than presence (which were mere mysticism). It is God in power, in moral power, in historic and sempiternal action. It is a God real in a historic act, which is perpetual in its energy, achieved at one point but throbbing at every other, a timeless act, parallel with every human action, and mutually involuted with it (if one may so say), but involved in the way of struggle and conquest rather than mere permeation – an Eternal Cross rather than a universal Spirit. It is this act that is prolonged as the arduous emergence through history of that Kingdom of God, which, for all its immanence, is much more a gift to history than its product. The last authority is God in His supreme, saving act of grace to mankind in Christ's Cross, which is the power of God addressed to what is at once the power and the weakness in us, our will, conscience, and total moral self. Our last authority is something we can only obey by subjugation, reconciliation, and worship, and not by mere assent. It is that saving act of God which makes all our best moral action possible. It is an invasion of us, however inward, it is not an emergence from us; nor is it merely the stroke upon our hard shell which releases our innate divinity. It is an invasion, creative more than tonic, redeeming rather than releasing, putting into the soul a new mainspring and not disentangling the old which had caught.

But, invasion as it is, it is, yet no assault on the sanctuary of our personal freedom. We are mastered but not concussed. For it is the one influence, the one authority, that gives us to ourselves, and puts us in possession of our moral freedom. The true freedom of man springs from the holy sovereignty of God, which we only know in Christ, in redeeming action. There our freedom has its charter and not its doom. Even if we started psychologically free, the result of the choice of evil is to impair freedom; and an impaired freedom goes on to a destroyed freedom. Who doeth sin is the slave of sin. But God's sovereignty is redemption. He is never so sovereign as there. He is never so absolute as in making freedom. Redemption is not a second best sovereignty, in the room of a best of all for ever lost. It is a deliverance which makes us choose supreme good. And to choose good is to be free; while to be good without choice is neither goodness nor freedom. To choose good is not like choosing evil. It is not immaterial to our freedom what we choose so long as we are choosers. If we choose evil, our very choice enslaves us. But if it be good we choose we acquire ourselves and our freedom. And if we choose good it can only mean that we choose it, not as our ally, but as our sovereign. That is to say, it is choosing God and God's choice. And God's authoritative choice of us is a choice into life and therefore liberty. His sovereign choice of us is choosing us to choose good and enlarge our freedom. The authority of our Redeemer then does not concuss our personality – as an authority would do which was institutional, impersonal, external in that sense, like a church, or even a book. For the authority of our Redeemer over our person is a personal authority. And the redemption itself is the greatest moral act of existence; and therefore it is the freest act. Therefore also it is the act most creative of freedom, and therefore most authoritative for it. Our inchoate personality bows herein to something more personal than itself, and not less, something not less spiritual but more, something in which it comes to itself. The authority as redemptive is a living power, person, and act, revealing, making, giving freedom. It is the holy and complete person, creating personality. It is not a truth, nor an ideal, nor an institution, with their external and aesthetic effect, but it is a personal act, the eternal act of an eternal person, with all the moral effect due to that. As a redeeming authority it says, 'Be free and obey.' It does not say, 'Obey and be free.'

*

Thus, if the classic religion is Christianity, the classic type of Christianity is the experience of moral redemption and not merely ethical reform. Or rather it is the experience of a redeemer. Because it is not the *sense* of the experience that is the main matter, but the *source* of the experience, and its content. It is not our experience we are conscious of – that would be self-conscious piety – but it is Christ. It is not our experience we preach, but the Christ who comes in our experience. We preach not ourselves, but Christ.

*

4.   Christ, I have said, is the source of our experience. Let me, in addressing preachers, dwell on that. The age in which we live shows a singular conjunction in its return to the historic Christ, on the one hand, and its devotion to a subjective type of religion, on the other. Its allegiance is distracted between the historic Christ and the Christian spirit – meaning thereby the Christian style, manner, ethic, or temper – between Christ's person and the Christian principle. At one moment it pursues its quest for a biography of Christ; at another it says that this were but the Christ according to perishable, passing flesh; and it devotes itself therefore to the worship and culture of a perennial principle of which Christ was but the supreme expression. And faith then becomes a devout and altruistic frame of mind, a subjectivism, instead of

an act diffused through life, a life-act of self-committal into Christ's hands and Christ's Act of Grace. Attention is withdrawn from the contents of faith to the mood of faith. If we press for attention to the content of faith we are ruined by the charge of theology. For the mere temper of faith is comparatively indifferent to its theological veritable content. Let us have sweetness and charity at any cost to reality. And its machinery works whether you drop into the slot the legitimate metal or an iron disc.

Well, you can have no adequate Christ without theology when you turn seriously to realize or explain Him. But Christ is not there simply as the theological content of faith. That would not give Him His authority. He is not there simply as the substance of our belief, nor simply as the object of faith. He is there, above all, as the standing *source*, nay, the *creator* of our faith. This is where our sense of communion with Christ differs by a world from any alleged converse with Virgin or Saint. They are at most but the helpers, and not the fountain, of our faith. If our Christian experience tell us anything, it is not about ourselves in the first place, nor about our creed, but about Christ. And it tells us of Him as the Giver of faith, the source, the creator of the experience. That is what is meant by saying that our very faith is the gift of God. It cannot be worked up by us, nor by any one working at us. It is evoked by contact with Christ, who is the gift of God. That is why we must preach Christ, and not about Christ; why we must set the actual constraining Christ before people, and not coax or bully people into decision. If we put the veritable Christ before them He will rouse the faith before they know where they are. Our faith says, then, that He is the Creator of our faith. He is not simply its datum. You do not simply explain your faith by a historic, or a psychological reference to Christ as postulate. You do not use Christ to account for your faith, in a reflective, dialectic, hypothetic way. Your faith is faith in Him as acting, rousing your faith, creating it, and not merely receiving it. In your faith you are more conscious and sure of Him than you are of your faith. For your faith, you well know, may fail Him, but you know still better that He will not fail your faith. And you are more conscious and sure of Him, as the source and cause of your experience, than you are of the experience itself, which you forget to think of. The very apostles never asked us to believe their experience, nor to believe on the ground of it, but to believe with them in Christ. What your experience tells you is that both the frame of mind and its stateable contents were produced, and are produced, by Him and His act. He, as the creator of your faith, is more real to you than the fabric of your faith, or the sense of it. He is not behind your faith in the sense of being a datum which you must assume for it, and which one day you will verify. But he is realized in your faith as its effective cause and permanent reality. That is in the very definition of faith. He is not only objective there, He is initiative. He is known not simply *in* the experience, but as the creator of the experience. He is not simply reached by faith, He brings it to pass. It is the very life and movement of the faith to worship Him as its creator. That *is* faith, it does not flow from faith. Faith does not imply Him, it answers Him. Faith is nothing else than myself believing. And it is Himself I meet. And it is me He saves and re-creates. I do not infer Him, therefore, from my faith. My faith is myself, my moral self, finding Him, and finding that He first found me. It does not simply bear upon Him, it flows from Him. And our Christian experience is not merely an appreciation, or even an appropriation, of Christ, but the life action of Christ in us, and His action as Redeemer appropriating us. We are 'potential Christs' only in this sense – not that we grow into Christs, but that by faith Christ is formed and grows in us, and we live not, but Christ lives in us. And in this capacity He is our one authority, to whom we are not our own. And the preaching of our faith is what I venture to call the prolongation of His action and His Gospel.

Our experience of Christ is thus quite different from our experience of an objective world. Our moral sense of an agent, and that agent a Redeemer, is a different thing from the inference or postulate of an objective world behind sense to account for our impressions. That may be a cause but this is a Creator. When the objective announces itself as a heart and will, which not only chooses, or influences, me, but saves me, then the response of my active will, of myself as a person, is a different thing from the commonsense that instinctively places an object behind passive sensation. The relation of a cause to a sensation is not analogous to the relation of a person to a person. And our relation to Christ is no less different from our attitude to an auxiliary presence, like Saint or Virgin, which aids but does not redeem, and which is not my master because I owe it something much less than my eternal self.

*

These are not metaphysical considerations, however trying they may be to our loose religiosity, but they are positive, practical and experienced religion taking itself in earnest, bringing itself to book, taking a census of itself. I but make explicit in the statement what is implicit in the experienced fact, and present there though all unknown. And its testimony is that Christ does not stand as the crowning, stimulating, releasing instance of the best that is immanent in man. He is not the divine virtuoso, who thoroughly understands his human orchestra, and can bring out of it what none else can. He is not the sublime divine comrade, full of endless cheer, because he has been through it all before us, and has come out on the other side. He is not the herald of God's forgiveness for sins that but hamper our development or soil the surface without tainting our core. But, for all the classic Christian experience, from the New Testament down, He is the Redeemer of our total personality from its radical recalcitrance to God's will, and from its impotence to obey it, even when it has moved to desire it. The natural man is a *nisus* against God, against a God he cannot but feel. And the world's treatment of Christ shows that the higher and better God's will for us is, the more man repudiates, rebels, and fights against it. The authority which is really in question is the will of God. It is personal. And that is why our personality resents it. We yield far more readily to a process or an idea, because it makes no such demand on our self-will as the will of a personal God does. There are many attractions for self-love, vanity, or ambition, in Monism with its vague lack of moral realism and severe imperative. Everything leaves us with a subtle sense of superiority and self-satisfaction but the Will of God, which breaks us to our true peace. And the only means of reducing us to acknowledge the place and practicability of that will is by Redemption. To assert it was useless; to magnify it failed. It had itself to redeem us in Christ, and to bring such a remission of past guilt as should change our total attitude towards self and God, give us a confidence in self despair, bring us into loving communion for life, and confer on us the Gift of Life Eternal.

There is but one Authority therefore for human life – that life being what it is. It is its historic Redeemer, in the one critical and creative moral act of its history. All the amateur philosophandering of the hour is fumbling to escape from a historic, positive, evangelical Christianity, and to preserve before God a remnant of self-respect, self-possession, and self-will. But the prime content both of Christian and human experience is the Saviour, triumphant, not merely after the Cross, but upon it. This cross is the message that makes the preacher. And I have tried to make good what I said at the outset of this lecture, that the preacher is the organ of the only real and final authority for mankind. As to creed in its form and detail, if all men accepted that practical and absolute authority for their moral selves there would be no lack of either an inspiration or a standard for their belief, thought, action, of affection, throughout. An authority absolute in our experienced religion will marshal to its place by an inevitable moral psychology, our theology, philosophy, and politics alike. The King alone can make the Kingdom. The Christ of our faith will organize our life. The power that makes the soul will make the Church. What makes the faith will make and remake the creed. And the Gospel that made the book will bless the book, and give us the freedom in it that it gave us through it. If the Son make us free we shall be free throughout, and free indeed. To be the slave of Christ is to be the master of every fate. And this is as true for Humanity as it is for every soul.

Three

The Preacher and his Church, or Preaching as Worship

The modern neglect of the idea of the Church – The Church as the great preacher in history – The preacher's place in the Church not sacerdotal but sacramental – A sermon as an act involving the real presence of Christ – A preacher's first business is with the Church – His work interpretive, not creative, of Revelation – The preacher as the Church's means of self-expression, and as the mandatory of the great Church for the individual Church and for the world – The corresponding responsibility of the preacher and his need for sober knowledge – Some consequences in regard to (1) the preacher's private views, (2) questions of Biblical Criticism, (3) the demand for short sermons.

I have been complaining (in the close of my first lecture) that Christians do not know their Bible. But even if they did, the preacher would still be at a loss in another way. He has to face the modern man's neglect of the Church no less than of the Bible. He meets impatient reformers who take a tone of superior realism, and coarsely speak of Church life and the edification of believers as a mere 'coddling of the Saints.' He lives in an age when the Kingdom of God engrosses more Christian interest than the Church of Christ, and Christian people are more devoted to the busy effort of getting God's will done on earth than to the deep repose of communion with God's finished will in Christ. It is characteristic of much of the Christian activity of the last half-century that it aims not so much at a Christocracy, where Christ has a household and is master of it, as at a Christolatry – a mere λατρεία of Christ, where he is worshipped mainly through the service of the public. It is needless to point out to the student of the New Testament how flatly this contradicts its genius. And it is useless to urge the point with those who treat the New Testament as archaeology.

Some of us who are greatly in sympathy with these churchless efforts, like the Salvation Army, may yet believe that if they became the ruling type their end would be lost. We may believe that, by the will of Christ, it is only through a real Church, truly Christianized, that Humanity can be served and saved for the Kingdom. We may feel that the love of Humanity could not survive apart from not only our love of Christ, but also from the personal communion with Christ in a Church which feeds that love. The φιλανθρωπία is only possible through the φιλαδελφία. Do good to all men, *but especially to those that are of the household of faith*. Our fellow Christians have claims on us that may precede those of our fellow-men. The Communion of saints is more to God than the enthusiasm of Humanity. The neighbour, in the New Testament, is not the same as the brother.[1] The brotherhood of the New Testament is indeed meant to cover the race at last, but it is the brotherhood of Christian faith and love, not of mankind. The victory which overcomes the world is not humane love but Christian faith. It is won not by the natural heart but by the recreating Cross. The goats in the parable were condemned not for being of the world; for they were a part of the Church; they were not wolves or dogs. But they were false to the love which makes the Church, the love which crowns true faith in Christ with kindness to the needy ones of the sacred flock. The tragedy of the race is too awful and sordid for any salvation that is not constantly fed by the Saviour ever rising through His community from His Cross and grave. Devoted men and women, who go on now by the impulse from centuries of the cross, would break down under

---

[1] This point would richly repay working out in the interests of a true Social Christianity.

the horrible conditions of life where it most needs saving, if the habit of a faith and fraternity bred in the Church alone were to die out.

Many of us realize that. But great numbers of people, even Christian people, do not realize it. They call roughly upon the preacher to spend less time and concern upon maturing the converted, or edifing comfortable believers; and they urge him to go straight to the world – to Society or to the masses, to the natural man, cultured or coarse. It is a large question that opens here. I cannot do much more here than place myself on the side of the sound principle that it is the Church that is the great missionary to Humanity, and not apostles, prophets, and agents here and there. If a preacher is to act on the world he must, as a rule, do it through his Church. And his Church, if it be not built up in its faith, will in due course cease to exist. Many Christians are like Peter. They need several conversions (Luke xxii. 32). And a neglected Church will lose that collective wisdom which alone forms a sound judgment on the difficult moral issues of Society. Practical wisdom speaks only amid the full-grown; and our souls mature only in a living Christian community. Of course, if the preacher so preaches that his Church cultivates the snugness of pious comfort instead of the humble confidence of evangelical faith, then also the Church is in decay, and it will in due time become but a religious circle. But for all that the minister's first duty is to his Church. He must make it a Church that acts on the world – through him indeed, but also otherwise. He is to act at its head, and not in its stead.

In this matter the preacher must refuse to have his duty dictated by those without, who have little or no Church sympathy or responsibility. I have observed that the demand on the preacher to ignore his people and go straight to the world, is largely made by the world, by influences, at least, which voice the verdict of the world rather than the insight of the Church, by religious parliamentarians, eager socialists, or by people who are willing to utilize the Church but quite evade its responsibilities. Some are, like many sections of the press or of literature, voices that stand aloof from the Christian burden and speak often in severe criticism. Or they are that end of the Church which is more moulded by these influences than by Bible or Faith. They speak as if Christ's first obedience had been to human needs and not to God's will. And they are not much entitled to an opinion as to what the proper method of the Gospel is, or the consequent duty of the Church. The genius of the Gospel is after all best understood by the personal believers in the Gospel. And that genius certainly is to go to the world; but it is to go there through the Church, and the Church's Word. It goes through the common action of believing men, who are mature enough in their educated faith to have measured both the world and the Gospel, and to be sure, beyond cavil, that their Gospel is the tragic, desperate world's one hope. They are men who have been evangelized to good ripe purpose. The Gospel of a moral salvation will never seize the world through men who are but thinly sure, or personally neutral, and have only an admiration for Christian ethic. The act of Grace can never be conveyed by men on whom it does not act. As little will it capture the world through men who are converted and no more, who are not built up by the spiritual education and insight of a living Church.

*

The one great preacher in history, I would contend, is the Church. And the first business of the individual preacher is to enable the Church to preach. Yet so that he is not its echo but its living voice, not the echo of its consciousness but the organ of its Gospel. Either he gives the Church utterance, or he gives it insight into the Gospel it utters. He is to preach to the Church from the Gospel so that with the Church he may preach the Gospel to the world. He is so to preach to the Church that he shall also preach *from* the Church. That is to say, he must be a sacrament to the Church, that with the Church he may become a missionary to the world.

You perceive what high ground I take. The preacher's place in the Church is sacramental. It is not sacerdotal, but it is sacramental. He mediates the word to the Church from faith to faith, from his faith to theirs, from one stage of their common faith to another. He does not there speak to un-faith. He is a living element in Christ's hands (broken, if need be) for the distribution and increment of Grace. He is laid on the altar of the Cross. He is not a mere reporter, nor a mere lecturer, on sacred things. He is not merely illuminative, he is augmentive. His work is not to enlighten simply, but to empower and enhance. Men as they leave him should be not only clearer but greater, not only surer but stronger, not only interested, nor only instructed, nor only affected, but fed and increased. He has not merely to show certain things but to get them home, and so home that they change life, either in direction or in scale. It is only an age like the present age of mere knowledge that tends to make preaching the statement of sound and simple truth, interesting but powerless. It is only an age which starves the idea of revelation, by its neglect of the sacramental idea, that reduces preaching to evangelizing alone. It is only an age engrossed with impressions and careless about realities that could regard the preacher's prime work as that of converting the world, to the neglect of transforming the Church. It is only such an age that could think of preaching as something *said* with more or less force, instead of something *done* with more or less power. We spend our polemic upon the Mass, and fitly enough in proper place. But the Catholic form of worship will always have a vast advantage over ours so long as people come away from its central act with the sense of something done in the spirit-world, while they leave ours with the sense only of something said to this present world. In true preaching, as in a true sacrament, more is done than said. And much is well done which is poorly said. Let the preacher but have real doings with God and even with a stammering tongue and a loose syntax he will do much for life which has never yet been done by a finished style. The preacher may go 'lame but lovely', to use Charles Lamb's fine phrase. His word may lack finish if it have hands and feet. He is a man of action. He is among the men who do things. That is why I call him a sacramental man, not merely an expository, declaratory man. In a sacrament is there not something done, not merely shown, not merely recalled? It is no mere memorial. How can you have a mere memorial of One who is always living, always present, always more potent than our act of recall is, always the mover of it? What he once put there might be a memorial, but what he is always putting there is much more than that. It is at least his organ. It is, indeed, his act. It is something practical and not spectacular. A revelation may be but something exhibited, but in a sacrament there is something effected. And the one revelation in the strict sense is the sacrament of the Cross, the Cross as an effective act of redemption. A revelation of redemption is a revelation of something done; and it is only a deed that can reveal a deed. If the preacher reveal redemption he does it by a deed, by a deed in which the Redeemer is the chief actor, by some self-reproduction by Christ, some function of the work of the Cross. He has to reproduce the word of the beginning, the word of the Cross which is really the Cross's own energy, the Cross in action. No true preaching of the Cross can be other than part of the action of the Cross. If a man preach let him preach as the Oracle of God, let him preach as Christ did, whose true pulpit was His Cross, whose Cross made disciples apostles, in whose Cross God first preached to the world, whose preaching from the Cross has done for the world what all His discourses – even His discourses – failed to do.

The preacher, in reproducing this Gospel word of God, prolongs Christ's sacramental work. The real presence of Christ crucified is what makes preaching. It is what makes of a speech a sermon, and of a sermon Gospel. This is the work of God, this continues His work in Christ, that ye should believe in Him whom He hath sent. We do not repeat or imitate that Cross, on the one hand; and we do not merely state it, on the other. It re-enacts itself in us. God's living word reproduces itself as a living act. It is not inert truth, but quick power. All teaching about the truth as it is in Jesus culminates in the preaching of the truth which is Jesus, the self-reproduction of the word of reconciliation in the Cross. Every true sermon, therefore, is a sacramental time and act. It is God's Gospel act reasserting itself in detail. The preacher's word, when he preaches the gospel and not only delivers a sermon, is an effective deed, charged with blessing or with judgment. We eat and drink judgment to ourselves as we hear. It is not an utterance, and not a feat, and not a treat. It is a sacramental act, done together with the community in the name and power of Christ's

redeeming act and our common faith. It has the real presence of
the active Word whose creation it is. If Christ set up the sacrament,
His Gospel set up the sermon. And if He is real in our sacramental
act still, no less is His deed real in our preached word which
prolongs that deed. And it is known to be real by the insight of
faith, however many counterfeits there are, with no insight but
only zeal, and sometimes with nothing but stir.

Our Catholic opponents charge us with having cut ourselves
off from the true Church by having lost the sacramental note. And
I will confess to some fear that it may be true, though in another
sense than theirs. For them the centre of gravity in the sacrament
is in the elements – in the change effected on them, and, through
them, on us. But for us the centre of gravity in any sacrament lies
not in the material element but in the communal act. That is the
site of Christ's real presence. It is not metaphysical but moral and
personal. It is not corporeal but collective. We do not partake of
Christ's body in the form of any substance, however refined and
ethereal. For us the body of Christ means the person of Christ,[2]
and the whole person of Christ is gathered into His saving, atoning
act. And what we perform is an act of communal reunion with
His person in its crucial and complete act. His great act of
Redemption renews itself in His Church. We re-enter by act the
communion not of Christ's substance but, as the apostle says, of
His death – that is, of His saving act. It is in the Church's act that
the real presence behind it takes effect, the real presence of Him
who was above all things the will and deed of God, God's eternal
will and new testament. It is the Great Act of Christ finding itself
anew in the act of the Church.

Now this is really what occurs in another aspect in the Sacrament of the Word, in the Church's preaching of the Gospel. To
be effective our preaching must be sacramental. It must be an act
prolonging the Great Act, mediating it, and conveying it. Its
energy and authority is that of the Great Act. The Gospel spoken
by man is the energizing of the Gospel achieved by God. Its
authority is not that of the preacher's personality nor even of his

---

[2] 'All flesh' = all persons. 'One flesh' = one dual personality.

faith, nay, not even of his message alone, but that of the divine action behind him, whereof he himself is but as it were the sacramental element, and not the sacramental Grace. If our preaching is not more sacramental than the Catholic altar – I do not say more eloquent or more able, but more sacramental – then it is the altar that must prevail over all our No-Popery. For religion *is* sacramental. Where it is not it becomes bald. And the only question is, where the sacrament lies. We place it in the Word of Gospel. *Accedit verbum et fit sacramentum.* Nothing but the Word made Sacrament can make a Sacrament out of elements, and keep it in its proper place. But what a task for our preachers to fulfil!

It is this sacramental note that I fear our preaching often loses. It is this objective power, overruling both the temperament of the preacher and the temper of his time. We speak freely and finely about the Gospel, but does the Gospel come to its own in it all? Does it preach itself through us with power? Are our sermons deeds, 'action-sermons'? They cost much labour, and what do we take by it? They are not without some effect, but are they real causes in the religious life? If they are not, is it because they lack will-power, because they are exercises more than acts, productions more than powers, which aim at impression more than at change? Is it because they lack behind them the volume of a Church's conviction, a Church's faith, the impact of a whole Church's will? Is it because we are more eager to have in our pulpits the manly man than the new man?

*

True preaching presupposes a Church, and not merely a public. And wherever the Church idea fades into that of a mere religious club or association you have a decay in preaching. Wherever the people are but a religious lecture society the pulpit sinks. When it is idolized it always sinks. It does not lose in interest, or in the sympathetic note, but it loses in power, which is the first thing in a Gospel. If the preacher but hold the mirror up to our finer nature the people soon forget what manner of men they are.

But you point out to me that the preaching of the Apostles was addressed to the public, that it was very largely of the gathering, of the missionary, kind. Yes, but even that began and worked from the faith it found. It began with the susceptible among the Jews. At first it was not so much converting for Gentiles as stirring for Jews. It was always with the local synagogue that Paul began when he could, with the votaries of the Old Testament Word; and while he could he worked through them or their proselytes. Jesus Himself began so. His relations beyond Israel grew out of His relations with Israel. It was His earnest dealings with Israel that provoked the Cross, which alone universalized the Gospel. So the preacher has his starting point in the stated and solemn assemblies of the Church, though he does not end there. Through these, he works also on his public who are present, though not of the Church. Then in the end he goes to the world without. But his first duty, if he is a settled pastor, and not a preaching friar, is to his Church. Nothing could be more misplaced, when a young preacher enters on a Church, than a neglect or contempt of its corporate life and creed, or a sudden inversion of these in order that he may get at the world. He has no right to stop the building that he may start elsewhere. He has no right to use his Church merely to provide himself with an outside pulpit. It is together that they must go to the world, he and his Church. What Christ founded was not an order of preachers, nor the institution of preaching, but a community, a Church, whose first charge His preaching should be. It is Church and preacher together that reach the world.

The preaching even to the Church, being in the presence of the public, has of course due regard to their presence. The sermon is not a mere homily to an inner circle. It is gospelling. The Church is addressed in the presence of people who are not of the Church. The preacher indeed renews for believers the reality of the Gospel; but he does it in a large way that concerns also those who have not confessed their faith explicitly. He dwells for the most part on the large and broad features of the Gospel rather than on individual and casuistic situations. He declares the whole counsel of God; that is, the counsel of God as a whole. If he handle individual cases, it is as illustrations of wider truth. He leaves cases of conscience to private intercourse. He is not in the pulpit a director of conscience so much as a shepherd or a seeker of souls. And he may give expression to his own private experiences only in so far as is seemly and useful for the more public aspects of his Gospel. If he is ever beside himself, it must be privately to God; for the people's sake he is sober and sane. Preaching is not simply pastoral visitation on a large scale. Teaching from house to house meant for the apostles not visitation, but ministering to the Church gathered in private houses, as it had then to be.

The first *vis-à-vis* of the preacher, then, is not the world, but the Gospel community. The word is living only in a living community. Its spirit can act outwards only as it grows inwardly and animates a body duly fed and cared for. The preacher has to do this tending. He has to declare the Church's word, and to utter the Church's faith, to itself, in order that he and the Church together may declare them to the world. The Church may use, but cannot rely upon, evangelists who are evangelists and nothing else. When the preacher speaks to believers it is to build them *up as* a Christian community; when he speaks to the world it is to build them *into* a Christian community. And the Church is built up by taking sanctuary, by stopping to realize its own faith, by the repetition of its own old Gospel, by turning aside to see its great sight, by standing still to see the salvation of the Lord.

*

Its own old Gospel! It is not needful that the preacher should be original as a genius is, but only as a true believer is. What he brings to the Church is not something unheard of, and imported from outside, to revolutionize it. He has to offer the Church, in outer form, the word which is always within it, in order that the Church, by that presentation, may become anew what by God's grace it already is. He must be original in the sense that his truth is his own, but not in the sense that it has been no one else's. You must distinguish between novelty and freshness. The preacher is not to be original in the sense of being absolutely *new*, but in the sense of being *fresh*, of appropriating for his own personality, or his own age, what is the standing possession of the Church, and its perennial trust from Christ. He makes discovery *in* the Gospel, not *of* the Gospel. Some preachers spoil their work by an incessant strain after novelty, and a morbid dread of the commonplace. But it was one no less original than Goethe who said the great artist is not afraid of the commonplace. To be unable to freshen the commonplace is to be either dull or bizarre. Yet to be nothing but new is like a raw and treeless house shouting its plaster novelty on a beautiful old brown moor. The artist may treat revelation as discovery. He may create what he finds but as chaos. He finds but power, and he issues it in grace. But it is otherwise with the preacher. It is the converse. He finds revelation in all discovery. He finds to his hand the grace which he has to issue with power. His word is to send home a Word which was articulate from the beginning, 'What we have seen and heard of the Word of life declare we to you.' The artist's grace is not the preacher's. Nor is it true without modification that 'all grace is the grace of God.' The preacher has often been compared with the actor, and often he has succumbed to the actor's temperament, or to his arts. But there is a point of real analogy. The actor creates a part, as the phrase is; but it is only by appropriating a personality which the dramatist really created and put into his hands. And that is what the preacher has to do. He has to work less with his own personality than with the personality provided him in Christ, through Christ's work in him. He has to interpret Christ. Moreover, the actor's is a voice which is forgotten, while the poet's is a voice that remains. So also the preacher's originality is limited. By the very Spirit that moves him he speaks not of himself. He must not expect the actor's vogue. Self-assertion or jealousy are more offensive in him than in the artist. It is enough if he be a living voice; he is not a creative word. He is not the light; he but bears witness to it.

Je ne suis pas la rose, mais j'ai vécu près d'elle.

There is even less room for originality of idea in the pulpit than elsewhere. What is needed is rather spontaneity of power. This is quite in keeping with the conservatism that must always play a part so much greater in the Church than in the State. The preacher not only appeals to the permanent in human nature; he is also the hierophant of a foregone revelation; he is not the organ of a new one. His foundation is laid for him once for all in Christ. His power lies not in initiation, but in appropriation. And his work is largely to assist the Church to a fresh appropriation of its own Gospel. It is not to dazzle us with brand-new aspects even of the Gospel. God forbid that I should say a word to seem to justify the dullness that infects the pulpit. Alas! if our sin crucify Christ afresh, our stupidity buries Him again. But the cure for pulpit dullness is not brilliancy, as in literature. It is reality. It is directness and spontaneity of the common life. The preacher is not there to astonish people with the unheard of; he is there to revive in them what they have long heard. He discovers a mine on the estate. The Church, by the preacher's aid, has to realize its own faith, and take home anew its own Gospel. That which was from the beginning declare we unto you – that fresh old human nature and that fresh old grace of God.

What a strength we all receive from self-expression! How we pine if it is denied! How we die if it is suppressed! It is life to a genius to get out what is in him; it is death to be stifled or neglected. If we can but express what is in us to ourselves it is often sufficient. If we can put pen to paper, paint to canvas, or the hand to clay, it may save us, even if we do not get a market or a vogue. Otherwise it is solitary confinement, or death. The flame dies for want of air. In like manner also our private prayer receives for ourselves a new value when in our solitude we utter it aloud. The aspiration gains mightily from the spoken word. The very effort to shape it in words adds to its depth, precision, confidence, and effect. It is well to sigh our prayers, but it is better to utter them. With the heart man believeth unto righteousness, but with the mouth we confess unto salvation. Righteousness is well, but it must be established and confirmed as salvation. Just so the preacher's address to the Church is really the Church preaching to the Church. It is the Church expressing itself to itself. The Church is feeling its own strength, and by the feeling it is growing in godly self-confidence, and in power to say to the world what the whole world resists.

The Christian preacher is no prophet sent to the public till he is a voice of the Church to the Church. He is but a part of the Church, yet he speaks to the whole. We tend our body with the hand, which is but an organ of the body. So the preacher tends the Church as a part of it, moved in his act, not by the part's life, but by its share in the life of the whole. He is over against the Church only as the organ is over against the organism. It is the body that turns the hand upon itself. The Church in the preacher becomes explicitly conscious of itself. Its latent faith becomes patent. It knows how much greater it is than it thought. It is amazed with itself. It realizes what a mighty matter its faith is. The flush rises to the face of its love. The gleam shines in its eye of its hope. And it *must* reach this self-expression. It is not merely the better for it. The expression is part of the reality. The form is part of the life. It is part of the joint action of the Word which is the Church's life, and of the faith that meets that Word. The sermon is an essential part of the worship.

*

The preacher, therefore, starts with a Church of brethren that agree with him and that believe with him; and in its power he goes to a world that does neither. What he has to do is not to exhibit himself to the Church, nor to force himself on it. He offers himself to it in the like faith, as a part of their common offering by the Eternal Spirit to God. And the stronger the Church is, so much the more it needs preaching, and the more it desires preaching, preaching not only *through* it but *to* it; just as genius demands self-expression in passionate proportion to its power. Only note that while the genius demands expression for itself the Church demands it for its Gospel. It demands expression for its positive, objective faith and not its consciousness; its message and not merely its experience. The Eternal Word that always makes the Church has to speak to a Church whose experience is largely below the level of the faith of that Word. What makes the Church is not Christ as its founder but Christ as its tenant, as its life, as its power, the Christ living in the faith of its members in general, and of its ministers in particular. But it is a Christ that only partially comes to His own in the Church's actual experience. The faith within the Church has to speak to its half-faith, its bewildered faith, its struggling, or even its decaying faith.

What is done in preaching to the Church, therefore, is not to set out its own consciousness. At any rate, it is not the consciousness of the Church at any one stage – even the present. It is the Spirit speaking to the Churches. It is the past Church speaking to the present, the whole Church to the single Church, the ripe Church to the unripe, the faithful Church to the faltering Church, the ideal Church to the actual, the unseen to the seen. It is the great, common, universal faith addressing the faith of the local community. And, in so far as the preacher is the voice of the Church, he is the voice, not of his own Church, but of the Great Church that envelops his own. The preacher reflects the faith of the great true Church, but neither the faith nor the views of those around him. He is not giving expression to the average opinion of his congregation, or his denomination. The preacher is the mandatory of the great Church, which any congregation or sect but represents here and now. And what he has to do is to nourish that single and accidental community with the essence of the Church universal; that the members of the Church may rise to the level of the Church, to its true nature, its ideal holiness as the called of God. When he addresses the Church it is the ideal Church addressing the actual, the upper Church the lower, the Church of the ages appealing to the Church of the hour, the Church universal to the Church on the spot. The inner Church addresses the outer, that the outer may realize itself anew, and apprehend that for which Christ apprehended it. Nothing in the service goes to the root of the Gospel (and, therefore, of the Church) like preaching. And this makes preaching the chief part of our evangelical ritual, the part which gives the law to all worship, since the message is what stirs worship and makes it possible. Our chief praise is thanksgiving for the Gospel. And our prayer is Christian only in the name of the Gospel. Preaching is 'the organized Hallelujah of an ordered community.'

But when the preacher turns from the Church of which he is pastor to the world to which he is missionary he must speak in the name of the whole Church as a unity. Hence the slowness of missions while the other parts of the Church fight and devour each other. Hence, too, the unifying reaction of missions on the Church. Hence, also, the missionary must preach in chief those great things which are the objective power of the Church, and not a subjective or merely experimental piety. Let him preach the

Gospel, and leave it to make its own experience in the new races, by its own creative power. Their form of experience may be very different from what has grown up in the train of our civilization, with the mentality of the West. No preacher (I have said) is only the representative of the Church's consciousness; and the missionary preacher is so least of all. He is the organ of the Gospel that created the Church's consciousness at the first, and has developed it all along.

Therefore, it is not the Church that he or any evangelist preaches. Wherever the Church is preached, the Gospel comes short. We have then Catholicism, and we cease in due course to have the Gospel at all. The preacher has not even his commission from the Church, but only a licence at most, only his opportunity. The Church supplies not his authority but his pulpit. He has his commission from God, from the Church only his permission. He is an officer, not of the Church, but of the Word that the Church has in stewardship. And all the Church has to do is to discover if he has the commission, by the wisest, and even severest, tests, by a prolonged training, perhaps, which is also a probation. But it is a commission the Church cannot bestow. It can only discern. It cannot convey the apostolic spirit, it can but wait upon it. The Church has no rights in the matter of ordination, and can confer none. It has but a duty to recognize the spirit's movement and the purity of the Word, and to facilitate the Gospel in the most effectual way.

*

Preaching, then, is part of the cultus. That is the Protestant idea. To treat it as a gratuitous adjunct to the service is Catholic. To regard it as the mere exposition of a minister's views is neither Protestant nor Catholic. It is not even Christian. It is a rationalistic way of regarding the matter, and it causes the sermon to differ by no whit from a lecture more or less popular, or from a manifesto, more or less interesting, of the preacher's personality. The sermon has always been regarded as an integral part of the service by a Protestantism which knew what it was about. It is the Word of the Gospel returning in confession to God who gave it. It is addressed to men indeed, but in truth it is offered to God.

Addressed to men but offered to God – that is the true genius of preaching. Christ sees in it joyfully the travail and the trophy of His soul. Like all the rest of the worship, it is the fruit of the Gospel. May I call it again 'the organized Hallelujah' of intelligent faith.

In so viewing preaching, Protestantism has reverted to the New Testament idea, and to the first Church. There more attention (to say the least) is given to the proclamation of the Word, than to the worship. And quite as much as is given to the Sacraments – which were sometimes outside the personal concern of an apostle like Paul. He thanks God he had baptised but two in one Church. Our Lord, we are told, baptised not. On the other hand, the apostles could not but preach. It was an essential part of their grateful, worshipful response to the Word of Grace which had found them. It was a creation of that Word. 'It pleased God to reveal His Son in me that I might preach Him among the Gentiles.' That is to say, the preacher's commission was given in the very nature of the revelation which made him a Christian. The revelation by its very meaning left him no choice. The self-same act of the cross which made him worship Christ, made him preach Christ as part of the worship. And by a consequence, that hearing of the preaching was also part of their worship to whom he spoke. Real preaching then was bound up with the worship of Christ, with a faith that could not but worship. The testimony to men was as truly an acknowledgement to God of His gracious Gospel as was any express act of confession or praise. And the men who heard had a part and a responsibility as great as the preacher's. The confession of sin, which all call a part of worship, did not mean so much as the confession of holiness in a Saviour – which is the preaching of the Church.

Further, if preaching is a main part of the Church's worship, it is a part especially of the minister's own personal worship. It is for him an act of worship, in a far more intimate and real sense than anything he may do in the serving of tables, the organizing of work, or the carrying of help. Nothing tends more to lower the quality of preaching than a loss of this sense on the preacher's part. Nothing will destroy public respect for it so fast as the preacher's own loss of respect for it. And that respect is lost when, for the preacher himself, the preaching is more speech than action, when he feels its practical value to be more in what it leads to, than in what it is. If great art is praise, true preaching is so no less. Much preaching that is not popular is still true worship.

Preaching is thus the creation of the Gospel, and not our mere tribute to the Gospel; therefore, it has one great note which should appeal to the modern mind – the note of inevitability. It was the inevitable word, so prized now by the connoisseurs of style – the authentic Word. It was the triumph of the Gospel genius, the royalty of the Gospel way. It came forth with the ease, aptness and weight wielded by full and conscious power. However verbose preachers may be, preaching is not the verbosity of a Word whose truer nature would have been reticent like a ritual sacrament. The preacher may be illogical, but preaching is there by a spiritual logic, and a psychological necessity, in the Gospel itself. It was the Church's great spontaneous confession of its faith both to itself and the world. There was something almost lyric about it – as the great creeds were at first hymns. They expressed not merely belief, but triumphant irrepressible belief. Nay, it was more. It was the belief of men more than conquerors, more than triumphant. They were the harbingers and hierophants of the world's foregone but final conquest. They were more than victorious, they were redeemed. They were victorious only because redeemed. They could not be parted from Christ's love by any tribulation, anguish, peril, or sword (Rom. viii. 35–9) – not because they had overcome these things, even in His name, but because He had, already and in advance, put them under His feet for good and all, for Himself and His people. They were trophies of Christ's conquest more than victors in their own. And it was more joy to be a trophy and captive in the triumphal procession of Christ than to sit with Cæsar in his car. What made them preach was a victory gained, not by them, but in them and over them. And they sang their joy in preachings that captured the world for which they were themselves also captured in Christ.

Preaching then is the Church confessing its faith. And it is as surely a part of the service as the reciting of a creed could be. It is another aspect of the same response to the Word given. It is less organized, but no less collective than the great creeds. And in the Churches where there are no formal creeds it takes their place. The place of the sermon in the more democratic and non-Catholic Churches is due, in part, to the absence in their ritual of a recited creed. It is all that some of them, like the Congregationalists, have for a creed.

*

This fact, of course, lays a corresponding responsibility on the preacher; though it is a responsibility that is sometimes ignored or resented by preachers, who claim for themselves a freedom that properly belongs only to the Church. For the minister of a Church in its pulpit is not a free lance (I say in *its* pulpit, not in *his*). He is not a mere preaching friar, a vagrant Evangelist, gathering his audience in streets and lanes, hedges and highways, as he can find them. He enters on a position of trust which he did not create. He is licensed to it when he is called by its custodian, the Church. Any call to a minister is, in substance, a licence conferred on him, however much in form it may be a petition addressed to him. He stands on a platform, an institution, which is provided for him, and he owes practical regard to the Church that provides it. He bespeaks men's attention, not in virtue of his personal quality merely, but in virtue of a charge and Gospel, given both to minister and Church, which both must serve. He is not free to vend in his pulpit the extravagances of an eccentric individualism, nor the thin heresies of the amateur. He is not entitled to ask men to hear with respectful silence the freaks of mere mother wit or the guesses of an untutored intelligence. When a man is entrusted with the pastoral care of a Church from its pulpit he accepts, along with the normality of Scripture, the obligations, limitations and reserves of the pastoral commission. He that sweareth by the altar sweareth also by that which is upon the altar: and he abuses his position if he simply unload upon his charge certain startling views by way of relief to his own egoist conscience. To the older members of the flock that can be upon occasion the heartlessness of intellectualism, or the cruelty of youth. A man speaking his genuine experience in the experimental region of religion is always worth listening to.

But if a man takes leave to assault the great doctrines, or to raise the great questions as if they had occurred to him first, if he knows nothing of what has been done in them by experts, or where thinkers have left the question, he is out of place. No man is entitled to discuss theology in public who has not studied theology. It is like any other weighty subject. Still more is this requisite if he set to challenge and reform theology. He ought to be a trained theologian. He need not have been at college, if he show sufficient evidence of real study. To read theology is not enough. Reading may be no more than the browsing of a mental epicure at will. The subject must be studied, and studied at fountain heads. No man should ask for a public hearing on a theological question unless he has mastered his New Testament at first hand, together with one or more of the great classics which are landmarks and points of new departure for theological thought. If we had more honest work behind our theological talk we should not, for instance, have popular clap-trap like the statement that the Athanasian Creed is a jumble of Greek metaphysics, when its whole substance registers the vital effort of the Church to overcome metaphysic in the interest of a historic redemption; as it were to be wished the victims of metaphysic would do who essay to reform our creed to-day. But it takes a mastery of metaphysic to escape from metaphysic. And it takes a real knowledge of theology to lead theology on its broadening way, and at the same time preserve the depth and intimacy of its Gospel.

A man is not invited into a pulpit just to say how things strike him at his angle, any more than he is expected to lay bare to the public the private recesses of his soul. Nor is it the preacher's first duty to be up-to-date, to be in the van of tentative thought. He can do his work well without the very newest machinery. The professor should know the last thing written, but the preacher need not. If he is young, and has not been well trained in his subject, perhaps better not. He is there to declare the eternal, which is always in the van, equally present, equally real for every soul, everlasting, final, insuperable for every age. He is not in the pulpit, primarily, as the place where he can get most scope for his own individuality, and most freedom for his own idiosyncrasy. He is there, as the servant both of the Word and the Church, to do a certain work, to declare a certain message, to discharge a certain trust. He is not in the pulpit as the roomiest place he has found to enable him to be himself, and develop his genius. Some young preachers are more concerned about their own freedom than their people's service. They are prone to think they must get freedom to develop their individuality before they have any positive idea what they are to do. But you cannot develop your individuality except obliviously, in the doing of some definite objective thing. Without that you are taking yourself too seriously. You are but 'pottering at the pyramid of your own existence,' or modelling yourself in clay. No, you 'are taken into Heaven backwards.' You must grow in the doing of some definite thing, to learn which thing and the handling of it your individuality ought to go to a very severe school. Your duty is not to be yourself. 'To thyself be true' is not a Christian precept. It is automatic for the Christian man, whose one concern is to be true to Christ. The first thing due even to yourself is to go to school. Learn. Find a master. Let the past and its trust make you yourself! The first duty of a man is not to assert a freedom, nor to use a private judgment, but to find an absolute master. There is put into the preacher's hands a trust, a message, which is not merely like the artist's, the subjective trust of genius with a responsibility as to how it shall be used; but it is the objective trust of the Gospel, of a positive word which he must deliver however it may affect his self-culture. Any genius that he has can but enrich his Gospel. He is given the word of a foregone and final revelation – not its idea but its word, not its surmise but its arrival, not its conception but its visitation, not its intuition but its revelation, something which is his because of its insight into him rather than his insight into it, something wherein he is known rather than knows, something finally done which is the root of all our best doing. The Kingdom of God is among us, and has long been among us. Such is the standing message of the Church, and it is at once the source and the limit of her theological liberty. It is the Gospel of the achieved more than the call to achieve. It bids us not to make, so much as to rest in something we find made. It teaches us that all good we do is but the energy in us of the best already done. It is an *opus operatum*. That is the standing word of Gospel. And the business of each preacher in charge of a flock is to translate to his small Church this message and content of the great Church, that he may integrate the small Church into the great, and that he and it together may swell the transmission of the Word to the world. That is the true Catholicism, the universalizing of the universal Word. That is the principle which makes a Church out of a sect or conventicle, and puts a preacher in the true apostolic succession. The true succession is the true inheritance of the eternal Word, and not the due concatenation of its agents. The great apostolate is one, not in the heredity of a historic line but in the solidarity of a historic Gospel, not in a continuous stream but in an organic Word.

*

We have thus some guide to answering the question whether a minister's first duty is to his Church or to the world. If we must choose, in what is perhaps a false dilemma, it is to his Church. The duty to the world is a joint duty of preacher and Church. Churches are always forgetting this, and reducing preachers to priests in spite of themselves by making everything turn on the preacher. It is part of the price that we pay for popular preachers that we fall into a way of thinking as if, when a gifted speaker appears, the main duty of the Church is to give him his platform, or even his pedestal, and then stand out of his way. Hence manifold mischief to preacher, Church, and Gospel; the cossetting of the preacher's selfwill, the elimination of the communal will, the deflection of the will of God. The task of the great preacher is at bottom the task of the smaller preacher who can but be faithful. It is to act upon the world through his Church and not merely *from* his Church. His Church is not the arena for his individualism (far less the pedestal of his vanity) but its school. A man who is truly, through the Word, the agent of the great Church will never become the mere exploiter of his own Church. The captive of the Gospel will never lord it in the Lord's house, nor simply use the flock he is there to feed.

*

There are some consequences that follow, if we grasp the great principle that the sermon is an essential part of the worship.

1. The minister (as I have said) may not use the pulpit merely for the exposition of his own views. Any views of his must be given as such, and be used, directly or indirectly, for the ruling purpose of the message from God. In proportion as he puts in the front views and opinions of his he may expect public abstention, or contradiction, from those who have differing views. Farther, the minister may not sacrifice the pulpit to mere instruction, mere lectures, or intellectual or aesthetic treats. Let the lecture room or the Bible Class be used for that. Of course I speak of such habitual use of the pulpit, not of exceptional occasions.

2. As a corollary of this it is the preacher's duty, in most cases, to touch questions of Bible criticism only in so far as they clear the ground for a real and positive Gospel. The structure of the Bible may be discussed in the pulpit only in so far as it affects the history of revelation, and not merely of religion. The popular religion of Israel is one thing, and the divine revelation that gradually emerged through it and subdued it is another. And though it is no part of the preacher's work to treat of the religion of Israel for its own sake, yet it is his to disentangle those parts of the Old Testament where the revelation of God is forcing its way through the popular religion, in ways which even the writers themselves but dimly understood. Still the preacher is not an academic; he is an evangelist. The minister's conscience is not scientific but pastoral. For this purpose he must often exercise a discreet reserve as to scientific truth in the interest of higher truth, or truth on the whole.

> Although we hold the doctrine sound
> For life outliving hearts of youth,
> Yet who would preach it as a truth
> To those that eddy round and round?

The thinker and the scholar have a freedom, and even a duty, which do not belong to the pastor who has a cure of souls. The savant may owe to the public, or the lecturer to his class, what the preacher does not owe to his charge. To rend a Church on a point of speculative theology mostly argues some tactlessness on the preacher's part, or a misconception of his office, or an egoistic sense of duty. There may be many points on which he should keep silence, partly because he or his people are not ready, partly because these are points which do not directly concern his Gospel. He should not allow his hand to be forced, especially by outsiders. No outsider has his responsibility, nor, indeed, any insider either. He should be the best judge about his own reserves as pastor. And he should not force the convictions of his people. Of course if the first charge on him were the integrity of pure doctrine (as was once thought) if he were one of the theologians he derides, then perhaps he ought to treat his Church as a class and at once indicate his departure from tradition. But his charge is to educate those people not in a correct theology, old or new, but in a mighty Gospel. He is a minister of the Gospel, not a professor of scientific theology. 'There are truths we must say to all, and truths we should say to some; and there are truths we can only tell to those who ask.' It is not the preacher's duty to tell everything he knows about the Bible; but it is his duty to tell everything he knows about the Gospel, and, in this reduced yet enlarged sense, in this plenary but not exhaustive sense, to declare the whole counsel of God. He has to give the Gospel its divine place in knowledge, and not knowledge a supreme place in the Gospel. The whole counsel of God, not the whole results of scholarship, is the preacher's burthen – these last only when they remove obstacles from the Gospel, or enrich its message. It is no business of the preacher, at the stated occasions of worship, to enlarge on the stratification of the Pentateuch, or the postexilian origin of the Psalms; unless he is engaged in opening larger sweeps of God's method of revelation, or expounding Christ's true relation to the Old Testament, as its fulfilment, and not its professor.

3. We discourage the position of those who are impatient of the sermon, who walk out when it comes on, or who paralyse preachers by a demand for brevity before everything else. I speak of those who do so on the ground that they go to Church to worship God. I should like to say here that in my humble judgment

the demand for short sermons on the part of Christian people is one of the most fatal influences at work to destroy preaching in the true sense of the word. How can a man preach if he feel throughout that the people set a watch upon his lips? Brevity may be the soul of wit, but the preacher is not a wit. And those who say they want little sermon because they are there to worship God and not hear man, have not grasped the rudiments of the first idea of Christian worship. They but represent the indifference of the natural man, his Catholicism. They but swell that Protestant Catholicism which is preparing so rich a harvest in due course for Rome. For remember that Catholicism is the Christianity of the natural man. It is easy with human nature. You cannot quench the preacher without kindling the priest. If the preachers are not satisfactory, let the Church take steps to make them so. If they bore the people, let the people not be too patient. But let us not go wrong as to what preaching is for the Gospel, or for any Church that is in earnest with the Gospel. A Christianity of short sermons is a Christianity of short fibre.

Four

The Preacher and the Age

The relation of the preacher's message to the mental vernacular of his time – Two observations thereon: (1) In its greatest ages the Church marked by an attitude to the world of detachment; the example of Gnosticism; (2) our creed to be minimal and our faith maximal, belief to be reduced and emphasis redistributed – The need of forcing a crisis of the will – The old Theologies to be interpreted completely and with sympathy – Reduction not Repristination necessary – The casualness of the Public – The value of pessimism as a corrective – Ibsen – The danger of a false humanism – The severity of Christ.

The question raised in the last lecture as to the preacher's attitude to the world is worth closer definition. Is his mental attitude to the world, to all that passes as civilization, or culture, to be one of isolation or accommodation? I am not asking now whether he should know the results of contemporary culture, nor how far, if he knows them, he ought to press them on his own people. I am asking whether he should do much or little in construing his own conception of his message in the mental vernacular of his time. It is not here a question of pedagogy with his charge, but of his theology and his truth. It is a larger question than concerns his procedure or style with the public. It concerns his Gospel and its intellectual content. Shall he become here all things to all men; shall he use here the opportunism that he may freely use in practical affairs, where he has to work *with* other men rather than *upon* them? Or shall he, at the other extreme, deliver a message manifestly, and almost aggressively, independent of the fashions of thought, with small concern whether men hear or forbear?

Shall he use the old categories and terms of the Gospel like redemption (always, of course, in a living way, and not as a dead orthodoxy)? Or shall he be eager to discard such terms as being 'the language of Canaan'; and shall he seize on the latest thing in thought or action, and force his message into wholly modern terms? Shall he discard redemption and take up with evolution? Shall he reject atonement and speak only of sacrifice? Shall he cease to think evangelically if only he think ethically? Shall he give up speaking of faith, and talk of spirituality? Shall he forswear revelation for the God-consciousness, and drop from his vocabulary a word like incarnation to make room for immanence? Shall he be silent about the Church in order to speak of the Kingdom of God, or say little even about that, that he may not repel those who will only hear about the brotherhood of man? Should he give up alluding to the bond of the Spirit, and dilate upon sympathies and affinities? That is to say, are the intelligible terms of his message to be given it chiefly by current thought? Is its substance so poor, its matter so impotent, that it has been unable to frame a permanent terminology for its own spiritual experiences, and is forced to borrow and adapt the current language of the cultured natural man? Is the preacher's terminology to have regard only to men's business and their bosoms, to the vocabulary of commerce and affection? And must he cast off the specific language created and consecrated by classic Christian experience because it is theological and non-natural? If he keep any theology, is it to be adjusted entirely to modern thought without any call made on modern thought to adjust itself to a theology given in the Gospel and peculiar or inevitable to it? Is his mind, for all its heavenly birth and lineage, to be entirely naturalized in the better quarters of the world? Or is he to be palpably less at home in the world's ways of thinking and writing, a stranger and a sojourner as all his fathers were?

An acute form of the difficulty occurs when a preacher is faced by the question, Shall I preach to the modern age, whether by my theology or my methods, at the cost of rending my church? Well, with a man of real culture, sympathy, and good sense (I have said), probably the dilemma need not occur. In very many cases where such crises arise they arise from the preacher's lack of sympathy and judgment. Either that, or he lacks a sense of responsibility for anything but what I have called the unloading of his own egoistic conscience. But if the crisis do come, if a headlong policy of vigour and rigour call for a decisive answer, it would be this, in my humble judgment. A man whose action on public affairs promises to rend his church should resign his church, and seek one that will go solidly with him. I know it is a very difficult question. But the church is not there with political or social reform for its prime object. And when a Free Church minister has to fight his people for his position it is time to leave it. Victory is mostly sterile for him; and defeat may be heartbreaking, without the dignity of the Cross. His church is not there, as I have said, to be his platform merely, but the body of which he is the head; he must animate it with his principles and not dissolve it. The brain must not quarrel with the nerves. He is the church's organ rather than the church his. His first duty is to the church. His whole manhood goes primarily to the church. If his duty to the public threatens to destroy his church, then he should release himself and his church likewise. The order of obligation for a preacher is first to the Gospel (in its nature, not its particular applications), second to his church, third to the great Church, and then to the public. He is not first a prophet of social righteousness but an apostle of the Gospel. He is not merely an agent of the ethical kingdom. Every Christian is that. But when he adopts the ministry as a life work, he adopts what is an office of the Church. He becomes something else than a prophet, and something more. He represents the Spirit which abides like a dove and does not swoop like an eagle. He accepts the conditions of a stable society, its position, its aid, and, along with these, responsibility to it. His place is not a prerogative of his own. It is not a right that belongs to him by his mere subjective sense of a Charisma. He is not a wandering seer.

*

In all such cases the line a man may take will be much affected by his idiosyncrasy. And I do not say that it ought not, so long as we understand that idiosyncrasy is not the decisive thing. It is a question here of the principles that prescribe the general attitude of the Church to the world, not of a man to his circle. For these large principles prescribe the preacher's attitude, in so far as he is more than the victim of his temperament and becomes the servant of the Gospel in a church. And from this point of view there are two things to be said in answer to the question with which I set out.

1.   First, in the great and crucial ages of the Church she saved herself and her word by taking the attitude of detachment – not to say intolerance – rather than accommodation. She faced the world with a boon but also a demand. Is there no intolerance in the Johannine writings? She served a world she would not obey, in the name of a mastery it could neither confer nor withstand. She did not lead the world, nor echo it; she confronted it. If she borrowed the thought, the organization, the methods of the world, she did so voluntarily. And she only used them as a calculus. She was but requisitioning the ladders by which she escaped from the world, and rose to its command. She used the alloy not to debase the metal, but to make it workable, to make it a currency.

The mention of the Johannine writings reminds us that the first and greatest of these crises was the conflict with paganism, and especially with gnosticism in the early centuries. And what was it that then saved the Church for the future and for the Gospel? It was not the apologists nor the line they took in presenting Christianity as the noblest of all the cultures, the most comprehensive of all the philosophies, the most efficient of all the ethics, the consummation of prophecies immanent in pagan humanity, and the apotheosis of all its latent powers. That was a line that developed the gnostic tendency, as it is the leading line in the gnosticism of to-day. But the situation was saved by the other line, by Athanasius, who developed everything that distinguished his position out of the principle of the experienced redemption of a ruined world. To express this unutterable reality he had to do as Paul did, to capture and transform the speculation of the day; and he had even to coin a new metaphysic. He converted the past more

because they are outside the literature by which classicism has become known to us for the most part. It represented that element in paganism which was not contributed by cultured Greece so much as held by Hellenism in common with other paganisms, held by it outside the literary class, and chiefly developed in the dreamy East. It stood for the deep human passion to be redeemed; though it did not realize, as historic Christianity alone did, the moral depth of the need, or the holy passion in God to redeem. The redemption which was the passion of Asia was a much more intense though a much less positive and effectual thing than that demanded by the more free and ethical West. It moved among spiritual processes rather than moral and historic acts. And it steamed up, like slow and spectral vapours, from the cauldron of the prisoned, seething world, rather than issued in the effectual shape of a hero and a deed.

Now, had this early Gnosticism had its way it would have stifled the young Church in its cradle; whereas medieval Aristotelianism only infected a Church whose evangelical constitution was shown by the Reformation to be now too mature to succumb. In the early period the very affinities of Gnosticism with the redemptive idea in Christianity increased the danger by their plausible advances to the burdened soul's demand; and they gave the gnostics a huge advantage over the whiggish apologists and their liberal Christianity, which ignored that idea. But the Gospel triumphed, and, thanks to Athanasius, by the middle ages the evangelical idea had become so imbedded in the constitution of the Church that Aristotle could not smother it, and it leaped to life in the Reformation. Doubtless the Reformation issue was one of life and death. But not so profoundly as in the gnostic strife. It was between two sections of the Church; it was not between the Church and the world, the Church and civilization, the Church and humanity, God and man. Everybody in civilization then belonged to the Church. And even after the Reformation it was only a question of which Church a man belonged to; it was not whether he belonged to Church or world, whether he was Christian or pagan.

But to-day it is the latter question that we ask. The bulk of the civilized public of Europe, practically, either belong to no Church, or they are indifferent to which Church they belong. And most culture is rather with the world than with the Gospel. We are thus in the most critical time since the first centuries. And, if history teach us rightly, does it not teach us that the main policy of the Church must be the same now as then? It must be self-sufficient, autonomous, independent. I say the main policy, for the accommodations to modern knowledge and modern criticism must be many. But amid all these adjustments to the world of natural and rational culture, the Church must in principle be detached. With all her liberalism she must be positive. She must insist on the autonomy of faith in the matter of knowledge and certainty. She must descend on the world out of heaven from God. Her note is the supernatural note which distinguishes incarnation from immanence, redemption from evolution, the Kingdom of God from mere spiritual progress, and the Holy Spirit from mere spiritual process. She must never be opportunist at the cost of being evangelical, liberal at the cost of being positive, too broad for the Cross's narrow way. And she must produce that impression on the whole, that impression of detachment from the world and of descent on it. The minister may be licensed by the Church, but the Church, as Christ's great minister for the kingdom on earth, depends on no licence either from the schools, the world, or the state. The Saviour of the world was not made or moulded by the world; and the world knew, and still knows in Him a presence that must be either obeyed or destroyed. He always looked down on the world He had to save. He always viewed it from God's side, and in God's interest. He always stood for God against the men he would save. It was indeed with divine pity he looked down, and not contempt; but it *was* with pity, it was not with co-equal love. It was not the love of give and take, but the mercy which gives all and claims all.

And this must be the note of the pulpit. It must of course be liberal. That is to say, it must not be obscurantist. It must give knowledge its place and modify accordingly. It must leave to the region of knowledge much that used to be held part of saving faith. If you are not humane, as civilization understands it, you do not speak the language of the time. You must wear the intelligible forms of living faith, the fair humanities of kind religion. But still more must you be divine and positive, else you do not declare the Word of God which is Humanity's one hope. We do not approach men in order to interpret them to themselves, as a genius might do, but to interpret to them God in Christ. Christ is ours not because He represents our best but because He redeems our worst, not because He set a seal to our manhood but because He saves it, not because He elicits it but because He gives it. You must not tell men that the way to understand God is to understand the human heart, nor that the way to be true to men is to be true to their own selves. We are not true to men till we are in Christian relation to them; and that comes from being true to Christ and to the Word of His grace. As angels of the Churches you must descend on men. That must always be the ruling note of your word and work. If you wash His disciples' feet it must be not merely as a poor serving brother but with the kind dignity of the agent and apostle of Christ. And you must always so speak as the oracles of God, as the ambassadors of Christ, and king's messengers. You must always tell men that they can never be right with each other except as they are right with God in Christ and in the atoning Cross of Christ.

*

2. So the second thing to be said is this. If we accommodate ourselves to the world in one way we must be exigent in another. Our demands must never be submerged by our sympathies. The more kind we are, the more lofty we must be with our kindness. The goodness of God must never minish the severity of God. His gifts of love must never obscure the prior claim of holiness. His grace must never abolish His judgment. Fatherhood is not the fatherhood of Christ's God if it erase from our faith the necessity of an Atonement offered not to man alone but to God. The love by which God's offspring are called sons of God is not His kindness to His creatures, but it is a special manner of love bestowed upon us with the gift of Christ and not with the gift of existence, by a Redeemer and not a Creator (I John i. 3).

But the particular bearing of the principle in my mind at the moment is this. – If we so accommodate ourselves to the world as to reduce the bulk of our *creed* we must insist on more serious attention, more concentration, by the world upon the quality of our *faith*. Reduction of belief on our part must be balanced by concentration of faith on the part of the public.

Reduce the burden of belief we must. The old orthodoxy laid on men's believing power more than it could carry. That orthodoxy, that Protestant scholasticism, was in its way thorough. It went in its way as Ibsen's Brand did in his – it was all or nothing. It moved altogether if it moved at all. It attracted the all-or-nothing spirits, whose tendency was to move like a prairie fire, covering the whole area but spreading only in one plane. It was comprehensive and acute rather than profound and subtle. It threatened to organize the faith clean out of belief. It seemed to sacrifice colour to drawing, and life to form. It had no atmosphere, no flexibility. And, great as it could be, it came at last to be more vast than great. It brought to men more to carry than power to carry it. And like its predecessor, the medieval scholasticism, it was disintegrated by its own subtlety; it crumbled through its own acuteness; it died of its own insatiable dialectic; and fell of its own thin and ambitious imperialism.

This appeared conspicuously in regard to the claims made for the Bible as replacing the Church. 'The whole Bible or none,' it was said. 'Take but a stone away and the edifice subsides.' This came of the Bible having been reduced to a fabric instead of an organism. And how many sceptics that course has made! How many Pharisees! How many spiritual tragedies! If I were a Secularist I would not touch by assault the doctrine of plenary verbal inspiration and inerrancy. I should let it work freely as one of my best adjutants. But this all-or-nothingness applied also to the whole system of Protestant scholasticism. Dislodge but a pillar of the porch and the house fell in. Lop a bough and the tree died. Train a branch another way and it pined.

The habit of mind, I say, was in its way thorough. And, indeed, I often wish we had the like thoroughness of design and excellence of building on the foundations of the present. But we now build with a sense that systems do not last, and so we do not build well. We build but to house a generation or a couple. The systems we frame are all revisable, all on lease; and the framers naturally leave much to the tenants and inspectors of the future. It was otherwise with our fathers. *In aeternum pinxerunt.* The systems they built aimed at finality. Every part was of the same steel. The nuts and screws were of the eternal. *Nuance*, evolution was an unheard-of thing. So that when the end came it came for many as it has been immortally symbolized for us by the American spirit of comedy in Olive Wendell Holmes's *The One Hoss Shay*. That must be the end of every system which aims at being universal and final.

But in such systems we have ceased to believe. Finality is but in God and His act. With a final system we should have no God. The finality would then not be a living soul but a scheme. We believe, on the one hand, that scientific theology lives the growing life of every other science, in respect of its element of knowledge or statement. And we believe, on the other hand, that salvation is not a matter of scientific theology, but of personal relation to the Gospel. And the truth of the Gospel is portable in proportion to its power. 'Few things are needful – or one.' The one principle of holy grace carries in it all Christ and Christianity. A few mighty cohesive truths which capture, fire, and mould the whole soul are worth much more than a correct conspectus of the total area of divine knowledge – and especially for the preacher. A minimal creed, an ample science, a maximal faith – that is our aim.

*

There is one misunderstanding I should like to avert. When I speak of a reduction of belief I do not mean an attenuation of belief. I do not mean to discredit an ample theology. I do not think of consigning the greater part of faith's area to the region of Agnosticism, and compelling the mind to be satisfied with a few general principles. By the reduction of belief I mean reducing the amount of our claim upon the belief of the public, shortening the articles of association, so to say. I do not mean that every truth of theology should be capable of verification by experience – the pre-existence of Christ is not. Theological truth is far wider than experience. But I do mean that we should not base the Church's appeal to the public upon truths which are outside experience – meaning Christian experience. In asking people to concentrate more upon what we offer we cease asking them to attend to what they have not means of understanding. We ask them to go in upon their moral experience with more earnestness and resolution. We would remove their interest from things they are incompetent to solve, and kindle it on matters that appeal to their own soul, conscience, and destiny. So that what we offer is not so much a new system of theology as a new pronunciation of theology. It is theology uttered with a change of accent. The stress is differently distributed. The emphasis falls on other parts of the great Word We certainly would escape from the monotone of a whole system of equal value and obligation in all parts. And we would dwell with but minor force upon some truths which are not so much saving truths as their corollaries. If I took an example of what I mean, I would say that we ought to restore to Christ's Atoning Cross much of the popular interest so easily arrested by His birth and its manner. We should lean but lightly on the Virgin Birth, which does not make a moral appeal to us, but too often appeals to a ready interest either in a baby or a miracle; and we should bear far more heavily on the centre of all moral action and regeneration in the Cross, which the popular mind so readily shuns because there the world is crucified unto us and we unto the world. And a like transfer of emphasis should take place from the truth of Christ's pre-existence, which is outside the range of our experience, to that of His risen and royal life, wherein we ourselves are made partakers of His resurrection and vouchers of His real presence. So that in the order of importance we should go to the world first of all with the Atoning Cross which is the Alpha and Omega of grace; second, with the resurrection of Christ which is the emergence into experience of the new life won for us on the Cross; third, with the life, character, teaching, and miracles of Christ; fourth, with the pre-existence of Christ, which is a corollary of His Eternal Life, and only after such things with the Virgin Birth, which may or may not be demanded by the rest. It is not a case of denying any of these points or even challenging them. They may all be accepted, but let it be in their true perspective, the perspective of faith. And they are offered to the public, and belief is claimed, in the degree of their relevancy to a vital Christian experience of the one Christian doctrine of grace. For when we carry reduction to its length we condense upon that one principle and power of grace which has in it the promise of the potency of all the soul's life and all Christian truth.

*

We must therefore practise a reduction of belief and with it a redistribution of emphasis. We must call in our main army from lining the long ramparts. We must rally at the great strategic forts; and from them command with our new weapons, firing quick and carrying far, the whole region we have to defend. To do this will give us fresh impetus. The change from walls to guns means the change from defence to attack, from form to life, from system to power. It is a change which brings immense gain. How much moral force we have squandered! We have to admit frankly, if sadly, that a great deal of what lives were once lost for, and hearts broken, and torture endured, is not worth the while. What an awful course history has had to take, to teach us things that seem so simple now. What an irony it all is! Does He that sits in Heaven laugh? At least we cannot be surprised that some should think He does. Heine spoke of the great Aristophanes of heaven. Arnold asks, Was Heine one of those enigmatic smiles? Is the irony of Christ in the Gospels still in the face and grace of God over human history? Truly, our great simplicities are most costly and elaborate things. The reason why they seem so simple now is because they were so hard and bitter then. We do now almost automatically what meant once labour and sorrow. We enter into the labours and deaths of others; and we see clearly only from the shoulders of greater men than ourselves, who had to keep their eyes on the paths for our sakes, and did not see the land.

*

But now if we do thus narrow the demand on the world for belief, are we not entitled to require that this retraction of claim on our part shall be met by a corresponding concentration on the part of the public? If we bring intellectual relief we must plead for moral attention, the narrowness of intensity. What marks the modern man is the mobility and dispersion of his interest. And what does that mean but weakness of will, the lack of power to attend, to decide, to choose? Such irresolution is the chief of all reasons for the lack of response to Christ, or even to Christianity. That is why such large sections of culture have no part or lot in Christ; why they have no more than an interest about Him. For culture in many cases not only does not exercise the will, it dissipates it, it narcotises it. Men are stupefied morally by all the thousand impressions of the hour. They are quick to feel, and keen to know; but they are not only slow, they are averse, to decide. Yet it is for decision that Christianity calls, nay, it is for decision that the energetic universe calls, far more than for a mere impression in response. We are not set in such a world as this simply to return its note as artists or esthetes, but to act. And Christ asked for faith, which is an energy of the will, far oftener than for love, which is a movement of the heart.

And in this respect Christianity can endure, not by surrendering itself to the modern mind and modern culture, but rather by a break with it: the condition of a long future both for culture and the soul is the Christianity which antagonizes culture without denying its place. Culture asks but a half Gospel; and a half Gospel is no Gospel. We must, of course, go some way to meet the world, but when we do meet we must do more than greet. A crisis has from time to time to be forced, a crisis of the will. And the world, which is not unready to profess itself enchanted with Christ, must be converted to Him, and subdued, and made not merely a better world, but another world reconciled and redeemed. A new departure is not enough; there must be a new creation. Refinement is not reform; and amelioration is not regeneration.

We are not being fairly met if the public bestows upon the few things we now hold crucial no more attention or effort than if they were merely a sample handful scooped at random from a mass of loose or languid truths.

It is very singular that on the most grave concern of life a serious man so often makes up his mind in an offhand way. His religious views are of the most casual kind. He seldom really takes pains with the matter. He does not attend to it. His opinions are a sort of spontaneous deposit on the surface of his mind. If it were a business matter he would go into it. If it were a scientific question he would train his mind, and then examine. He takes business and science seriously. But his religion he does not. Scientific people who begin to desire some acquaintance with theology will betake themselves, not to the masters of that discipline as they would with any other science, but to popular socialists who happen to have a vogue. It is not a matter worth study, as history, literature, philosophy, economy, or the markets are. I do not say a man's religion must be the result of professional or technical study, like these subjects. But it should receive no less earnest attention, and engage him no less seriously and personally, and not be taken at haphazard. That casualness is the source of most of the confusion of the time. Every important topic of human discussion seems a pathless thicket to the person who gives it no attention. It is only after you have taken it seriously for a year or two that it opens into clearness and order. Religion is confused and pathless chiefly to those who treat the greatest concerns with most levity. And it is clear and great not from without the Church, but from within. To look at a building like the Albert Hall, or even St. Paul's, from the outside, you would have no such impression of its vastness or grandeur as you receive from its interior. And so with Christian truth. It is really and mightily true only from within.

Now in reducing the bulk of belief we do far more than scoop up a chance handful from a heap. That is not how we arrive at the few mighty beliefs we select. That is not the proper principle, or the proper method, of treating the ponderous systems. We must proceed by a serious and laborious process. A coherent system which has grown obese cannot be reduced, like a statue, by chipping, or paring, as the ignorant critic of vigour and rigour thinks. A criticism which is mere surgery is out of place when we are dealing with great organic systems of belief. The methods must be more medical, more psychical, more sympathetic, more in the nature of moral regimen, and less in the way of amputation. We must not cut down, but work down. This reduction exercised on the old creeds is a moral act or process. It is not merely eclectic. Reduction is the right word. It is working the huge tissue of

orthodoxy down to its normal bulk and place. It means acting on
it naturally through its organic centres. To throw beliefs over-
board, like superfluous cargo, is only too easy. Any ship's boy can
jettison the past like that, or as much of it as he can lift. Thousands
of thin rebels against orthodoxy stand to prove how cheap that
is, and how sterile. Your pert witling, destitute of historic reverence of scientific competency, can entertain a whole company by
stripping belief to the nude, and whipping it through the town in
the wake of his lean team. But you cannot dismember at will
systems whose parts are neither packed together, nor nailed
together, but developed from a centre with some concinnity of
thought. And such these orthodoxies were – both the medieval
scholasticism and the Protestant. The development may have
proceeded under a mistaken idea, but it was done with great
intellectual power, with rare acumen, and wonderful sequence.
And it cannot be undone simply by smashing the machine and
throwing it on the scrap heap. The idea of a total collapse of the
old systems is all very well for poetic effect, humorous point, or
popular purposes. Rather, however, if we speak mechanically let
us speak (with a friend of my own) of reversing gear.

But it is still better not to speak of an organic system which
proceeded from a living Church as a machine. Let us treat it at once
more sympathetically, and more scientifically. Let us treat it as an
organism – as an overgrown organism, if you will, and too inert,
but as being earnest in its intention and serious in its answer to
problems which are real. If we cease to feel these problems we lose
far more than we do by cherishing an inadequate answer. So long
as the problems are real an inadequate answer such as the systems
gave is better than the antagonism of none. It took much grave and
able toil of spiritual men to rear those fabrics we so lightly crush.
They did not do it to amuse their leisure, or to occupy an idle life.
Had they been less serious there would have been less temper about
it; and, after all, the *odium theologicum* is better than the spiritual
insouciance of many who cultivate the modern mind and a sentimental charity more than they pursue reality and truth. These
systems grew in the hands of the mental *élite* of their day. In labour
they were born, and they should not die in contempt. If they were

worked up they must be worked down. At least, they should be worked at. They should not be the target of the man in the street, as if they were in the public pillory. In their decay they are decayed gentlefolk, somewhat heartless, perhaps, like the French aristocrats of the Revolution, but not ignoble, and too distinguished for the missiles of the mob. They should not be disintegrated in their hour of eclipse by tearing their seamless robe and gambling their vesture away. If their form must be reduced, I repeat, it must be worked down. It was competent moral effort that put them there, and it must be moral and competent effort that removes them. It was the science of the day that reared them, and it is competent science in their own kind that should deal with them. They should be tried by their peers. They should not be broken down but trained down – if I may use the phrase. If it was development as they rose, it must be by development that they subside. They should be shed and not shot. In evolution a living thing sheds its superfluous parts; it is only disease that demands amputation. And it is only the raw procacity of the hour that speaks of theological science as a disease of the Church. But quackery is the worst heresy.

*

The word I should prefer to use for the process would be distillation. As the revelation is distilled from the Bible rather than dissected, so we should treat the theologies of the past, and so we should reduce their aged bulk. The creed is to be distilled from the confessions. The treatment must be honestly applied, and with insight. We must divine the creed within the creeds. It is not simply imbedded in them, as if the debris could be dug away by any youth with a pickaxe, or yokel with a spade. It rather pervades them as an organic principle. We must unsphere the spirit of Calvin and Edwards rather than disentomb their remains. We must first know them, then 'appreciate' them. A modern theology must be an appreciation of the old, done lovingly and sympathetically, and with scientific continuity. If we need positivity in the present we need also to reach it by the interpretation of the past. And to interpret we must know both languages equally well. We must interpret with an informed sympathy. The great authors of these systems loved and trusted God at least as deeply as we do who never have the word love off our lips – at least *as* deeply, and, on the whole, perhaps, *more* deeply. They had among them some of the spiritual giants of the race. They thought in an atmosphere of Christian experience. Their theology was like the wounds of Christ, graven on their heart and on the palms of their hands. To denounce and ridicule here is sheer heartlessness. The call is for interpretation. The need of the hour in respect of past theologians (if we would escape vulgarity) is informed and sympathetic re-interpretation. We must ask what their profound and solemn minds aimed at, and what they strove by their system to guarantee; though we may modify their way of securing it.

*

Let me take an illustration. You would not venture to preach at this time of day a sermon on predestination. You say the idea is either exploded or it is left behind. Where it is not entirely discarded it is so out of date as to be too far in the rear of the religious mind for your purpose.

Well, but it may be your duty on occasion to rescue some great beliefs from their oblivion by an age which freely casts God, heaven, and hell into the rear of its concern. You are there not simply to speak what people care to hear but also to make them care for what you must speak. And as to this matter of predestination, is there no way of preaching it so that even to-day some will listen, some will listen gladly, and some few even with a rising soul and a swelling heart?

Men will still hear of the soul if it be a true soul that speaks – no smatterer, and no self-seeker. They will still hear of the great value of the soul. They will even hear of its absolute value, its pearl of price for whose sake all other pearls are but a currency, and all other ends but means. Tell them that this is the Christian, the New Testament faith. Say, also, that in New Testament times, when it was desired to emphasise the absolute value of anything, they spoke of its pre-existence. The Jews with their beliefs spoke thus of their Law, and of their Temple even. If your audience follow you so far, one at least will want to interject that to speak thus of the absolute value of the soul would lead to speech about its pre-existence. To which you would reply that it did so lead.

Even Plato, and many since, took and followed that lead. But that was because, instead of thinking of the soul as a moral subject, they thought of it as a finely vitalized substance, finished in its kind, with an immortal existence innate in itself. The Hebrew idea was different. The Jews thought of the soul as immortal not in itself but in a destiny conferred on it. They thought of its immortality and perfection as given by God. Its destiny was there as the result of the will and choice of God. That destiny was due to the divine purpose, and it existed there, not in the soul's fibre, so to say. It was written not in the soul's creation but in its Creator, not in its germ but in its Maker.[1] Accordingly what was said to pre-exist was not the soul in its independent nature, as a sort of fiery particle forming an exception from the great universe of inert existence, but the will of God for the soul, its destiny as a purpose and choice of God. And as the purpose is that of God, to whom all things future are present, therefore in Him our destiny is an ever-present and ever-living reality. Thus the soul's absolute and final value was found in Christ, in the pre-existent Christ, eternally chosen, God's personal purpose, eternal and unbegotten, in whom we were and are created.

You will not of course preach in exactly those terms, but by such thoughts you may satisfy and clear and stablish your own minds, so that you can put the matter freely in a more popular way, People will listen to that – often indeed too readily, deeming sometimes of the Humanity eternal in God almost as if it were an independent entity in God which God existed to serve and magnify; so that they speak and think as if God loved Christ for the sake of the humanity He embodied so perfectly, instead of loving humanity for the sake of Christ, who redeemed it so perfectly in God's saving purpose.

---

[1] You see how near this comes to our modern idea about moral personality being the nature and meaning of Soul, and about personality arriving as a growth out of experience and providence by the moral discipline of our faith. I have already pointed out how sonship is not a natural feature of the Soul but is conferred on it, though from its beginning, as a destiny, a gift from God's hand, an adoption from before the foundation of the world by God's calling and purpose.

I am not going further into that. I only want to point out that
the pre-existence of the soul in Plato became, for a Christian
thought based on positive revelation, the preexistence of Christ,
who was the personal embodiment of God's personal purpose and
choice with persons, the Captain of the elect, the eternal object of
God's choice, and God's own perfect and perpetual answer to His
own will. I only want to say that, if you put it to people in the
appropriate way, and not exactly as I put it to you who are trained
men, they will listen with at least an imaginative interest. For these
realities are great poetry, and when well handled they satisfy and
pacify. And people who rise above a material, selfish, impatient
and over-practical Christianity will listen to preaching about the
soul's destiny, about its being so absolute and precious that it was
predestiny, bound up with God's timeless thought, will, and
purpose – a purpose pre-intelligent and pre-active and pre-re-
deeming (Rom. viii. 28 ff.) – a purpose in which God foreknew
what He was about, fore-ordained the soul, the race, unto salvation, and fore-saved and justified it before our day, and indeed
before the day of Time. People can be made to rise above the
vulgar contempt for such interests. They can be made to respond
to efforts of this kind to translate a material and temporal
valuation of life into a spiritual and eternal, to deliver them from
polemical dogmas about the number and specification of the elect
to the presence and sober joy of thoughts beyond time concerning
the fundamental gift and absolute reality of a redeeming salvation.
It is in our forgiveness that we find our soul and its destiny. Faith
in an eternally slain Christ is the foundation for the Church of all
certainty of salvation, all divine destiny for the soul. From the
beginning, from the heart of God, from Christ, we were destined
for God's will and redemption. We were for ever in His purpose
in Christ our Saviour. We were from the first where Christ, by
God's eternal will, ever is. And so we arrive at the great world-
conquering and world-reconciling conviction which lifts the soul
to a heavenly rock above the flux and storm of Time. It is the
conviction that Christ in us is the hope of glory, that any hope we
have of a glorious and transcendent future rests upon the finished
reality of a glorious and transcendent past, not only in Calvary

but in the very bosom and will of a Holy Father Almighty to save and Eternal to seal.

*

If we catch no echo in these considerations of mighty happenings beyond the light of common day, if we hear no hint or music of them from behind the veil, if, while we prepare (as you are here doing) to play our part upon this stage of time, we hear nothing of the murmur of that eternal cloud of witnesses expectant on the other side of the curtain, and if we do not rise to their interests or their thoughts, then we cannot quit ourselves well (as they would count well) when the time comes. And if people will not hear of such things, because they are stale lumber well banished to the attics of the Church when it was refurnished in modern taste, then their revolt is not from orthodoxy, dogma, or polemic but from the serious, the Christian, the spiritual, the eternal world of life and reality.

It is easy for any soft humanist or hard witling to hold up to horror or ridicule our fathers' doctrine of predestination, or reprobation. It is easy because we believe in man (if we do) where they believed in God. We are supremely concerned about human happiness where they were engrossed with the glory of God. We are preoccupied with human freedom, and are not interested (as they were above all) in the freedom of God. We are greatly interested in freedom of thought, and little in the freedom of grace; much troubled about freedom of thought or action, and little about freedom of soul. But we are not just to those great spirits till we have the same prime concern, the same perspective of interest, the same sense of final values. We are not just to them till we realize that what moved everything in them was concern for that glory and freedom of God which is the supreme object of existence, and which prescribes the final interests of humanity. Nothing can make man free which does not secure in advance the freedom of God. The old theologians saw that as I wish we could see it. And that was what led them to positions which can seem absurd and inhuman only to people who care but for the glorious freedom of man, and who use a God but as its minister. It is easy for any *littérateur* to sweep Calvin out of doors of a morning, and take in a suite of theological furniture in completely modern style.[2] But it is not easy, it is a great moral effort, to think our way out of Calvinism into truth more modest and no less mighty. It is not easy, it is laborious moral effort, as well as mental energy, which enables us to keep in the front of our interest that issue of God's freedom, and yet to secure it by other doctrines than those which have now become untenable. They have become so partly by the growth of the humane idea, but still more by the growth upon us of the revelation latent in a historic Christ and His Gospel.

*

I should like to point out farther that the labour of this reduction cannot be avoided by attempts, like Tolstoi's or other naïve spirits, at what we may call mere repristination – a violent return to revive Christianity in its earliest and most primitive form. We cannot do with our Christian ideas and institutions what we can do with our personal faith. We cannot go back to the fountain head and simply ignore the 2,000 years of Christian evolution. We cannot do that now in the matter of polity. We cannot restore the exact conditions of the New Testament Church. Nor can we in the matter of creed, of mental construction either of man or the world. It seems easy to the uninstructed person who has the Bible put into his hand to say, 'Why not return, in mode of life and form of thought, to what is so normative there?' He omits to note that the normative in the New Testament is not a pattern. It is there in a historic context, not on a desert island. We cannot even go back the shorter journey to the Reformation in this sense. It would be destructive to man's spiritual life, even if it were psychologically possible, which it is not. Nor is it historically possible. We have not sufficient data about that very early state of affairs. Those who suggest such a thing are devoid of the historical sense. They have no idea of the dimensions of the problem – which is a sure sign of incompetency. And it is therefore as difficult to convince them of the impossibility as it would be to perform the feat. To couple up directly with the Church order of the first century, with

---

[2]   I was amused, while delivering these lectures, to see over an American shop the sign of the 'Hegel Furniture Company.'

its literal precepts, with its mental concepts, would be in truth to break with the past in its more inward reality. We may re-interpret and re-organize, but we cannot restore it. We know what the result of Church restoration is in art, in architecture. And it is no less unhappy and impossible in the inner fabric of our faith. It is impossible for Churches to turn this mental somersault, even if individuals tried it, or sects arose upon the effort. All such attempts have been failures, and, more or less, waste. The future must grow out of all the past. Neither Church history nor Church piety is a continuous fall from the first century, where each age feels itself at the bottom, and must start scrambling up. Rather the whole of history converges and ascends through the present. And we must interpret the originality and normality of Christ and the New Testament consistently with that. We have to solve our own problems as the whole past presents them. We have to draw from an eternity which is brought to our door by the whole course of history up to now. We have to ignore the growing bulk of the question, to fix on its spiritual core. We have to interrogate eternity through the unity of history, past and present. We must practise divination, and especially at the point where that unity is condensed and narrowed in the Cross of Christ.

Well, if such be the spirit and method of our theological reduction, are we not entitled to call on the public (for whom we are really acting) to meet us in the like earnest spirit? The work done by theologians is not done for a small. group of people with an interest in that hobby. It is not sectional work at all. It is first done for the preachers and their preaching, and through them for the public, on the question of most universal moment. And we are entitled, especially we preachers who stand between the theologians and the public (as the theologians stand between the critics and the preachers), to expect from it some effort to correspond. We may ask it to make moral effort, and to treat more seriously that more portable and potent creed which we distil from the creeds rather than pick from the poets, or from the poetry even of Scripture. A generous theology should not be associated with mere mobility of sympathy and shortness of spiritual fibre. Let our public put aside the habit of discursive attention and sustained distraction which marks the restless, casual age. Let it deliberately call in its vagrant thoughts, and give itself and its mind to those prime matters of the soul. If they deserve any attention they deserve our best. Let it give to this high business of eternity at least some of the same effort as it gives to the grave business of time. Let it give to life some of the intense and capable energy it gives to living. Let its religion cease to be merely a refuge and a balm for men so jaded with the pursuit of the world as to be fit on Sundays for no more than a warm bath or a sacred concert.

Moreover, let the religious public at least have some consideration for its ministry, which it irritates and debases by trivial ethics, and the impatient demand for short sermons and long 'socials.' Let it respect the dignity of the ministry. Let it cease to degrade the ministry into a competitor for public notice, a caterer for public comfort, and a mere waiter upon social convenience or religious decency. Let it make greater demands on the pulpit for power, and grasp, and range, and penetration, and reality. Let it encourage the ministry to do more justice to the mighty *matter* of the Bible and its burthen, and not only to its beauty, its charm, its sentiment, or its precepts. Let it come in aid to protect the pulpit from that curse of petty sentiment which grows upon the Church, which rolls up from the pew into the pulpit, and from the pulpit rolls down upon the pew in a warm and soaking mist. There is an element in the preacher's eloquence which only the audience can give. Let it do so by being, not less exacting but more – only, exacting on the great right things. Let it realize that for true eloquence there must be great matter, both in him who speaks and in those who hear. The greatest eloquence is not that of the man but of the theme. There is no such supporter of a minister as the man who, he knows, studies the Bible with as much earnestness as himself, if with fewer facilities. Such supporters add immeasurably to the staying power of a Church. If our people are experts of the Bible we shall have none of the rude remarks of philanthropy about the time the minister wastes on theology. I say that, in the present state of the Church, and certainly for the sake of its pulpit, its ministers, and its future, theology is a greater need

than philanthropy. Because men do not know where they are.
They are only steering by dead reckoning – when anything may
happen. But theology is 'taking the sun.' And it is wonderful – it
is dangerous – how few of our officers can use the sextant for
themselves. Yet what is the use of captains who are more at home
entertaining the passengers than navigating the ship? The theology of the Bible is but the moral adequacy and virility of the word
of the Cross, and the thews of a powerful Gospel. A theology
chiefly curious, or speculative, a secondary theology, may be left
to the leisure of the schools; but a theology of experienced Grace,
primary theology, is of the essence of the Gospel. And it is not
merely of the *bene esse*, it is of the *esse* of the Church.

The Church, then, may adjust itself to the world in reducing its
demand to those experimental but rational limits which the New
Testament prescribes. But within those limits it must descend on
the world from the side of God and the glory of his throne, whether
it come, like the Spirit, as a rushing mighty wind, or, like the New
Jerusalem, sailing down beautiful as a bride. In the last matters of
the soul it is the Church that gives the law to the world; it is not
the world that gives the law to the Church. But it is the Church as
prophet, not as King. It is not the imperial Church but the serving
Church, the Church not as judge but as witness. It is the Church
not as an organization, far less as a monarchy, but as the company
of the faithful, the communion of saints and the fellow heirs of the
Gospel; the Church as the trustee of the Word of saving Grace, not
as the nuncio of an imperious prerogative; as the meek, mighty
apostle of the Redeemer, not as the gorgeous vicar of Christ.

*

Meantime let us welcome and use any signs that the age presents
of the frame of mind we desire to see. Let us be quick to read and
interpret not only its unrest, not even its compunction, but its
deep, though hidden, sense of guilt, and its keen, though stifled,
sense of despair. Let us recognize that men are brooding on their
moral condition much more than they own. Let us realize how
they are being forced, by mightier influences than ours, upon the
moral problems that set up the real crisis of the soul. Let us not
be the victims of the conventional phases of sin, penitence, and

prayer; of those forms of them which religious speakers work to death and rob of solemn meaning. Let us learn to discover the thing itself where the traditional expressions of it do not appear, and the ecclesiastical symptoms are wanting. If we get deep enough with the public mind – at any rate in the Old World – we shall find that men are less satisfied with success than would appear from the plaudits of the day, less the victims of things as they are than the press would indicate, and more preoccupied with their inward moral failure than their bravado will admit.

It is true, when the conscience begins to act we often find no more than a vague sense of imperfection before the Christian standard, or a dim disquiet. But that is not all. We find also an inner schism and a real sense of retribution, however vague, when conscience does bite. The curse comes home. But it is not the fear of hell, scarcely of God. It is the fear of judgment, indeed, but the judgment of exposure to man, not of inquisition by God. It is the judgment of being found out, whether by self or society. And the torment of being found out by yourself, and carrying about in yourself a living fraud, a moral corpse, can become to some as great as the exposure to the world. What comes home is the nemesis of guilt in the course of life, not in the judgment outside life. It comes home either in visible tragedy or in inward desiccation and calm despair. The sense of guilt is still there, it is often more active than we are allowed to know. And it cannot be escaped. It is very actual. Read Ibsen, for instance. You will find the dramatists much more to your purpose than most of the novelists. They get closer to life's moral realities. Read him again. Mark and learn his unsparing ethical realism. Could that remorseless insight of his through the shams and clothes of ordinary society miss the grim dull ache of guilt? For him, as for all the rest of the tragic poets, guilt is the centre of the tragedy. 'Guilt remains guilt,' he says. 'You cannot bully God into such blessing as turns guilt to merit, or penalty to reward.' No, God can be neither bullied nor blandished into that. Yet the blessing is there. The one thing needful is there – not the merit but the mercy. The forgiveness is there, and there from God, there of His own free gift, at His proper cost. And to realize how awful that cost is use such as Ibsen. To save your soul from sunny or silly piety, to realize the deadly inveteracy of evil, its dereliction by God, its sordid paralysis of all redeeming, self-recuperative power in man, its incurable fatal effect upon the moral order of society, read Ibsen. Yea, to realize how it thereby imports the element of death even into the moral order of the universe read Ibsen. It inflicts death on whatever power you call God. Unless, indeed, that power have the secret (unknown to this great prophet) of transforming the death which it cannot evade. Within the moral order there may reside (Christ says there does reside), a moral power to make itself effective, not only in spite of the wound to it, but by means of that wound. A holy God has power to make good the moral law by a personal resource which both honoured its affronted but infrangible majesty, and surmounted it in saving love. Such searching, fundamental things a man like Ibsen enables us to realize, and compels us to face. Our thought of evil is too shallow till these keen, hard ploughshares tear to the depths. Our attention is too slight and volatile, our hearts too happy, light, and credulous. These pessimists are a gift of God to us. Their bitter is a tonic to our time. They are the protest of a self-respecting conscience against an idyllic, juvenile, sanguine, and domestic tyranny of life. It is the great dramatists that are the great questioners, the great challengers, the great and serviceable accusers of current, easy, and fungous sainthood. It is not the learned critics that present the great challenge which draws out the last resources of a Gospel. They are too intellectualist. It is the great moral critics like Ibsen, Carlyle, and their kind. They lay bare not our errors but our shams. It is true they have no answer to the question they raise, no covering for the shame they expose. Ibsen does not believe that God can be bullied – that He can be mocked, as the Bible puts it. I wish more of us shared his belief there. But he also does not believe in a God that cannot be foiled, in a holiness that must establish itself upon everything, in a God of grace, in grace with all the creative power of God turned to redeem, in God as Lord of the moral order also, and able to deal with it and its mockery. A creed that can cope with such sceptics is the final creed of the world. Why does Ibsen not so believe? Because, while he reads one book with uncanny penetration, the book of Man, Church, and Society,

he has never turned the same piercing eye on the other book, the
New Testament, and never taken Christ as seriously as he takes
man. He is grimly, ghastly interpretive but not redemptive – like
his analytic age. It is the fault, the bane, of almost all the great
critics and accusers. But consent still to learn from them what they
have to teach you – you who are already taught by Christ, and sure
of your Gospel – perhaps too slightly sure, and too lightly per-
suaded you are, or are making, Christians. Preach to Ibsen's world,
and there are few that you will miss. Only do not preach his word.
Christ's Gospel has the same radical, unsparing, moral realism,
tearing to the roots, and tearing them up with relentless moral
veracity. It has the note of *thorough*. You find it chiefly in the
exactions, the irony, and the wrath of Christ's love. And next to
them in the Apostle of love, in the Epistles of John. 'If any man
love God and hate his brother he is a liar.' Learn, then, to shun
every hymn that has the word 'sweet' in it, to find other sources of
'greatness' than the 'gentleness' of God, and to look for something
else than lightness in the burden of Christ. Let your song be of
mercy, but the mercy of judgment. And learn not to say so much
to your people of a day of Judgment sure though far. The farness
destroys the sureness. Ethicize the reality of judgment. Moralize
the eschatology. Couple it up to the hour. Drop, if need be, the
drapery of the remote assize. The judge is at the door. Everything
comes home. It comes home in calamity if you do not take it home
in repentance. Life needs far more for most people, for all people
when you get as deep as that, far more than filling out. It needs
remaking. It needs divine, decisive action, forgiveness, atonement,
the cancelling of guilt, salvation in that sense, rescue from the moral
nemesis, the breaking of the guilty entail. It needs more even than
redemption, if by redemption you mean but Buddhist rescue from
the tragic ills and clogs of life. It needs, before all redemption,
reconciliation, the reopening of communication, the dissipation of
guilt's cloud which darkens for us the face of God. It is unfortunate
that so many who preach reconciliation lose sight of redemption,
while the preachers of redemption are apt to lose the note of
reconciliation.

*

Beware, of course, of censoriousness, which is a frequent trap for the young moralist. But do preach a gospel where salvation is in real *rapport* with deep guilt, and redemption with holy judgment. For God's sake do not tell poor prodigals and black scoundrels they are better than they think, that they have more of Christ in them than they know, and so on. The conscience which is really in hell is the first to be angered at ingenuities and futilities like these, the more exasperating because of the poetic quarter-truth they contain.

This is where we suffer from the word of a pseudoliberalism and humanism. It seeks to be modern by the way of extenuation rather than realism, by palliation rather than penetration, by moral tenderness rather than by moral probing, by poetry rather than prophesying, by nursing where surgery is required. So much of our modern liberalism, even when ethical, is more kindly in tone than positive in power. And, therefore, it fails to grasp much beyond the milder sins and the milder sex. It is shy of the only thing relevant – a divine atonement, or it empties it of virile force and mordant meaning. Those who so speak seem never themselves to have resisted unto blood striving against sin, nor to have been snatched from self-contempt and despair. But I venture to think John Newton's 'I asked the Lord that I might grow'[3] one of the greatest and most realistic utterances of Christian experience. And it represents the course our sunny liberalism must take as it passes from a trout stream of the morning to the river of God which is full of deep water. Our young lions suffer hunger.

Do you realize that it was the severity of Christ that made the agony of Christ, His love of God's holy law more even than of His brother men? Do you realize how, first to last, He stood on God's side against men? There was in existence in the Judaism of Christ's day a mild, humane, and attractive school of the law, in contrast with those teachers who pressed it into unsparing detail. And has it occurred to you to ask why Christ did not ally Himself with that kind and genial school, and work from its midst? Nay, how was it that He stood as opposed to it as He did to the other

---

[3] See Hymn, page 237.

extreme? Because His freedom in relation to the law lay not in getting rid of it, not in easing it. He preached no mere emancipation. He was not antinomian. What He brought was not a general dispensation. The imperative note was always in the front of His preaching. He always recognized the law as the will of God. His complaint was that both extremes tampered with it; not that the Pharisees were legalist, but that they were inconsistent with their own legal version of it. 'What they bid you do, do, but do not as they do.' In his own relation to the law He was not so much under it, or against it, as above it. He handled it as God would. His obedience to the law was not free like the Sadducees by reducing its claim, nor slavish like the Pharisees by not rising above its claim. It was the obedience of the Son in His Father's house. He pressed the law's validity by expanding its scope. His modifications were to increase its obligations. Love was more searching, and therefore more imperative, than precept. Law for him (as for Paul) was always exigent, never outworn. The Sabbath was made for man. The greater man grows the more imperative is a Sabbath, the more serious the penalty of its neglect. Traffic in the Temple was what roused Him, not its priests nor its ritual. Commercialist piety was far more unholy than sacerdotal. As Christ's love to God was greater than His love to man, so His love for God's law was more intense than His sympathy with man's weakness. True, His love to men was part of God's love to men. But that shows that a divine love of man is only possible if divine holiness is loved as God loves it. Always the obedience to holy God was precedent with Christ to the service of needy men. He served men chiefly out of obedience to God, and His love to them was because of His love to God. His teeming pity flowed from His love, and His love was fixed upon the Holy One. The hallowing of God's name always came first. And for Christ the law was no piece of Judaism to be overthrown with Pharisaism, but it was the expression of God's holy will to be honoured in His Son. The original thing in Jesus was His peculiar way of honouring the law, and not His discarding of it. The claim of God's holy will was never ended till it was met. He was not, as I have said, among the liberals of the Jewish Church. He pressed the claim of holy law, only in a new construction. He was neither orthodox nor liberal. It is even bad taste to apply to Him such terms. He had the word of living grace and searching power. That note is what we call positive to-day. And, therefore, He was adjudged by both dull parties to be unintelligible or a traitor. And it was only when Christ had honoured in full the holiness of God's claim upon the Cross that Paul could take the attitude to the law he did, and speak of Him as its end.

The guilt, the Pharisaism, that saturates the Europe or America spread out before men like Ibsen, can never be dealt with by pressing a social ethic, or a moral order, or an enfolding sympathy for man, while pooh-poohing the holy demand of God. It can only be dealt with by a conception of God's action in Christ, which shall do more justice to God's inexorable holiness than the Judaisms of orthodoxy, or the genialities of humanism. It can only be dealt with by making room for the judgment grace of God in Christ's cross – applying it as judiciously as you will, and remembering always the strength of reserve and the reverence of the holy name hallowed in silent action there.

But to this subject I shall be compelled to return by the pressure of that idea which underlies, subdues, and goes on to absorb all I say in this series of discourse.

Five

The Preacher and Religious Reality

The Reformation not to be regretted nor renounced, but reformed by its own principle of faith and its demand for moral reality – The need of facing as fairly as the Reformers the moral, social and political situation, – the supreme demand to-day is for spiritual reality – The three diseases of the Church and their cures: (1) Triviality, demanding a new note of greatness in our creed; (2) Uncertainty, demanding a new note of wrestling and reality in our prayer; (3) Complacency, demanding a new note of judgment in our salvation – The root of moral reality, personal religion, and social security only to be found in the consciousness of guilt produced and transcended by the sense of vicarious redemption.

There are two ways of treating the Reformation – one is to complete it, and one is to escape from it. And there are two ways of escaping from it. One is the way of deploring it with shame as the grand defection of modern history, renouncing it as the grand schism, and returning to the medievalism it abjured. That is the Catholic way. And the other is the way of deploring and renouncing it with regret as a lapse into theology and violence, when all that was needed might have been done by culture and reform. That is the way of Erasmus, and Goethe, the way of the Illumination. Goethe expresses the mind of many refined Protestants when he says that Luther's Reformation threw back the progress of culture by centuries.

I would express the conviction, against both of these ways, that the proper treatment of the Reformation is to finish it – to reform and complete it. And, still further, it is not to correct it by an extraneous principle like culture, but to reform it by its own intrinsic principle of faith. We are but half way through the Reformation. So mighty was that conversion of Christianity, that second birth of the Gospel. Remember, it was in its nature the Church's reforming of itself. So it goes on still as the self-reformation of the reformed Church. It was evolved from the Church, it was not thrust on it. It was the reward to the Church for the evangelical fidelity that had long been struggling in it. It began at the Church's self-reformation by the Spirit. That is its genius. Therefore, it goes on so. That is to say, the modernizing of our theology, as of our evangelical methods, is something demanded by the reformed faith itself. A new theology is to express the growth of faith and give room for more.

I have mentioned and applied several of the modern ideas to which we have to adjust our message – the idea of authority, the idea of morality, the idea of immanence. There is another modern passion which we must go out to satisfy, one inherent in faith itself – the passion for reality – and especially moral reality. By which I need hardly say I mean much more than ordinary sincerity.

The history of the passion for reality would be the history of the whole modern mind since medievalism was outgrown. And that indeed is not so very long ago. The medieval period did not really expire till, in the eighteenth century, the Illumination killed its legatee in scholastic Protestantism. But the history of the movement on its moral side began with the Reformation. That was a vast assertion of ethical realism. It pursued the actual moral condition of the soul into the recesses of the conscience, and dealt unsparingly, effectually, with it there in the shape of sin. It is true that almost immediately that mighty wave began to ebb – just as Judaism surged swiftly back on Pauline Christianity, and submerged it in Catholicism till the Reformation. The great moral *vis* of the Reformation subsided into the renewed intellectualism of the seventeenth century dogmatists, so able, so acute, so elaborate, and so irrelevant to life. Correction then became inevitable; and it came from the Illumination, the rationalist, humanist movement of the 18th century, with its science and its romance, its enlargement both of interest and of heart, its sense of the world and of humanity, its concrete realism. As Luther had faced the reality of the moral situation, the Illumination faced the reality of the intellectual situation. And the result now is that we are driven back to the early moral genius of the Reformation, to its evangelical prime, to rescue us from a mere eager intellectualism. We are forced back, beyond all eagerness or even earnestness, on the thorough-going moral realism which is the first interest of the Gospel. We are driven there for a refuge from the Illumination; both from the intellectualism which overdoes its rationality, and from the sentiment which overdoes its romance. At the present hour romantic religion has submerged evangelical, the religion of affection and temperament has obscured the religion of will and conscience, the religion of love or lovelessness the religion of holiness or sin. Romantic religion lives in the sentiments and sympathies, but evangelical religion – faith – lives in repentance, forgiveness, trust, and self-committal to the Redeemer. When Paul was in his seventh heaven, and heard things not to be spoken, it was a romantic, mystic moment in his life. But he did not boast of that, but of Jesus Christ, and the Cross, and the faith of the Cross, where was now no condemnation but peace – by which he meant not calm but the life-confidence of reconciliation and co-operation with God. His Christianity lay not in his romantic experiences but in his evangelical. We need a more searching evangelical realism to protect us from orthodoxism, rationalism, and the temperamental *littérateurs*. And we find it in the old faith (when we take the word faith quite seriously) with its realist demand for a new theology.

*

If we are to preach with Gospel effect to our time we must give up the idea of dragging men back to the dogmas of scholastic Protestantism. It is no more wise than the attempt to drag them back to the dogmas and institutions of the medieval Church. The worship of orthodoxy is Protestant Catholicism, Protestant Romanism. And it is what none of the great men did who have chiefly made Christianity what it is. Christianity did arise on Jewish soil;

but the fathers did not try to force the world back into Judaism, or to any oriental creed. They poured the wine of Christianity into the bottles of the Greek and Roman spirit. They met with their Gospel the real intellectual problems of their time. The misfortune was that their successors did not know when that time was by. And so it was also with the great Reformers. Luther met with the Gospel his time's moral need, Calvin its social and political. That touch their successors lost. But in completing this work we can only do it by facing the situation around us as really as the heroes did theirs.

For instance, we must meet criticism of the Bible with a hospitable face. We have learned much from it, and we have much to learn. We preachers, especially, must realize how it has redis-covered the Bible, as Luther rediscovered the Gospel. We must use all wise and tender means to give our people the results of that rediscovery, and to make the Bible for them the real historic and living book which it has so widely ceased to be. We must avoid irritating them with discoveries of what it is not, and statements of what is upset; and we must kindle them with the positive exposition of what it is now found to be for heart, history, faith and grace. We must get rid, as we wisely can, of the amateur and fantastic habit of laying out the Bible in diagrams and schemes, which treat it like a public park, and which ignore historic and critical study. We must give up the allegorical interpretations by which some attempt to save its verbal inspiration, now hopelessly gone. And we must restrain ourselves in the fanciful use of texts at the cost of the historic revelation which the whole context gives. These practices have a show of honouring the Bible, but they really treat it with the disrespect that is always there when we presume people to mean another thing than they say. If you treat a text mystically make it clear that you take a liberty in doing so. Preach more expository sermons. Take long passages for texts. Perhaps you have no idea how eager people are to have the Bible expounded, and how much they prefer you to unriddle what the Bible says, with its large utterance, than to confuse them with what you can make it say by some ingenuity. It is thus you will get real preaching in the sense of preaching from the real situation of the Bible to the real situation of the time. It is thus you make history preach to history, the past to the present, and not merely a text to a soul.

*

Again we must cultivate reality by preaching to the social situation, to social sin. It is impossible to preach with reality to an age like this and ignore the social crisis and demand. We must face the questions put to the Gospel by a time which is passing from one social epoch to another. It is to the Gospel these questions are put, though they are addressed to the care of the Church. I hope the Church will see that they reach their destination. We are at the junction of two ages – the Capitalist and the Socialist. And we who live in the supreme society of the Church, and who possess the word of moral power for every age, must not be unprepared with a relevant word, even if we have not yet the final word. It is a work to be done with the greatest judgment. And it is not honestly done without due knowledge. We must know the ethic of the Gospel on the one hand, and the economics of the age on the other. You will not be so ill-advised as to make this the staple of your pulpit. Some should not touch it there at all. It is not for every preacher, and it is not for the preacher alone, but for the preacher co-operating with men of affairs who will add his knowledge to their own. Neither the preacher alone nor the laymen alone makes the Church, as the great collective preacher, should have some social word that deserves public attention and respect, even if it cannot secure immediate belief. The realism of the Gospel and of the age alike require that. But the subject is so large I will not embark on it. It is one I have not ignored elsewhere. I but use it to illustrate my wider plea, and to enforce the demand for reality in our preaching.

*

I would, however, go on to press upon you at more length the demand for spiritual reality, a spiritual reality which is no more mere sincerity than spiritual veracity is mere plain truth-telling. I mean the practical recognition of the fact that the actual predicament of the human soul is its moral case, that its moral case is need and not strength, that its need is a moral more than a sympathetic need, that it is a matter of conscience and holiness more than of heart and affection, of sin more than wrong – though, of course, it is both.

And here I will venture to confess that the condition of the Church may well cause to realist faith something less than high satisfaction. Let me not be accused of being dull to love and pity if I say that these have been developed by the Churches we know best at the cost of the spiritual life, of the moral soul, and of a Gospel of holiness. I assure you I have the affections of other men, and a passion mostly too keen to be safely loosed and let go. I have a sense of wrong in things that would fill many of these lectures with violent, and perhaps some bitter, denunciation. It is a grief to me to walk the streets, and to see, with eyes too dim to see, the needy waifs, the dear, poor women, the lean, weary, great-eyed children. O, these sheep, what have they done! Love and pity are to me a daily pain. And yet it was not the sorrow of the world that broke the heart of Christ, but its wickedness. He was equal to its sorrow, and His power was never below His pity. He began by being the world's healer. But what broke him was its sin. That mighty heart, so capacious to receive, and so swift to pity, had to end as the moral Saviour. His witness of the loving God had to become His work for the Holy. And the greatest thing He could do in His love and pity was to redeem us. He lived benignly among the poignant realities of human sorrow, but what killed Him was His realization of human sin and guilt. The healer of our pain had to practise a more radical realism than pain stirs, and become the destroyer of our wickedness. Only so could the love and pity prevail at last. The brotherhood of man could only come by the communion of Saints in the household of faith, of men who by the awful Cross were scarcely saved. Yet to-day this Cross, with its moral realism dredging the very bottom of the conscience, and descending even into hell, is the centre of much more sentiment than repentance, and of far more celebration than surrender.

We suffer from three things, I will say. The Church, of course, has always suffered from whatever was the great world-power of the age, and suffered either by oppression from it, or, worse, by infection. It suffered so from pagan Rome. It has suffered from the dynasties of modern Europe. And as the world-power of to-day is the money power the Church to-day suffers from the plutocracy. I do not say from the plutocrats. Many of them mean well, and do well. But it suffers from the plutocracy. But this, again, is a matter too large; and I want to come nearer home to the matter of our spiritual realism. I will say then the Church suffers from three things.

1. From triviality (with externality).
2. From uncertainty of its foundation.
3. From satisfaction with itself

And to cure these the Gospel we have to preach prescribes –

1. For our *triviality*, a new note of greatness in our creed, the note that sounds in a theology more than in a sentiment.
2. For our *uncertainty*, a new note of wrestling and reality in our prayer.
3. For our *complacency*, a new note of judgment in our salvation.

And these three remedies cannot be taken by way of mere outward enterprise (which will, indeed, collapse for want of them). They can only be taken inwardly, by means of more religion, more positive religion, and more personal religion. I believe that a Church really sanctified would develop more power, light, and machinery for dealing with the tremendous realities of the world than is possible while we are groping in the dark, picking our timid path in economics, or flogging up the energies of a flagging faith.

*

1. As to the triviality from which we suffer.

I am afraid that, for the general public, religion has become associated with the small and negligible side of the soul. Nowhere has mediocrity its chance as it has it in religion. Nowhere has the gossipy side of life such scope. Nowhere has quackery of every kind such a field and such a harvest. I know very well that this is a perversion of the tenderness of religion for the weak things of the world and for the individual case. But a perversion it is. The weak things are not only considered, they take command. They claim to give the law. They make a majority. They trade upon Christian love, and belittle it. Eternity and its issues go out of faith as love comes in. Churches and preachers are choked with a crowd of paltry things kept in place by no sure authority, and dignified by no governing power. Both ministers and churches have as much of a struggle to get time for spiritual culture as if it were none of their business. Christian ethic suffers from what I may call inversion. I mean this. When Paul, the persecutor, goes the length he does in considering the weak brother it is a very great trophy of the moral victory of Christ, and it prescribes a principle of Christian ethic. But it is a total inversion of that ethic when the weakling sets up a claim, and demands as a right what the apostle gave but as a grace. That is overweening in the weak, and it is fatal for the Church. It turns consideration to pampering, and makes Christian pity the factory of moral paupers with the paupers' audacity. Or, on the other hand, the Church's worship, which should gather and greaten its soul, is sacrificed to its work. You have bustle all the week and baldness all the Sunday. You have energy everywhere except in the Spirit. The religious material is tugged and stretched to cover so much that it grows too thin for anything and parts into rents and rags. We are more anxious to cover ground than to secure it, to evangelize the world than to convert it. It is faithless impatience, of the youngest thinnest kind. A bustling institution may cover spiritual destitution, just as Christian work may be taken up as a narcotic to spiritual doubt and emptiness. The minister's study becomes more of an office than an oratory. Committees suck away the breath of power. Socialities become the only welcome sacraments. The tea-meeting draws people together as the communion table does not. The minister may talk the silliest platitudes without resentment, but he may not smoke a cigar in some places without causing an explosion. And religion becomes an ambulance, not a pioneer.

But why need I go on with a diagnosis which is only too apt to describe tendencies as if they were results, and treat extreme cases as if they were the rule? Let us turn from observation to experience. Let us look within. Do our hungry souls not tell us faithfully that much of our vivid and ingenious talk about statistics of Church attendance, about advanced and popular methods is well, is eloquent – but 'tis not true? It regards the Church as a going concern rather than a communion of saints. It has the tone of the press rather than of the Gospel. It has not the accent of the Holy Ghost, not His solemn rushing wind, nor the piercing of His discerning sword. It is not the truth, the kind of truth, that goes to the reality of the spiritual case. It treats symptoms rather than diagnoses the disease. Suppose Christ had read no deeper than that the predicament of man and Israel! Suppose He had pierced no closer to moral reality than that! Suppose He had measured His success by His supporters! Suppose His great and first object had been conversions!

*

For that state of things, that πολυπραγμοσΰνη both in the Church and the world, there is no outward remedy. What we need most is not the re-organization of society. That is a topic so actual that the press will discuss it freely. But the actual is one thing, the real is another. The actual is the present hour, the real is the eternal power. And the reality of the situation it is hard to make people face. A business man learns the habit of facing fully his financial position, and noting it almost daily. But we have not learned the habit of facing fully and courageously the moral situation. When we do, we find that the re-organization of society is a small matter compared with the re-organization of the soul. And no new methods will do that. No reformation of our *modus operandi* will do that. You cannot do that by institutionalizing our religious agencies. The re-organizing of the soul is Redeemer's work. We have to secure our foundations anew. We Protestants have always to be securing the foundation anew. It is our genius to plant every man on the Rock, and to plant the whole man there. He has continually to refer himself to Christ, and to appropriate Christ's salvation anew. We have constantly to acquire what we inherit. The branch must ever draw from the trunk vine. We must keep in close contact at one end with spiritual reality. If we do not we are cut off and withered. That is, we become sectional and shrunk, sectarian and trivial. And churches may become hives of little bees, with the due proportion of drones and stings, instead of fraternities of godly, great, wise, and worthy souls.

We must regain our sense of *soul* greatness, and our sense of its eternal price. If we measure things by the Cross, which is the price of salvation, and the touchstone of spiritual reality, God cares more that we should be great than that we should be happy. He cares more that we should trust and help than that we should enjoy. Christ's love (which was God's) was all help and no enjoyment. Whereas for most people, Christian people, it is the other way. A religion that makes men right and real seems to have no chance with one that makes them feel safe and 'good.' But the Churches can do nothing permanent and nothing final for human welfare till the soul gets its own. The Church is not 'first of all a working Church.' It is a communion of saints and lovers, a company of believers, a fellowship of spiritual realists. It is there first to feed the soul with eternal reality, to stablish, strengthen, and settle the soul upon the Rock of Ages. You cannot expect ill-fed people to devise much wisdom, or do much good. And many in our active churches are very hungry as to the soul. They are anæmic in the Spirit. They are fed upon sentiment and not on faith. They have hectic energy – and leanness of soul.

*

If the soul is to realize its greatness, and its union with God's eternity in the world, it must be nourished with more congenial food. What shall that be? The philosophies, the humanities, the mysticisms? Can the soul be settled on reality by philosophies of its own cosmic place? Can it be stayed on psychologies of its mystic structure and volcanic subliminal depths? Do we come into tune with the infinite by mystic immersion in the sea of Being? Does our reconciliation consist in recovering a forgotten sense that human nature is always in unbroken continuity with the divine? Can we cultivate moral reality by a mere transcendent ethic? Many a gross Pharisee is a mighty moralist; and he believes himself sincere with it. The deadliest Pharisaism is not hypocrisy; it is the unconscious Pharisaism of unreality. Can we escape that by mere moral vigour and rigour? Can we greaten the soul for good by literary contact with epic heroisms, or asthetic spectacles of its dramatic fate? Can we even dilate and confirm the soul into eternity by loftiest speculation upon the nature of Godhead and the psychology of Trinity?

No. However these things move us they do not make us. They may alter us but they do not change us. They refit us but they do not reform us. The greatness of the soul, the greatness of faith, cannot be sustained upon any scrutiny of the soul, whether created or increate, human or divine, not by any psychology of man or of God; but only upon the experience of the soul redeemed. The mere contemplation of Christ will not save you. You must appropriate Him. You must know the fellowship of His death. But that means that it is moral action that is reality. God Himself is an ἐνεργεία. And it is by the fellowship of the supreme moral action of the spiritual world in Christ's Cross that our soul comes to reality, to its true self, its real depths, and its eternal destiny. And most of all we share the last realism of life by the sense, so gone from our practical creed, *quanti ponderis sit peccatum*, what it cost the Redeemer to redeem. No estimate of the soul which may be reached by itself is so true and great as His estimate, who counted and paid the whole cost of the great war for its recovery. That estimate of sin is expressed in the Cross. And if the preachers do not feel this (as they often do not) the Church must, and must force the preacher's hand. But to learn the Cross so is no mere matter of Bible class or of theology. We must give it time and scope to act upon us, as we do not now do, before we can presume to act with it upon the world. And then perhaps we may cease to hear so much of that talk which paralyses the preacher about short sermons, incessant visits, or religious bustle. Justification is far more than visitation.

*

It is impossible to banish sentiment from religion without impoverishing it, but it is quite necessary to teach it its true place; and never so necessary as to-day. It cannot be allowed to lead, as in so many cases it does. What imagination did in medieval Catholicism, that sentiment does in contemporary Protestantism. And the one is a guide no safer than the other. Both tend to the unreal. But there is this difference, that the Bible, which is full of imagination, has no sentiment. Such an episode as that of the alabaster box is not sentiment but passion. It is certain that sentiment occupies a place with us which is quite out of the perspective of New Testament faith. It makes the language of the faith unintelligible. It can be for the hour, and for our democratic Churches, a foe as dangerous to reality as dishonesty is. It creates a demand for emotions which become too facile in the supply, and, therefore, thoughtless and unreal. Unreality is worse than dishonesty. And we even have in our religion what has been called the Pharisaism of the publican. One has often to note in history the total lack of sound judgment that goes with extreme pietism, or the absence of reality, and even veracity, that *may* go with the saintly type. We have, moreover, the modern and most insidious type of Pharisaism – the unconscious hypocrite, the man or woman not of fraud but of pose, not of deep and dark design but of subtle egoism, prompt certainty, and facile religiosity. The mischief lies in the unreality of their faith and character rather than in a calculated hypocrisy. The victims are fair and fickle, rather than hollow and hard.

I would trace the undue place which modern religion gives to sentiment to the undue subjectivity of the whole modern type of faith, and its loss of hold upon the mind. And, definitely, I would trace it to the loss of a real positive authority, the loss of an objective grasp of the world's moral crisis in the Christian centre of the Cross. So long as the chief value of the Cross is its value for man, so long as its first effect is upon man and not upon God, so long as its prime action is not upon reality but upon our feeling about reality, then so long shall we be led away from direct contact with reality at our religious centre; and we shall be induced to dwell more upon our experience of reconciliation than on the God by whose self-reconciliation we are reconciled. There is something fatal to a real and thorough religion in a view which makes the finished work of God to depend for its fate upon human experience. It makes God a mere offerer, proposer, or promiser, until we have become receivers. It might even descend to present

God in a light little different from that of a candidate for the suffrage of our faith. 'It generates a religion of words, and not of purposes and facts, having its reality in the creature and only its proposal of reality in God' (Ed. Irving). To regain our spiritual reality and its moral tone we must go back from our subjective experience, not only to the objectivity of a historic Cross, but to the objectivity and the cruciality of God's spiritual action behind that historic Cross, to a central action within His own nature. Our spiritual reality and its ethical results, both for private and public righteousness, mean a fresh grasp by the Church of the work of Christ upon the holiness of God and upon the principle of evil. That is the spiritual condition on which alone we can restore the note of moral realism that has died from our sympathetic piety. I allude often to that frequent combination of rationalism with sentiment which marks both a hard orthodoxy and a hard heresy. The sentiment then represents the effort on the part of intellectualism to make up by feeling, cultivated if not forced, for the great and real emotion that flows of itself from contact with the supernatural issues involved, and from a share in the central moral drama of existence.

*

2. Besides the triviality and externality I have named, we suffer from uncertainty. For the hour perhaps the Church has more need to cultivate certainty than sanctity. It is only the certainty we lack that can give us the sanctity we desire. If we are duly certain about God's holiness our own will follow. It is only the certainty of the Cross that can give us the sanctity of the Spirit. For the fountain head of the Spirit is the Cross. An established or a Catholic Church can flourish upon mere assent; but for our purposes we need certainty as a personal experience, certainty at first hand from God in Christ. One has truly said, 'The grand remedy for the present epidemic of doubt is a personal interest in the struggle against evil.' We do not get the full force of these words till we interpret them of Christ's decisive battle with evil in the Cross, and our part and lot there. The certainty which criticism is sapping can never be regained by more positive criticism. The whole situation is being changed by the new movement; and we are being

forced on a new basis of certainty – or rather forced anew on the old, on the evangelical basis of personal salvation, personal forgiveness, experienced from the Cross of Christ as the redemption of the whole moral world.

For holiness of the evangelical type we surely need this certainty – for the true holiness, which grows upon our faith and we know it not. The forms of sanctity in vogue are a little too self-conscious, and too directly cultivated. It is always dangerous to make religion one of the professions. And to work at holiness can be fatal. Yet some forms of sanctity much admired seem to me to be pursued as a spiritual luxury rather than worn upon faith like a spiritual halo as unfelt as our hair. When Moses came down from the Mount he wist not that his face shone. We languish after 'peace, perfect peace' when we should be at godly war. The sinlessness we admire may be no more than poverty of blood. And we sing mawkishly about 'Angels of Jesus, angels of light' when we should be wrestling with them for the new name. It is so easy to do Christian work, and so hard to pray. *Magna res est, magnum omnino bonum, cum Jesu conversari*. It is not hard to be devotional, but it is hard to pray. *Orare est laborare*. What is called a gift in prayer is not uncommon. What is harder to come at is the gift from prayer, the prayer that prevails. Men may even take up Christian work to evade the arduous toil of spiritual concentration. And outward work often does cost us our spiritual insight, certainty, and reality. But without soul-certainty neither our work nor our principle has any meaning. It is soul-certainty that the world needs, even more than sound principles – not soul-facility but soul-certainty, not ready religion but sure. And it is soul-certainty that the ordinary able preacher, of busy effort, good cricket, vivid interests, actual topics, recent reading, and ingenious prayers cannot give you. Knowledge may give you convictions, and thought ideas; conscience will give you principles, and the heart sentiments; but that soul-certainty, that saved certainty, which is Eternal Life, can only arise from something very objective and positive, which turns the truths of the preacher to the word of authority, sets him in the Evangelic succession, and clothes him with the apostolic power. Our preaching has lost the note of

authority – though not the air of authority, the note of authoritativeness. That note, indeed, may be a phase of our Pharisaism. But
it has lost the stamp and effect of authority. The minister is more
strongly induced to be the friend and comrade of his people than
their moral authority and guide. And he is tempted to care more
(as the public care more) for the happy touch in his preaching than
the great Word.

What we need is not so much something pious as something
positive which makes piety. We need fewer homilies upon 'Fret
not' or 'Study to be Quiet,' fewer essays on 'the Beauty of
Holiness,' or other aspects of pensive piety. And we need more
sermons on 'Through Him the world is crucified to me, and I to
the world,' or 'Him who was made sin for us.' There is the real
incarnation, the emergence of God's reality, the reality of God as
an energy. There is the incarnation which puts us at once at the
moral heart of reality – the Son made sin rather than the Word
made flesh. The incarnation has no religious value but as the
background of the atonement. And here is the real righteousness
of God. It is our practical, experiential incorporation into the holy
Christ. It is not our success in doing God's will in a Christian spirit.
That is a Gospel of whose ineptitude I confess I am tired. It is at
the root of much of our present impotence. Christ's Gospel is the
gift (through the gift of Christ) of a totally new righteousness,
which is identical with faith, rises in forgiveness, emerges in
repentance, acts in love, spreads in society, and proceeds in
Eternal Life. What is sanctity if it do not bring a deepening
repentance? It was when Christ came to closer quarters with
God's holiness that man's sin roused that in Him which is repentance in us, and crushed Him to death. And the repentance of the
young convert is the merest regret compared with that of the aged
disciple. What is our sanctification but a perpetual conversion,
the realization of pardon in detail? That way alone lies the reality
on which man's moral rests, and with his moral soul his social
future and his eternal destiny.

*

The soul of the age asks us to help it to footing. And we try – when
we can steady our own feet for a moment. And how do we often

proceed? Why, we are so ill-found in the autonomy and supremacy of faith, that, instead of a fresh recourse to Christ, we cry to the men of science in the other boat to help us. We are so incredulous of the knowledge contained in faith, we are so sure that real knowledge cannot come by the moral way of faith, but only by intellectual science of some kind, that we look with nervous anxiety for corroboration – nay, more, for verification – from the savants. We are actually relieved at the prospects of ghosts, to vouch, on the authority of the Psychical Society, for a sure immortality that we have ceased to find in Christ. And we are grateful to the original and delightful Professor William James and Sir Oliver Lodge for the way in which their fresh results make good the sad defects of our Christian faith as to the spiritual nature of the world, or the spiritual depths of the soul. They tell us the old materialism is dead, and we breathe again. They suggest that the old agnosticism is dying, and we are cheered. We look to them and our faces are lightened. For a time at least they are lightened, till some ingenious fellow suggests new misgivings. Then we become less certain that the new idealism will sustain the soul's life, and we grow anxious again. Or we find ourselves after a delightful evening with the subliminal self, at deadly grips with a ferocious and ignoble passion.

But we reflect, perhaps, that though we personally are weak and contrary, yet a new presentiment of the unseen has laid hold of the modern mind, and we think there may be hope for Christianity still. So when that modern mind asks us for help to a footing we still turn to men of science, to men often who evidently never in their lives read a theological classic or an authority on moral philosophy, who indeed might scout the idea, and we ask them to assure the inquirer, with a certainty beyond ours, that things promise well for a soul. We do this, instead of descending upon science or its imagination with a sureness which has nothing to gain in the way of certainty but everything to give, when it is a question of the certainty above and beneath all. Is it not a nervous and pusillanimous Christianity, devoid of self-respect? How can we hope to regain the influence the pulpit has lost until we come with the surest Word in all the world to the guesses of science, the maxims of ethic, and the instincts of art?

Meantime, all kinds of occultism exploit this groping hunger of the age in the interests of their hobby. They believe not Moses and the prophets, but they would believe if one returned from the dead. They have lost the sense of moral evidence, which is faith, and they are devoted to phantasmal, which is sight. The rubbish that is grotesquely called Christian science is the scoriae of a volcano. It means, being interpreted, that the upheaval of the hour is not due to the need for truth, formal and stateable, but for power. It is soul certainty and moral reality that we crave for more than any -ology or any -doxy. We demand the unseen not in the form of a doctrine, or even an idea, far less a system, but as an energy, a life principle of rescue, power, authority. Men ask us, not, 'What do you believe? but 'What helps you, really?' What does it matter about our belief if it do not help? And there is but one way to that reality. The reality that matters, and that helps the race is redemption. Our puny individualism is always asking, 'What helps me?' But we shall get no satisfactory answer even to that question upon the lines of mere subjective feeling – as we might say of a meal 'it does me good, I feel fed' – but only upon those ethical lines which include the whole race, though they may for our individual self sometimes bring us rather to heroic confidence than to happy peace.

The note of the higher age is moral realism. It is the quest for unfailing love, in the spirit of unsparing ethical realism, the quest, in a word, for holy love. It is the quest which is met in prophet, Christ, and apostle. And the focus of the whole answer is still the Cross, where the holy love of the Eternal spared not His own Son in face of the ghastly realism of guilt. We can *trust* love only as it is holy.

*

But I can still hear the pertinacious citizen of his own age, who is a Chauvinist or Jingo of his own century as some are of their own country, who is totally disqualified for reading either his time or his land because he knows no other – I can hear him say, 'Are not Abana and Pharpar at our own doors better than that provincial

old Jordan? Are not art, science, ethic, sentiment, and philanthropy, however defective, better than these Hebrew old clothes?
Is the answer to the soul still in the worn old past and not in the
modern spirit?' Yes, that is so. The answer is in the old past, in
the historic cross of Christ or nowhere. 'But even Paul was only
a Judaist of genius who disfigured Christ by rabbinic notions. And
we are so weary of the old theologies.' But I was not thinking of
theologies. I had in my mind a deeper weariness than yours, and
I was thinking of principalities and powers. When shall we learn
that Paul, for instance, was not a dogmatist but the apostle of an
act of grace which condensed in itself the moral energy of Eternal
Reality? He was the vehicle of a passionate soul-experience,
soul-certainty, and moral reality. He was saturated with theology,
as you are with (let us say) psychical science, but he was not a
dogmatician. He was afire with the faith which is a life, with an
experience which made his mere ideas possibly inconsistent but
still incandescent. I have already pointed out how, to find expression for these experiences from the Cross, he seized every likely
idea, and pressed it into service, whenever he met it – in Judaism,
Gnosticism, Roman law or elsewhere. I was thinking of the
weariness which the theologies were very earnest efforts to heal.
It is the old perennial curse that lies on us – and it is the old eternal
cure. If you feel the curse (and it is moral dullness not to feel it),
where do you find so deep a treatment of it, and so many cases
of cure, as in the theologies of the Cross? That which makes the
Church is still the key of the world. The act of the Cross is still
the soul's centre, the centre of human destiny, and the centre of
the real presence of God; it is not the centre of our worship alone.
It is the centre of that evil conscience which is the pivot of the
world's tragedy, and therefore, the world's destiny. You cannot
sound the great literature of the world, the great transcripts of
man's moral soul, without realizing that the Pauline issues are the
marrow of the great literature of the world. What moral realism
finds at the dregs of life is guilt. And as yet the only effectual secret
of guilt's treatment is the Cross. The reality of life is Christ – and
not Christ's beauty, pity, or self-sacrifice, but His love as God's
holy grace, His moral mercy, moral judgment, moral atonement,

and moral victory of redemption. To that we must return, if all the world go on and leave us. And not only so, but we preachers must steep our soul in that, till we become charged with the one power to which men bow at last, Christ's conquest of the whole crisis of man's moral situation, His power to redeem, and His authority to forgive. The pulpit has lost authority because it has lost intimacy with the Cross, immersion in the Cross. It has robbed Christ of Paul. But that Church will be the ruling Church which most frees man's conscience, – not his thought, or his theology, but his conscience – and which carries in it most of the power to forgive and absolve. Only with this Gospel, authoritative because evangelical, can we make the spiritual life a world power, take it out of corners and coteries, give it control of the world and its resources, and save it from convent, conventicle, and college alike, to be ecumenical, practical, and final. Our lack of authority is mainly due to our lack of piercing moral realism, the radicalism of the Cross. It is a power which goes not out and comes not home except by prayer, laborious prayer as the concentration of mind and will. 'The truth is not with the right, nor with the left, nor in the middle, but in the heights.' The secret of spiritual realism is personal judgment, personal pardon, and personal prayer – prayer as conflict and wrestling with God, not simply as sunning one's self in God. There is no reality without wrestling, as without shedding of blood there is no remission. If you are not called to wrestle it is only because the wrestling is being done for you. Somewhere it must be done, and we must do more than watch it. And for the preacher it is only serious searching prayer, not prayer as sweet and seemly devotion at the day's dawn or close, but prayer as an ingredient of the day's work, pastoral and theological prayer, priest's prayer – it is only such prayer that can save the preacher from histrionics and sentiment, flat fluency, and that familiarity with things holy which is the very Satan to so many forward apostles.

I speak to and of the ministry, which is at once our despair and our hope. If the preachers have brought preaching down it is the preachers that must save it. The Church will be what its ministers make it. A Church of faith like Protestantism must always be what its chief believers make it. And these foremost and formative believers are the ministers. The real archbishops are the archbelievers. If a Church has not its chief believers in the pulpit it is unfortunate. And if a whole denomination of Churches fail in this matter there is something fatally wrong. The ministers are in idea the experts in faith. They are the *élite* of prayer. If the Church is to be saved from the world it is the ministers that must do it. And how can they do it but as men pre-eminently saved from the world? And no man has the seal of that salvation on him except by action – by thought and prayer which become moral action. A man has the stamp of supernatural reality upon him only by such prayer. If another than the minister carry that stamp in any Church he is its true minister. The true minister, in the pulpit or out, does all his business in the spirit of this prayer. The man of commerce may say he cannot. I will not argue that now. I will only say that the minister has this advantage – he not only can but he must, if he know his business, and is to keep it going. And no man ought to take up this business unless he know it. A preacher whose chief power is not in studious prayer is, to that extent, a man who does not know his business. A stringent ethic would say he was in danger of becoming a quack. That of prayer *is* the minister's business. He cannot be a sound preacher unless he is a priest. Prayer of the serious, evangelical, unceasing sort is to faith what original research is for science – it is the grand means of contact with reality. It is the soul's fruitful contact with that which for the soul is Nature – God in Christ. It founds us there upon the rock, and withstands the gates of hell. The religious life, the life which has religion for a profession, is the most dangerous of all. There are so many temptations to unreality in it – especially in connexion with what is sometimes called the deepening of the spiritual life. The bane of much sanctity is its unreality. I do not mean its insincerity, so much as its lack of contact with world-reality, moral, historic reality. Our great peril is not the coarse hypocrisy, which the common critic can see and scourge amid cheers. It is the subtler, deadlier unreality which may settle upon the executioner of hypocrisy, which is hidden even from ourselves, hidden by our very peace of mind, or hidden by the cheers, hidden, it may be, by our very well-doing. It is not the amusing hypocrisy of Mr. Pecksniff but the alarming hypocrisy of Mr. Bulstrode, so much more terrible because more true to actual life, because it waits for us at our own door. The preacher feels the full force of these temptations. At least he receives their full force, whether he always feel it or not, from his exposed position. He is a dealer in words; and it is very hard to keep them full of the Spirit, and yet to keep himself their master. He is a popular leader; and it is hard to lead the people without being led by the people to yield to them. The winning of souls, or the leading of souls, often costs the soul. A man can be popular and real both, especially as a preacher. I do not know of any line of life in which the combination is more possible. But to continue to be popular and also to be real depends on much. And then the preacher has the sophistries of his own egoism, the egoism even of his own conscience, the seductions of his own vanity, and the insincerities of his own heart, which are always most dangerous in the guise of piety. Some preachers appear to have no humiliation, confession, penance, or absolution in their soul's habit or history. Ephraim is a heifer unbroken to the yoke. Many a fervent prayer in the pulpit, and many a thrilling sermon, has but deepened the perdition of the unreal soul that uttered it – heartfelt though it was for the hour. Against such things private searching prayer, prayer much alone with the Judge of the Pharisees, is the corrective – prayer whose *keynote* is the Bible, however its *motives* may be the experiences of the soul. It is better and safer to pray over the Bible than to brood over self. And the prayer which is stirred by the Cross is holier even than that which arises from the guilt that drives us to the Cross. What really searches us is neither our own introspection, nor God's law, but it is God's Gospel, as it pierces us from the merciless mercy of the Cross and the Son unspared for us.

*

3.   The third vice of the Christian hour is spiritual self-satisfaction, well-to-do-ness, comfort. The voice of the turtle is heard in the land.

This is the religious counterpart of that intellectual self-sufficiency in many sections of science, where men are quite sure they have, in the experience that deals so successfully with parts, a key to the infinite whole. Their science gives them a closed scheme of all existence, which only needs filling in with discovery or filling out with invention. They do not realize that the knowledge of a world, a whole, is a knowledge by faith and not by science. None has ever seen or realized a whole world by any scientific experience, only by an act of faith. The more we know things or men the less we understand them till faith explains them by their goal. We see not yet all things, but we see Jesus.

Such also, in its way, is the self-satisfaction of so much naïve religion, denominationalism, or Churchmanship, the religion of the plain man who is always saying he is Davus and not Œdipus, who hates riddles, and who talks to you of his sectional interests or idols as if they must be of equal interest and volume to all the world.

> Who takes the murmur of his little burg
> For all the mighty music of the world.

We live too happily on the middle register. It is all so interesting – the day's doings, the vivid world, the Church, the Bible, the meetings, the movements, the singing, the preaching, the books, the reviews, the music, the marrying, the giving in marriage. We enjoy the long picnic, by the still waters, in companies upon the green grass. The flood, indeed, is already in the hills, and trained and gifted ears hear it, and give the alarm. And yet we sit down easily and agreeably beside the modern man, with his mixture of refined materialism and scrappy culture, to whom religion is but a phase of his general interests, or the key-stone of the social arch. Religion is to-day debased to a mere means of human happiness, to a social utility, as it never was before. It was once a political pawn, it is now a social facility. And the result is unfaith, or, worse, an affectation of faith. We are so healthy, so poetical, so kindly, so optimistic. God's love and patience and mercy are all so much in line with life's innocent charm, all so much a matter of course and of congratulation. And we are so strange to heart-hunger, or soul-despair, or passionate gratitude, or heavenly home-sickness. Whole tracts of our religion are bare of spiritual passion, or spiritual depth. Christianity speaks the language of our humane civilization; it does not speak the language of Christ. The age, and much of the Church, believes in civilization and is interested in the Gospel, instead of believing in the Gospel and being interested in civilization. And we treat as fanatics those who tell us that there is no reconciliation possible between the Cross and culture, when each knows its own mind, except as culture itself submits to be redeemed. As if Christ did not come to redeem us not from sin only, nor from worldliness, but from the world.

I once addressed a meeting of ministers on the necessity of the evangelical consciousness, by which I meant the central or even daily life of forgiveness, repentance, humiliation, and their fruits, in contrast with what is vaguely known as the Christian spirit. And I created a good deal of bewilderment. For one of them came to me afterwards, and asked me if he had understood me right, as, to his knowledge, the experience was one that few ministers possessed. If that was so I need not say another word to account for the loss of pulpit power and authority. It is not more religion we need so much as a better order of religion, and a more serious idea of the soul, its sin and its salvation.

For an ill like this there is but one cure. It is a deeper, daily, though perhaps reserved sense, not only of our unworthiness, but of our perdition except for the Grace of Christ, the mercy of the Cross. And this deepened sense will not come. It must be sought, courted, entreated. The deepening of personal religion! It is something much more that we need. We need the humiliation in which we forget about religion, the faith in which we forget about either faith or works, the sanctity that has no knowledge of its own holiness. We need an experience of Christ in which we think everything about the Christ and not about the experience. We need that preachers shall not keep demanding either a faith or love that we cannot rise to, but shall preach a Christ that produces and compels both. And we need that the Christ we preach shall not be our brother, ideal, or King only, but also our judge. Nay, we read that He is chiefly our judge, because He took our judgment on Him for our redemption. Every great revival in the Church has gone with a new sense of Christ's vicarious redemption, and not merely with a new wave of pity. Our great need is not ardour to save man but courage to face God – courage to face God with our soul as it is, and with our Saviour as He is; to face God always thus, and so to win the power which saves and serves man more than any other power can. We can never fully say 'My brother!' till we have heartily said 'My God;' and we can never heartily say 'My God' till we have humbly said 'My Guilt!' That is the root of moral reality, of personal religion, and social security. It is only thus that we really meet the passion for reality, which is so hopeful a feature of modern time, because it is the ruling passion of a Holy God.

Six

Preaching Positive and Liberal

Authority the need of the hour – The preacher's authority being the objective personal content of faith, his first need a *positive theology* – The meaning of a 'positive theology' – Its irrepressible adjustment in each age – Its vital difference from Liberalism in its emphasis on historic and experienced grace and on the absoluteness of Christ – Creational rather than evolutionary – Its norm the New Testament Gospel and not the modern mind – Its adequacy to the human tragedy – Its emphasis on personality and sin – Its interpretation of Christ by incarnation, not by immanence – The seriousness of the issue to-day.

The first requisite for a Christian man is faith. That is what makes a soul a member of Christ and of the true Church – the faith that works and blossoms out into love. Being faith in Christ, how could it but work and flower out into love? The fact that so often it does not must mean that in so many cases it is not really faith, or not faith in Christ. It is not personal contact and commerce with Him. This faith it is that is the greatest thing in the world, having in it all the promise and potency of love, godliness, peace, and joy in the Holy Ghost. It is such living faith that makes a man a Christian.

But among Christians the preacher stands out in a special place and work. And the first requisite for the ministry of a Church is a theology, a faith which knows what it is about, a positive faith, faith with not only an experience but a content, not glow only but grasp, and mass, and measure. The preacher who is but feeling his way to a theology is but preparing to be a preacher, however eloquent he may have become. He may be no more than 'the hierophant of an unapprehended inspiration.' And that kind of inspiration may be mantic or romantic, but it is neither prophetic nor apostolic. The faith which makes a man a Christian must go on in the preacher to be a theology. He cannot afford to live on in a *fides non formata*. A viscous unreflecting faith is for the preacher a faith without footing and therefore without authority. In special cases it may have a certain infection about it, but it has not authority. Yet it is authority that the world chiefly needs and the preaching of the hour lacks – an authoritative Gospel in a humble personality. And for authority, for weight, we need experience, indeed, but, still more, positive faith.

It is but a little way that experience will carry the herald of the Gospel. He has to expound a message which, because it is eternal, far transcends his experience. He has to do more than set to his own personal seal. Every Christian has to do that. The preacher has to be sure of a knowledge that creates experience, and does not rise out of it. His burthen is something given, something that reports a world beyond experience, a world that is not of experience, though always in its shape. Experience is but in part, yet he has to dogmatize about the whole. He has to be sure of what ever is, and evermore shall be. Experience is in time, and he has to be positive about eternity. His experience covers but his own soul, or at most a few besides that he touches; yet he has to declare a certainty about the eternal destiny of the whole world, and the eternal will of the whole God. That is a knowledge far beyond experience. It is not realizable except in experience, but experience could not reach it, could not assure it. It is a knowledge that comes by faith. Wherever you have a universe you have something beyond experience, and accessible only to faith. Experience is not the only organ of knowledge, however it may be a condition. Experience deals with but the one, or the several; faith deals with a whole; for it deals with God, eternity and the world; it deals with a reality of the whole, which we experience but in a measure. There is a knowledge by faith as sound of its kind as the knowledge by experience, by science; and its kind is much higher, deeper, more momentous. It is the knowledge of a person in his purpose, not of a thing and its features, not of a force and its laws. It is not simply faith as a personal experience that is the burthen of the preacher, but faith as a knowledge, the inner objective content of faith, the thing in faith which always creates the experience of it; in a word, the person, will, and action of God in Christ. It is there, in the objective personal content of faith, and not in the subjective personal experience, that the authority of the preacher lies. His experience may make him impressive at times, but it is his faith that gives him permanent power. That power really lies not in the preacher but in his Gospel, in his theology. For the preacher it is most true that his theology is an essential, perhaps the essential, part of his religion. He may be quite unfit to lecture in theology as a science, but he is the less of a preacher, however fine a speaker, if he have not a theology at the root of his preaching and its sap circulating in it. And if he is a pastor, producing his effect not by a few addresses but by a cumulative ministry, all this is still more true.

*

The first requirement of the ministry, then, is a positive theology. But by that I do not mean a highly systematic theology, nor an orthodox theology. For a systematic theology easily becomes doctrinaire, and an orthodoxy soon becomes obsolete. It were well to banish antiquated words like orthodoxy and heterodoxy as anything but historical terms. They belong to an out-grown age, when a formal theology had a direct saving value for the individual soul; when there was but one true theology instead of many, as there was but one true Church; when there was an external authority, to make a standard, in an inerrant Bible, a final confession, or an infallible Pope. The one orthodox Church, the Greek Church, is the deadest of all the Churches. And we should have been as dead if orthodoxy had had its way with the West as it had with the East. For at its worst it is mere conformity; and at its best it is the regime of intellectualism. It reduces religion to an intellectualism with a divine charter. And its reaction in hetero-doxy is natural, equal, and opposite. Both are intellectualist and theosophic. Let us consider the words, therefore, as archaic and defunct for faith. And instead of speaking or thinking about an orthodox theology, which is canned theology gone stale, let us think of a positive theology which is theology alive, alert, and in power.

*

Again, by a positive theology I mean naturally the opposite of a negative. But when is a theology negative? Negative of what? Negative of a tradition? No, of a power. Negative of the Gospel. A positive theology is an evangelical theology. Positivity in this connexion has a chief reference to what I have often to describe as the primacy of the will. It is moral; but moral in a far higher sense than a mere imperative – moral as being not diffused in an idea or organized in thought, but concentrated in a personal act, in redemption. The love manifested by Christ in His life was positive in the sense that it was not merely affectional but rational and moral. That is to say, its great features were first that it understood the total situation – so far it was rational – and second that it condensed into one definite practical purpose – it was saving and moral. It understood God uniquely; no man knoweth the Father but the Son. It understood man to his moral centre, and needed that no man should tell it what was in man. And it was concentrated into crucial action both on God and on man. It was decisive and redemptive. Positive means moral in the great evangelical sense. That is to say, in the first place, it means that the supreme form of God's love was a real act, central in history and critical for eternity. It was a holy life not simply in the sense of being spotless but in the sense of being one vast moral deed, one absolute achievement of conscience, affecting the being both of God and man and the whole spiritual world. It was not merely impressionist. It was not an influence but an act, not a fresh stimulus but a new creation, not a career opened for the race but a finished thing. Holiness has no meaning apart from an act into which is put a whole moral person; and if there be an eternal person it is an eternal act, and not merely a past event, or the attribute of an eternal being, or an infinite presence, as the mystics dream. Accordingly, in the second place, God's gift was an eternal life, something beyond natural goodness, however good, and however refined. For what is morality, when we are at the height to which we have now come? It is not a mere obedience. That were in the end but some kind of Pharisaism, of which indeed Protestantism has been greatly the victim. No compliance with a mere law or creed, however good or fine makes a moral action. Morality is the expression of our personality; and to grow moral means to grow in personality, and not merely in a certain exercise of personality. It is our creative action. It is the soul co-operating with the holy energy of God and fulfilling its redeemed destiny. To live in the Spirit is not simply to walk in the light. The Spirit is creative energy; and to live in the Spirit is to exercise this energy. It is eternal life in its countless concrete forms of actuality, experience, and history – in worship, art, science, politics, in Church, State, or family. Positive Christianity then is Christianity which recognizes the primacy of the moral in the shape of life, and of holy life. It is Christianity which first adjusts man to the holy and then creates the holy in man, and does both through the Cross with its atoning gift of eternal life. It is evangelical Christianity – Christianity not as a creed nor as a process but as a Holy Spirit's energy and act, issuing always from the central act and achievement of God and of history in the Cross of Christ.

But the name of evangelical theology has often been monopolized by a theology which has not really escaped from the idea of orthodoxy, a theology not only elaborate but final, irrevisable, and therefore obscurantist, and therefore robbed of public power. By an evangelical theology I mean any theology which does full justice to the one creative principle of grace. Any theology is evangelical which does that. A theology is not evangelical by its conclusions but by its principles, not by its clauses and statements, not by its spirit or temper, but by the Holy Spirit of grace and power. It is the statement of a Gospel of Grace, it is not the scientific explication of that Gospel's corollaries and implicates.

*

Some forms of evangelical theology are too fond of describing a critical theology as negative. I do not like the word negative. There is a certain unpleasant suggestion in it which we should avoid. I would rather use the more correct and current antithesis of positive, and say liberal. Here again, however, we are in difficulties. For in the first place, if what we oppose is liberal, are we not illiberal in opposing it? And is there not an unpleasant suggestion in that? And in the next place, if we follow current use and say liberal as the antithesis of positive, do we mean that a positive theology is only conservative and incapable of modification with time to meet the progress of thought and knowledge? The answer to that, of course, is that a confession of faith not only can be, but must be modified in this way. The creed must take the expression which gives the best effect at the time to the grace which creates it. In this regard it reflects the almighty power of God which (if Christ be His revelation) is chiefly shown in His capacity for any self-limitation needful to give effect to His holy will of grace and love at a particular juncture. Theological form must be adjustable. The old faith demands a new theology. For, in the first place, its nature does, and in the second, its history.

First, its nature does. Christ, as the standing object of our faith, is the meeting-point of changeless eternity, and changing history. In Him the eternal emerges at a fleeting point. But, if He is the same yesterday, to-day, and for ever, this final utterance must be expressible at every other such point. His eternal revelation is vocal and relevant for every age. The changeless Gospel must speak with equal facility the language of each new time, as well as of each far land. If it be missionary to every soul it is also missionary to the whole soul of history. There is an ironic, socratic docility in the everlasting Gospel. It must be flexible if it is to search and permeate. It must be tractable and reasonable because it is so supreme and sure. It must have the power to vary, and to meet the forms of thought and life which it does so much to produce. We could never preach to the time if our Gospel had but a lapidary and monumental eternity. Remember Lot's wife.

There must be such a thing as a history of Christianity, not merely a history of the effects of Christian doctrine in the world. That doctrine is not a rock in a stream. The religion itself must have an elasticity of its own, a variableness and adaptability which do not alter its substance. It is not like a philosophic system which cannot reappear in a modified form, but can only be replaced by another system. Christianity must modify, for it is not a fixed quantity cut and dried. It has no existence outside of the life and the will of moving man. Therefore while it has a continuity it has also a history and not a mere persistence. No otherwise is it a living potent religion. Only the lowest religions, like the lowest races and creatures, are without a history. And Christianity has a history because it is under the constant renewing of the Holy Ghost. It is a new and independent power of life within the stream of time. It is not a mere section of civilization. And its history has a unity quite different from the development of religion in general. It is not simply a limb in the organism of spiritual evolution.

In the second place, the history of the old faith demands a re-interpretation of theology, even if we may not say a revision. For I have already noted how the greatest Apostles and fathers of the Church translated the Gospel into the current mind. And I note farther that in history fixed and final dogma constantly tends to produce a type of life quite other than that produced by the old faith. Where you fix a creed you flatten faith. Where dogma is idolized, life is sterilized. Where you canonise a system you demoralize men. But the effect of the faith of the Gospel is entirely the other way. It rouses, exalts, kindles men. A fixed and final system is therefore incompatible with the genius of the Gospel. That is the principle of the Reformation. Living faith means growing form. Orthodoxy, Catholicism, in different degrees tend to petrify life. Therefore they lose the power of the Gospel, no matter what the amount of zeal may be. Dogma is not an end in itself. And even doctrine is but the expression of life, it is not the life indeed.

The old faith of the Gospel, therefore, is not merely patient of new form, a new theology, but it demands it. It produces it. It fits itself in a masterly way to the shape and pressure of the time, unless we prevent it. The very power of its eternity, its supernatural power, shows itself in this, that it uses time and is not left behind. What is eternity but the soul's command of time?

*

But, if a positive Gospel thus asserts its positivity by irrepressible adjustment, why should we set in opposition positive and liberal? Well, as a matter of fact, theological liberalism has tended to destroy positive belief, distinctive experience, and aggressive Christianity. But perhaps the terms are not happy. Still, there they are in use. They are part of the accepted language of the discussion. And the word which is employed to express the adjustments native to a positive Gospel is not 'liberal' but 'modern.' A modern theology is one thing, theological liberalism is another. Ritschl represents one Gospel, Pfleiderer another. And they are disparate and incompatible. Paul and Luther cannot dwell with Hegel. The one is a function of faith, the other is a school of thought. I am not pleading for the terms. I am simply accepting them. They cover distinct things. It is the things I wish to distinguish. And I do so in the course of an attempt to make good my case that a positive and modern theology is a first requisite for a preacher of the Gospel. Of the Gospel, note. For the first requisite for a mere preacher is a temperament. And a temperament without a Gospel is more of a bane than a blessing to a public man. The more of a temperament a preacher has the more he needs a positive Gospel to carry it, and save it from shipwreck. Of course, I imply by my words that what is called liberal theology, as distinct from theology modern and positive, works on the whole against the preaching of the Gospel, and becomes little more than an enlightened Judaism.

I may here anticipate what I go on to say later by explaining in brief that by liberalism I mean the theology that begins with some rational canon of life or nature to which Christianity has to be cut down or enlarged (as the case may be); while by a modern positivity I mean a theology that begins with God's gift of a super-logical revelation in Christ's historic person and cross, whose object was not to adjust a contradiction but to resolve a crisis and save a situation of the human soul. For positive theology Christ is the object of faith; for liberal He is but its first and greatest subject, the agent of a faith directed elsewhere than on Him. It is really an infinite difference. For only one side can be true.

*

We need, for our pulpit efficiency, a theology that is new when compared with catechismal orthodoxy, a restatement of doctrine which may be either 'modern' or 'liberal.' Now which does the Gospel demand? What is the difference between a modernized positivity and liberalism, as I have defined the terms?

Let me name some vital distinctions.

1.   I begin with the most essential. *The positivity of the Gospel means the effectual primary of the given*. And this primacy of the given means two things. I have said that we can think modern and end positive. We can keep abreast of both thought and knowledge and yet emerge with the results of positive faith. We can still believe in the primacy of the given in these two aspects – first in respect of history or the origin of our religion, second in respect of theology or the nature of our religion.

First, in respect of the *origin* of our religion, when we say it is positive we mean that it is historical. The revelation is not primarily in my soul but in a fact which is in the chain of history. It is in Christ and His Cross. Positivity means therefore in the first place historicity. It opposes a religion whose genius is thought or idea instead of historic event. Christianity is founded *in* the historic Jesus, it was not merely founded *by* Him. In Him we have the revelation and not merely the first believer in the revelation. And in Him, in that historic figure, is the final and absolute revelation; He is not a mere stage in the history of revelation. His religion is not simply one among others and the best of them all. It is religion in the final sense of the word. And it is the religion that believes and worships Him; it is not simply religion that believes with Him, and with Him worships God.

Second, in respect of the *nature* of our religion, or its theology, positivity as the primacy of the given means that we take it seriously as the religion of grace. The Gospel descends on man, it does not rise from him. It is not a projection of his innate spirituality. It is revealed, not discovered, not invented. It is of grace, not works. It is conferred, not attained. It is a gift to our poverty, not a triumph of our resource. It is something which holds us, it is not something that we hold. It is something that saves us, and nothing that we have to save. Its Christ is a Christ sent to us and not developed from us, bestowed on our need and not produced from our strength, and He is given for our sin more than for our weakness.

That is to say, the first feature of a positive Gospel is that it is a Gospel of pure, free grace to human sin. (And you will find that liberalism either begins or ends with ignoring sin or minimising it.) The initiative rests entirely with God, and with a holy and injured God. On this article of grace the whole of Christianity turns. 'Christianity,' says an unfriendly critic, 'stands or falls with its doctrine of forgiveness.' A positive theology means the doctrines of grace – brought up to date by all means, but only so as to give larger scope to the Gospel of grace than to the claim of religious culture.

A liberal theology has most to say of God's love, a positive of God's mercy. The one views God's love chiefly in relation to human love, the other chiefly in relation to human sin. In relation to sin chiefly – because a positive Gospel is a revelation of *holy* love, and our answer to it is not merely affectional, but holy, obedient, and worshipful. If the great revelation of God is in the Cross, and the great gift of the Cross is the Holy Spirit, then the revelation is holiness, holiness working outward as love. It is not simply sacred love, as it comes, for most people, to mean; but it is holiness working out into love on God's side, as our faith does on our side. God's love is the outgoing of His holiness, not as exigent law, but as redeeming grace, bent on reclaiming us, all bankrupt and defiant, to His full, rich, harmonious, eternal life. The holiness of God is His self-sufficient perfection, whose passion is to establish itself in the unholy by gracious love. Holiness is love morally perfect; love is holiness brimming and overflowing. The perfection speaks in the overflow. It is in redemption. Love is perfect, not in amount but in kind, not as intense but as holy. And holiness is perfect, not as being remote, nor as being merely pure, but as it asserts itself in redeeming grace. Love, as holy, must react against sin in Atonement. Holiness, as grace, must establish itself by redemption in Satan's seat. It is not the obstacle of redemption but its source and impulse.

The primacy of the given, then, is only another way of expressing the final authority of grace. The question of the hour, for all life, and not only for the religious, is that of authority – the true effective authority. Where is it? At the last it is here. It is in God's eternal, perpetual act and gift of grace, met by the absolute obedience of our faith. Faith is absolute obedience to grace as absolute authority. Personal faith in the holy, gracious God of Christ's Cross is the one creative, authoritative, life-making, life-giving, life-shaping power of the moral soul.

Now a modernized theology is not only compatible with this old faith, it is inevitable to it. But the liberal theology, as I am describing it, is fatal to the old faith. For all its varieties have this in common. They are indifferent to a doctrine of the Holy Ghost. It is this doctrine that prevents us from describing the progress of Christianity as a mere spiritual *process*, or the spread of a movement. Any theology that places us in a spiritual *process*, or native movement between the finite and the infinite, depreciates the value of spiritual *act*, and thus makes us independent of the grace of God. Its movement is processional spectacular, aesthetic, it is not historic, dramatic, tragic or ethical. If it speak of the grace of God it does not take it with moral seriousness. It understands by God's grace no more than the Idea moving to transcend our error, or love acting in generosity, or in pity. It reduces mercy to a form of pity by abolishing the claim of holiness, the gravity of sin, and the action of an Atonement. It does not take either the measure of holiness or the weight of sin. It makes the Cross not necessary but valuable; not central but supplemental; not creative but exhibitive; a demonstration, but not a revelation; a reconciliation but not a redemption. It makes the Church a company of workers and not believers, the brethren of Christ rather than His flock and His property, a genial body rather than a regenerate, a band of lovers rather than of penitents. It attenuates the Fatherhood which it softens. It interprets it as His creating love. Now God the Father is indeed Creator, but it is not as Creator that He is Father. We are all destined to be sons of God; but the sonship is in our destiny rather than in our origin or state. A distinguished president of the British Association for Science recently described the child as 'a candidate for humanity.' And we are all but personalities in the making. We are sons by an election rather than a creation. We are sons not by heredity but by adoption; not by right but by redemption. In the Old Testament as in the New Testament the son is no created being, but a chosen. Israel in the Old Testament, and Christ in the New, are the Sons of God by His election and not by His creation. Christ is increate. The whole Bible use of the word Father refers it to an act of choice and a purpose of redemption. God is Father by His choosing will and not by His creative power, by gracious adoption and not by natural generation. Of His will begat He us, and by no instinctive process. We are sons 'begotten in the Gospel.' God is, directly, the Father of Christ alone. He is our Father only in Christ. God has but one Son; the many sons are sons in Him; and He is Son in none.

A positive Gospel, therefore, is given as a power to our Christian experience, while a liberal theology may bear little trace of Christian experience, and it may exist but as a truth in Christian reason. A positive theology is at bottom the theology of converted men, and not of academic intelligence brought to bear on the soul, the world, or history. It is faith giving a reasonable account of itself; it is not reason shaping, amending, or licensing faith. It carries in its body the marks of the Lord Jesus. Its datum is in history, not in thought. It has the stigmata of the Cross on its heart. The positive theology is more devout (I am not speaking of the theologians), the liberal is more doctrinaire. The one is more concerned with life, the other with truth. The one is pneumatic, the other dogmatic. The one is evangelical and moral, the other intellectualist. The one is part of the religion, the other is a view of the religion. Thus the liberal theology is the more theological, in the opprobrious sense of the term; for it is more engrossed with views and truths than experiences of faith.

*

2. *For liberalism the modern mind constitutes itself the supreme court*, and claims that nothing should survive in Christianity but what is congenial to it. Christianity, in so far as it is true, is simply 'the passion which is highest reason in a soul divine.' It is, as the old Apologists said, the practicable and effective completion of

the revelation that was labouring for outlet in Paganism. It is a new branch of culture. It is an immense, not to say infinite, extension of our old horizon. We are, on Christ's shoulders, lifted but not saved, not as lost sheep rejoicing in a new life, but as eager disciples rejoicing in a wider, deeper prospect of things. The way to God is thus really the world and not the word. His seat is the heart at its best, and not the conscience at its worst.

A positive theology starts with the experienced grace of God to sin as a historic gift in Christ and His Cross. It is a gift which is at once our source and our standard, a gift whose divinity is approved by faith's obedience on the principle that he who willeth to do God's will shall know congenially the moral quality of the doctrine. But the liberal theology starts from certain rational, metaphysical, or ethical principles existing in human thought, which determines by science, and not by obedience, whether any revelation, even Christ's, is divine. The one is theology, the other is theosophy. The one starts from the primacy of the ethos, the other from the primacy of the cosmos. The one is voluntarist, the other is intellectualist. The one is teleological, finding the world's destiny in the historic Christ as the source and surety of that destiny ('We see not yet all things, but we see Jesus'); the other is cosmological, engrossed with the world's structure or with its movement in reason. For positivity God's decisive revelation is in his action in Christ, and its effect is active in a Church; for liberalism it is in reason, and its effect is contemplative or theosophic in a school. The one acts historically, subjugating the world to Christ; the other aesthetically, subduing it to thought. The one modifies from age to age according to the intrinsic requirements of growing faith; the external *Zeitgeist* being but the occasion which releases the latent genius of belief. The other modifies wholly in the interest of scientific thought, whether physical, psychical, metaphysical, or critical, as if Christianity were a phase of civilization. The one regards the revelation of grace as autonomous, the other will have it licensed by the schools, or countersigned by the humane 'heart.' The positive starts with the holy and saving Christ, the liberal with Humanity, rational or affectional. The one handles sin, grace, and salvation according to the

world's moral mutiny: the other deals but with weakness, ignorance, and their evolutionary conquest, confirming the world in
its pride of power. A modern theology, in a word, is demanded
by an autonomous evangelical faith: the liberal is prescribed by
an aggressive, cosmological science. But we must start with that
faith; its synthesis with any kind of science is a hope for which we
wait and patiently work. The theologian, that is, can wait; but
you preachers cannot.

Now, when we preach on this liberalistic basis it is not Christ
preaching to an age so much as one age, or one part of an age,
preaching to another. It is not a message from God to man, it is
a message of the *élite* to the mass, a summons from the superman.
It is man trying to lift himself by his own collar. Positivity, on the
contrary, has its source and its standard in one, in the historic
origin of Christianity, the pure word and deed of God in Christ
and His finished grace. We preach a historic message from God
to humanity, and not a message of historic humanity to itself; a
real rescue by a hand from heaven at our utmost moral need, and
not a scaling of heaven by our intrinsic moral strength.

It ought to be said in justice that the rationalism of the liberal
position takes two forms, a Christian and an anti-Christian. And
it would not be fair to charge those who press the normality of
the Christian consciousness with the sterilities of scientific rationalism. It ought, however, also to be said, that if the Christian
consciousness of each age is the supreme court, the end is Catholicism – the supremacy of the Church's voice, of faith's latest stage,
over the Gospel. Of course a modern positivity admits the reason
as a critic of the Bible, of the mere sacred history, but not of the
holy Gospel. The Gospel which recreates our moral experience in
the end criticises us. We cannot judge our judge.

*

3. *Positive theology is creational, liberal is evolutionary.* For the
positive theologian the course of religious history has been
chiefly determined by the due intervention of supernatural and
incomparable factors. The spirit of man was invaded by the spirit
of God, as the whole Rhone shoots into Leman. Every doctrine
of God's immanence must be compatible with that supreme

moral experience, and licensed by it. Liberal theology on the contrary views the course of religion as an immanent evolution accounting even for experience. The action of God is not to recreate our spiritual power so much as to release and forward it. It is not a raising from the dead, but only a loosing and letting go. Religious experiences are inevitable products of the spiritual nature of man and the world as created and constituted by God. Whereas, according to a positive theology, they are produced, in the crucial cases at least, by a special action of God. What is uppermost is a person and not a process. The Church represents not simply the influence of Christ but His Holy Spirit. Christian experience, through that Spirit, must always be more than spiritual evolution. It comes from contact or communion with a living Lord; and faith is only explicable as His gift by the Spirit. In faith, we do not feel ourselves initiative or creative except as we feel ourselves a new creation. Now as preachers we must choose between these two versions of Christianity. In the preaching of a Gospel it is the one theology rather than the other that serves us. For the Gospel of liberalism, whatever it may be in theory, is in effect but man calling to men; while a positive Gospel is man called by God. You will observe that I am not trying to exhibit the extent to which Christianity may find room for evolution. That would occupy another inquiry. It is more needful in the interest of preaching to set out the antithesis. And here, the interest of preaching is the interest of the soul.

*

4. *As the most recent phase of evolutionary religion we have the historic-religious movement, challenging the absoluteness of Christianity.* Liberalism here rises from the study of the religions that abut upon the age of Christ with this question, 'Did they not make Him and the faith of Him? If they did not entirely create the historic figure of Jesus, did they not supply the ideas that Christianity thought were revealed in Christ? Did they not create the supernatural Christ, the pre-existent Christ, the propitiatory Christ, the Christ that should judge the world? If so, how can we speak of the finality of Christ, the absoluteness of Christianity? Is it not all relative to what went before, all a creation of history, all

just the past writ larger? Is it not relative to the future? May it not be superseded in its turn? How can anything historical be more than relative? How can it do more than serve its place and time, and then, when it has advanced these, retire to make room for something greater? How can we speak of the absolute and final value of Christ? How can we speak of Him as veritable God?'

To which a first answer is, that historical study certainly does compel us to include Christ in His time and world, and to alter in some points the fashion of His claim on us. In doing so it makes a real historic figure of Him, a real man, and not a magical prodigy. He shared the life of limited man, the life of His age, the life of His land. In the region of mere knowledge He was not infallible. He thought much in Jewish categories, He felt human finitude, He confessed to some human ignorance. We modify the impossible and Byzantine Christ into a national figure real and mighty, and only by doing so do we find His true universality. And a second answer would be this, that if the ideas that have been most active in Christianity were drawn from Judaism (which itself was largely shaped by the farther East) then the best Pharisees of Christ's day were more responsible for the foundation of historic Christianity than Christ Himself, which seems a *reductio ad absurdum* that I need not, perhaps, for my present purpose pursue.

But we go farther. We say that this limitation in Christ was the result, the expression of His absolute power. It was an exercise of His will. It was self-limitation, an effect of His self-emptying. It was the very power of God under conditions imposed not simply by human nature but by holy love, grace divine, and saving purpose. And therefore it was an expression of His absoluteness. By His own eternal self-determined will He became lower than the angels. He exerted power over both the natural and the moral world. For He overrode natural law, and broke the entail and Nemesis of guilt. His very obedience to nature was a voluntary and masterly obedience. And His 'becoming sin' for us was a voluntary act, a moral achievement of a kind possible only to Godhead. He parted with a physical omnipotence but never with a moral, never with the omnipotence of love, which is the Christian meaning of the Cross. The limitation of His consciousness was no limitation of His moral power, but its exercise. His ignorance of many things we know at school was part of His divine renunciation. His subjection to nature, to death, to dereliction, was the act of His free grace. ' 'Tis but in limits that the master shows.' And the absolute mastery of Christ was made perfect in the relativity He assumed. It was an absolute relativity as being self-determined. Otherwise I do not understand what Troeltsch means by 'a relative absoluteness.' The absolute is less than absolute if it has not the power of the relative. If the infinite could not be finite, it is less than infinite. For there is then a region outside its range. He had power to do anything perfectly that was due to love and to the will of God. The absoluteness of His obedience to that was the absoluteness of His moral power, which is the only absoluteness we have to do with at last.

No doubt the preacher of a Christ merely relative brings Him nearer to our *conditions*, but it is the preacher of the absolute Christ that brings Him nearest to our *need*. To be near our conditions makes a man interesting, but to be near to our moral need makes him a power. To humanize Christ is to popularize Him, no doubt. But it is His Deity that makes Him outstay popularity, surmount the desertion of the Cross, and become universal. What we need is a power to enter and save us which is possible only to the God we wronged; we do not need simply the most interesting of historic figures. Our trouble is not our ennui and not our ignorance, it is our sin. It is our Holy One that spoils our feasts and troubles our dreams. Is it not clear which of these two views belongs to a preached Gospel, and to our moral case? Our moral predicament, the actual need of the race, demands chiefly, not a more human Jesus, but a more divine Christ.

*

5.   *A positive theology finds the essence of Christianity in the core of the New Testament Gospel*, cleansed of those temporary hulls that clung to it in the first century. You may seek this core in the heart of Christ's teaching alone, or you may find it in the Cross as the heart of the whole New Testament Christ. That is a controversy which, for the moment, we may pass by. The point is that the source and norm is in the New Testament. The

simplification of faith is effected by going to its centre and origin. That is to say, it comes from a deepening of faith, and not merely from an easing of it. The maxim of textual criticism has a higher sense – *lectio difficilior potius*. Distrust the simple solutions of old problems. A simplification of Christianity which is not also a deepening of it is fatal to it. Its real simplicity lies at the centre, not on the surface. To simplify faith we must be taken to its heart. The simplicity *of* the heart may be very shallow, but the simplicity *at* the heart is deep. And history has driven Christianity to more simplicity chiefly by forcing it in on its centre, and not by thrusting it to the surface. The Bible has done much for history, but also history has done much for the Bible. It has driven us in on it. It has simplified not by lucidity but by concentration. It has clarified the issue by staking all on the centre, and by compelling us to feel in that deep core our infinite power. It has removed our first concern from the Bible to the Gospel within the Bible. It has forced us from the simplicity of clearness, obviousness, and ease to the simplicity of centrality, depth, and power.

I speak about Christ and the centre of Christ, which is to be found at the head of Christianity, in the Cross, as the Epistles exist to say in a very positive fashion. But the liberal theology finds the essence of Christianity to consist of the spine, so to speak, or marrow, or continuity, or, as Hegel would say, the 'truth,' of the whole development of Christianity which Christ but initiated. You must (it says) include the whole Christian history in your field of induction. The spinal cord has the same value as the brain it prolongs. The Church (viewed historically and not dogmatically) is essential for our definition of Christianity. You cannot read the Gospel aright except along with its results in a Church.

One objection to this is that, if that be so, the first Christians, like Paul, had next to no data to go on; and therefore they were less in a position than we are to say what Christianity really is. They had not the Gospel's results before them, but only the Gospel itself. This is also an objection which tells with equal force against the common and thoughtless saying that the real evidence of Christianity is the lives of Christians. God help us if that were so! It was not Christianity that made Paul a Christian, it was no church. It was not even the story of Jesus; it was the personal contact with Christ. It was his invasion by Christ. Paul had nothing to speak of before him in the shape of evidential Christendom. From the Church he had at most but testimony. He had to proceed entirely on Christ's evidence for Himself.

Another difficulty is that, on the liberal view, the field of induction has no limit. We cannot make the books up. The history of Christendom still goes on. The record of results is not yet done. In some ways it is not well begun. The region before us is indefinite. The half has not been told. How do we know that the weightier part of the evidence is not yet to come? As with an iceberg, the larger part of the mass is as yet under water. It is future and unseen. And there might be something preparing there which would change the centre of gravity and upset the whole fabric. Has God conquered sin, death, and the world in Christ? Or is it still an open question whether these will not foil, conquer, and mock God?

Were Christianity but an evolutionary spiritual process then it were right to look for the key at the close, and not at the origin. That is the principle of evolution. Man explains the monkey, not the monkey man. It is age that explains youth, and eternity time – 'the last of life, for which the first was made.' Were Christianity mere evolution we should have no key to it, since we have not yet its goal. But it is not a case of evolution; it is a case of positive revelation. Our destiny is given us in our new creation. Paul's apostolic commission, I have reminded you, was given him in his call to be a Christian. 'It pleased God to reveal His Son in me that I might preach Him among the Gentiles.' So the whole genius of Christianity is given us, not by an induction from its history (which would be sight) but by a deduction from its head (which is faith). We do not see eternity, but we realize it in Jesus, who is the substance of what we hope, and the reality of the unseen. In all the more spiritual products it is so. On the dawn of poetry we have Homer, the Eddas, the Kalevala, the Mahabarata. We have extraordinary precocity most abundant in the most spiritual of all the arts – music. In life we take the most momentous and formative decisions, as to a profession, or a wife, at the threshold of life. And conversion, on which Christianity itself essentially rests in one shape or another, belongs to the first part of life rather than the last.

It is not in the genius of Christianity that its essence should be distilled for us out of its whole history. The key is given in its source. Were it otherwise we concede the whole principle of an evolutionary Catholicism, as represented in the modern Romanism of Newman and Möhler, with its deep scepticism and lack of personal certainty.

*

6. All this is to say that positive Christianity has a historic standard in the New Testament. We have there the norm for every form. Liberalism has none, beyond a thing of fleeting hues, like the modern man, the modern mind, the modern conscience. But is it not hard to fix what the modern mind is? Shall Goethe represent it or Nietzsche, Wordsworth or Byron, Hegel or Haeckel, the metaphysicians or the psychologists, the optimists, the pessimists, or the naturalists? One says, follow impulse, man is essentially divine. Another says yes – man is essentially divine, and mainly so in his power to quell impulse. One says with Morris 'Love is enough – enjoy.' Another says with Goethe 'Die to live – renounce.' One again says 'Follow to the bitter end your individual conscience and its responsibility. Go, with Brand, for all or nothing.' Another says with Comte, 'No, the social conscience is lord with its hereditary and racial responsibility.' And a third translates this social conscience into Christianity as the Church, which relieves you of your conscience altogether and takes charge of it for you. Which of these represents the modern mind? Do we find it in life-vigour or life-weariness? In Bismarck or Amiel? in Roosevelt or Tolstoi? America or Europe?

Not everything new is modern, in the good sense of that word. That alone is worthily modern which really adds to the spiritual power of the race, and continues to develop from the old the real spiritual life of the world. 'Oddities do not last.' But still there is the question, What is spiritual life? and what is soundly progressive? What makes us sure in each case that we have more than a mere variant? How to tell a development from a sport, a purpose from a freak, a destiny from a whim? In the middle ages everything was modern which was outside the logic of the period, just as to many to-day everything is modern outside eighteenth century orthodoxy. There is much modernity in antiquity. How shall we discover and disentangle it? What is so modern, so fresh, so mighty in every age as eternity? How discern it? Where is the favoured haunt of the eternal voice, the region of its choice, where the soul owns its entire control? Do we not feel that amid our unexampled wealth of broad interests, new departure, swift change, teeming variation, and external mobility, life is flattening and starving to-day for want of the eternal stay of Christ, as a gorgeous tent slowly subsides to the dust as the pole decays? All our escape from tradition and from bondage, all the fires, feats, or freaks of freedom, the roses and raptures of romance, or even the heroisms of the great, do not permanently lift the tone or dignity of life. Where are we to take our bearings and find our north? Where shall we rest our lever? Where does the eternal well up through time to flood history? To such questions a positive Christianity has an answer in the Gospel of the Cross, taken seriously and objectively, the Cross where eternity springs up anew in every soul. But what is known as liberalism has none. It believes in the logic of the idea, or in human nature, divine human nature, man failing often but unfallen still, man as God made him. Human nature – where Iago succeeds and Brutus fails, indeed! Which wins at history's close? The only answer we have to that is in the absolute finality of the Gospel of the Cross. Human nature! It is indeed wonderful. But, alas!

> Unless above himself he can
> Erect himself, how mean a thing is man.

*

7.   *A liberal theology*, a belief in the unbroken unity of man with God, a creed of man's essential divinity superseding the need of redeeming grace, needing but benignant grace – such a theology *may suit those who are constitutionally ready to believe in good-ness* from simplicity of nature, or through lack of imaginative

lucidity, moral shrewdness, or knowledge of the world. It may satisfy those who can turn easily to life's varied interests and energies for relief from the bleeding wounds of the soul, or those who feel indeed the tragedy *in* the world, but have no power to realize the tragedy *of* the world. It may meet those whose reason serves them so well that revelation is not called for, who are young enough to rely on their own self-respect, and to trust their own self-help. But the modern man is inwardly more of a pessimist than that, in the old countries at least, where they have outgrown youth's happy knack of hope, and have long borne the white man's burden. The modern man represents the bankruptcy of natural optimism, and more and more craves for deliverance. He tastes life's tragedy and guilt, and pines for a Saviour, even when he disowns ours. 'O, had I lived,' says one of them, 'when Jesus of Nazareth walked in Galilee I would have followed Him, and lost all my pride in the love of Him.' Now, a positive theology comes to this jaded, impotent life with the note of a real, foregone redemption. It comes to modern Europe, the Europe of the Renaissance, and the Illumination, and the Revolution, and it comes to a Europe disillusioned of them all, as it came to the *débâcle* of classical antiquity. And man's extremity elicits the central resource of God the Saviour. As the time grows short God grows swift and keen. 'As the shorter time Satan hath, the more is his rage, so, the shorter time Christ hath, the more is His zeal for His saints and indignation against His enemies. His heart is set on it, and therefore it is we see in this latter age He hath made such changes in the world. We have seen Him do that in a few years that He hath not done in a hundred years before. For, being King of nations, He presses His interests; and being more near His kingdom He takes it with violence. We are now within the whirl of it and so His motions are rapt.' Thus even Goodwin the Puritan.

It is true a fresh young people, like America, has a somewhat different note. But it is useless to refer the weary Titan of Europe merely to the young Hercules of the West. The young men too shall grow weary, and their strength shall utterly fail. Nature has its due course to senility, and a natural optimism has its dying fall. It is the waiters on God that renew their strength. Christianity comes to-day as it came in the first centuries, to a paganism which is disillusioned about itself and is sinking into pessimism. In those first days Christianity took the world at its own estimate, and brought the message that the situation required. Even Stoicism then despaired of the mass of mankind in spite of its high conception of Humanity. It could not make a religion of that idea. It had the dream but not the power. It had not the Redemption, the secret of a new creation. This was the one thing the age craved, and it was the one thing Christianity brought. And it was to this outworn world Christianity came. It was not to the northern world of the fresh Teutonic races. Its method was not to save an old civilization by the infusion of a new and hopeful race. Or do you think that what saved antiquity was not the Christian redemption but the incursion of the Northern peoples? Well, Europe to-day is rapidly moving to where antiquity had come, to moral exhaustion, and to the pessimism into which natural optimism swings when the stress and burden are extreme. Do you think that situation is to be saved by the spontaneous resources of human nature, or the entrance upon the *Weltpolitik* of a mighty young people like America? Is there no paganism threatening America? What is to save America from her own colossal power, energy, self-confidence and preoccupation with the world? Her Christianity no doubt. But a Christianity which places in the centre not merely Christ but the Cross and its Redemption, in a far more ethical way than America is doing; a Christianity which is not only set in the presence of Christ's person but caught into the motion of Christ's work, which is not only with Christ but in Him by a total moral and social salvation.

For the time, however, your young optimism hardly realizes the tragic need for an absolute salvation. You are too Pelagian. I feel that Christianity comes with a less redemptive word, perhaps, to a fresh and dawning race; as to the vigorous Teutons of the fourth century in the north of Europe it came with a more Arian creed than was extorted from the Gospel by the desperate case of dying Rome. To youth the harmony of Christianity with the nobler natural man may appeal more strongly than does its blow to nature from the Cross. Your energy insists on synergy with

God. Your lack of tradition discredits a great theology. The transfiguration of humanity may be more attractive to you than its death and resurrection in Christ, because it is less deep. Hegel with his calm process of reconciliation may seem more Christian than the pessimists with their cry for redemption, and the iron quivering in their soul. It is easy to believe in man when the world is young, when every woman is a queen, and every goose a swan. It is easy to speak in pantheistic philosophemes of the essential divinity of human nature, and man's homogeneity with God. What has Christianity to do with that? That is for the philosophers. What brought Christ, and brought Him to the Cross, was man's alienation from God and his hate. To harp on continuity when we need communion, and for communion redemption, betrays that the moral eye has still its scales; that sin has not yet bitten; that there is not yet resistance unto blood; that the holy has not yet outgrown the homely; that grace is untasted still, however the heart takes its fill of love; and that the holy has not become the one reality. It indicates the ethical amateur brisk in his studies, though at times abashed; but not the broken man, the broken and contrite spirit, shamed, desperate, and delivered, lost and found. In such a Gospel as that of man's natural and indelible sonship we not only have no need that God be reconciled to us; we hardly seem to need to be reconciled to God. All we seem to need is to be reconciled to our inner truer selves. Be true to yourself, is the note of this youthful Gospel, and stir up one another to love. Cultivate the Spirit of Jesus. Believe and work for spiritual progress. Meet with a shining face the dawn of God who loves to see His children happy. Yes, but meantime, where is the anguish of the new birth? And where the stricken confession 'God be merciful to me a sinner'?

In a positive Gospel, on the contrary, everything turns on a real supernatural revelation, on a fundamental perdition, a radical evil, and a rescue from without as the one thing that makes a Christian humanity. Our salvation is not the mere contagion spread by powerful religious personalities. Nor is it the progress of a gradual spiritualization. It is a unique and finished work of God in Christ, to be taken, not made. It is not a piece of impressionism; it is a real redemption in the heart of things, in creative deed and not in stirring word alone. You cannot deeply preach without the note of a tragic and total redemption. To harp upon this as a truth is easy, I know, and it can be tedious; and the world has been well bored by it often. But to preach it, to saturate with the power and principle of it all thought and reality, that is a great life work, which puts the preacher's soul much upon the Cross, but also raises it continually from the dead.

*

Behind all the differences between a positive Gospel and religious liberalism there keep reappearing the two elements, *personality with its immortality and sin with its witness to holiness*. The liberalism I speak of consistently tends to erase the personal element both from God and from the human future. Its note is some variety of Pantheism, with all the spell and appeal of that issue to those who have but an intellectual history. And it farther erases, like all Monistic systems, the decisive factor in history, the factor of sin and of God's holiness. The holiness of the Spinosist deity is not holy in the Christian sense, nor in any sense which leaves us with a real conscience. Even Hegel tends to erase that. For such a creed sin is not outside the vast process of reconciliation whereby the supreme idea finds in the ideas below something intrinsically serviceable to its final purpose when the hour comes for them to be absorbed and preserved (*aufgehoben*). There is something in sin which can be preserved and utilized for the divine purpose. That is to say, there is something in it (as sin, and not merely as free volition) which is due to the divine purpose, and may be incorporated in the great reconcilement. One day we may see (if at that far day we continue to exist capable of seeing anything) how our sin was a negative contribution to the divine event, and had its place in the divine scheme of things. And we may even be ashamed of the pother we made about it.

All this is absolutely incompatible with the sin that brought death to God in the Son of God. Sin as we see it by God's holiness in Christ's Cross contains nothing that can be absorbed by that holiness and given an eternal value. It is outside the range of reconcileable things. It can only be destroyed as in principle Christ did destroy it. Doubtless it must be made to minister to God's greater glory; but never by any kind of exploitation; and only by entire destruction.

In all the efforts to subdue Christian theology to be a province of the empire of pure thought there is discernible an inability which seems constitutional to gauge the fact of sin at its moral value. There is some lack of a moral retina. There is an absence of a personal moral history. There is a poverty of moral realism and of soul history as distinct from the mind's. Yet I venture to think that there is more of a key to the divine method in the tragedies of remorse and the shame of guilt than in the fascinating processes of speculative thought. The greatest of modern popular orators, a master of laughter, tears, and all assemblies, often visited a friend of mine. One day as they stood on a height which commanded a noble view my friend missed him, and on search found him some yards away, prone on the heath, sobbing, with his head buried in his hands. When he had recovered somewhat, and assured his companion it was not illness, he said that from time to time some sight of greatness suddenly smote into him the shame of what he had been in the years of his dissipation and sin. And the horror of it never lost its freshness, nor did the freshness fade from the wonder of his forgiveness. Moments like these, and the men like these, have a key to the spiritual system of the world which the thinkers must fail to turn till they insert in its ring much more than their thought. And to have no such experience, or at least the power to understand it, is to be a minor in the moral life.

*

8. To gather the matter up. *The liberal theology finds Christ's centre of gravity in what He has in common with us, a positive theology in that wherein He differs.* The one urges us to a faith like Christ's, the other to a faith in Christ. The one bids us imitate the religion of Jesus; the other cannot attempt to imitate a Redeemer, or criticize the judge of conscience; and it takes Jesus for our religion. The one preaches as the principle of Christianity the principle of indefectible human sonship, the principle of man's incorrigible spirituality, with Christ only as its classic case and supreme prophet; the other identifies the principle with Christ, and

finds it secured only in the total act of His eternal Person. Liberalism dwells on Christ's preaching, positivity on a Christ preached. The one finds the most impressive thing in Christ to be His perfect human nature; the other is much more impressed by His treatment of human nature than by His incarnation of it. The one dwells on Christ as the expression of humanity, the other dwells on His business with humanity. For the one He consummates it, for the other He redeems it. Liberalism offers Christ to a seeking world as its answer, or to a suffering world as its healer; positivity offers Him to a guilty world also as its Atoning Saviour. The one treats the sinlessness of Christ as the expression of the essential, though soiled, sinlessness of man; the other treats it as the sanctity possible only to the Holy One of God. The one regards it as a relative sinlessness; the other as an absolute holiness. The one takes stand on love; the other declares that the divine thing in love, as it is in Christ, is holy grace. For the one the divine reality is a calm and mystic presence and he joys that God is near in love; for the other it is a perpetual deed, and the nearness is a terror except as grace for love scorned. A liberal theology discerns God's real presence in the mere *action*, process, or movement of the world; a positive finds it in the *act* of the world, the supreme act of history which consummates the world. The one is engrossed with the way God's *presence* pervades His world, the other with the way He realizes by redemptive act His *purpose* in the world. The one finds Christ to crown the *immanence* of the divine presence in the world; the other finds Him to be the *incarnation* of the divine will with the world. The one has the cosmological interest of evolution, the other the teleological interest of Redemption. For liberalism the world is God's arena, His sphere of energy, where His substance, forces, and ideas play; for positivity it is becoming His Kingdom, where His purpose rules. For the one the world is His organ, for the other it is His creature; and while He is immanent in His creature, He is incarnate only in His uncreated Son. If the world is the creature of His holy love, the Son is more; He is its eternal counterpart. For the one the world was created *for* Christ, or at least for Christ's ideal; for the other it was created *in* Christ.

*

Religion as it grows powerful grows positive. But the constant drift of liberalism is away from positivity, and it devotes itself to the scientific study of religions. Yet even that study might teach us that *the constant tendency of religion, as it rises in the scale, is to be more positive*, more historic, more defined, and more objective. There is no such thing anywhere as religion *per se*, religion apart from a specific form of religion – unless perhaps we find it in the decadents from the higher types, where you have a vague religiosity with the effort to detach itself from every form – Church, doctrine, or any other clear committal. But in the historic religions, as you rise in the scale of quality you grow in positivity. They become more historical, and more dogmatic, more explicit in regard to the gravest issues. They do not erase the frontiers, though they promote the coming and going of a freer trade. A positive religion is a concrete one. It is so intellectually; and still more so morally. Experience, I keep saying, makes an appeal to our will and choice. It puts us upon our moral mettle. It takes a line. It stakes life and eternity on selection, decision, committal. It calls us to moral verve and vigilance. There are mature lives to-day which are darker than they would have been had they not at the early stage fallen victims to a vague and pathetic fallacy of fatherhood, in which the holy had no meaning and judgment no place. But how poor, how remote it all is. As we live we are being tried for our life. And that is the issue you face as preachers. One of these tendencies will make you preachers of a Gospel, the other will make you advocates of a culture. One will make you strangers and sojourners in the world, the other citizens of the world, maybe men of the world. One will make you apostles of Christ, and one will make you champions of humanity. One will make you severe with yourself, one will make you tender with yourself. One will commend you to the naughty people, and one will commend you to the nice.

Now of these two tendencies one means the destruction of preaching. If it cease to be God's word, descending on men and intervening in history, then it will cease as an institution in due time. It may become lecturing, or it may become oratory, but as preaching it must die out with a positive Gospel. People cannot be expected to treat a message of insight from man to man as they do a message of revelation from God to man. An age cannot be expected to treat a message from another age as they treat a message from Eternal God to every age. Men with the passion of the present cannot be expected to listen even to a message from humanity as they would to one from God. And if humanity redeem itself you will not be able to prevent each member of it from feeling that he is his own redeemer. If we owe everything to man's innate spirituality, asserting itself in various forms of life or worship, we have, in this spirituality, something all too vague for a Gospel, too familiar for a message, and too little positive to give a real preacher his text, or his authority, or even his audience. For if it is all a matter of innate human spirituality it is too innate to each hearer to dispose him to hear it meekly. How should he hear meekly a word which is not engrafted but evolved out of the common spiritual stock? Each man's own spirituality is in its nature as good as anything another man might bring him.

Is it not all really a serious issue, and a grave choice? The less seriously you feel the issue the more serious it is for you. Not to feel the immense gulf it cleaves is not to choose with open eyes. Whichever side you go to, go with an adequate sense of what is involved. Do not treat the matter as if to men of sense and soul there were but one rational possibility. One respects far more a man who really grasps the situation and deliberately goes to the wrong side – far more than one who goes there for want of knowing his subject, or who good-naturedly minimizes the differ-ence and says we are all one at bottom. If we are so, it is either in a positive Christ, or in a pantheistic, monistic unity which is spiritually unmeaning and morally noxious. What we do not respect is the assumption of the liberal and superior note by men who have not wrestled with the subject, or measured the ground, but are the victims of epicurean reading, easy books, or popular expositors. This matter is really, for the preacher, an issue of the soul, a decision of the life, which turns study from a pursuit to a conflict, and makes the attainment of conviction a wrestling with God for your salvation. For the preacher, truly, the salvation of the soul is also the salvation of the mind. Your mind also must come to the obedience and service of faith. There is such a thing as the *sacrificium intellectus*. But it is not to an institution, it is to the conscience. It is the recognition of that primacy of the moral which views sin as the crux of the ethical, i.e. the human, situation, and redemption as its only solution. Your charter as preachers is not contained in what the world says to your earnest thought but in what the Word says to your sinful conscience. And the question is not 'What do you think of Christ?' but, 'How do you treat Him?' It is not what is He *to* you. It is more even than what is He *for* you. And still more it is what is He *in* you. And are you in Him? That last is in some ways the most crucial question of all. For by having Christ in you, you may mean no more than inheriting the results of His vast historic movement, and absorbing into your character the moral fruits of His legacy to men. So you might have Christ working on in you in a posthumous way. But when you ask yourself, 'Am I in Him?' you can say Yea to that, only if He still live, and live as Himself our spiritual world, made unto us justification, sanctification, and redemption.

Seven

Preaching Positive and Modern

The need of a modernized Theology:
I. Its positive doctrines (1) a Gospel of Jesus the Eternal Son of God; (2) a Gospel of Jesus the Mediator; (3) a Gospel of Christ's Resurrection.
II. Its recognition of modern principles. (1) The autonomy of the individual; (2) the Social Idea; (3) the development of personality; (4) the distinction between practical and theoretical knowledge; (5) the need of popularisation; (6) the principle of Evolution; (7) the passion for reality.
III. The issue not really critical but dogmatic – This illustrated in the case of the Bible and of Christ.
The vital need throughout of an experimental foundation in Grace – A living, positive faith in a historic gospel.

Theology, if it is to be of real use to the preacher, must be modernized. It is fruitless to offer to the public the precise modes of thought which were so fresh and powerful with the Reformers, or the schemes so ably pro-pounded by the dogmatists of the seventeenth century, and so severely raked by the Socinians. The nineteenth century was not a theological century, but it has not passed without leaving a great and good effect upon theology. It was a century of scholarship, of criticism, and of heresy. But do we not recognize now that competent heresy is a negative blessing to the Church and its truth? Only it must be competent. It is the dabblers on both sides that do the mischief. We must carry on the work of last century in modernizing theology.

But what does the modernizing of theology mean? Does it mean that its control passes into the hands of modern theories of the soul and the world? Does it mean that the Christian idea of a holy God shall be at the mercy of what is a mere philosophical ultimate? Does it mean that theology must be licensed by the cosmologies or psychologies of the hour? Does it mean that we start with a certain scheme of creation and cut off all that projects over its edge? For instance, nothing more worthily marks the modern Church than the idea of evolution, especially in connexion with its own history. But is our belief to be stretched on the pallet of evolution, for instance, and everything to be trimmed down which is beyond that scheme? The Higher Criticism is a gift to us of the Spirit which gave us the Bible. But is the Bible to be put on the rack of mere literary criticism, or historic, or even ethical, and nothing accepted from it but what it emits under such question? Are the scholars, the savants, the philosophers to be the Board of Triers for the Gospel? Is modern just equivalent to *à la mode*?

The result of that I have already discussed as mere theological liberalism, which, in the effort to discard dogma, only substitutes philosophic dogma for theological. The error is in its start and standard. It begins from the wrong end. It begins with a scheme of creation, a scheme of the world or man, with which, in truth, religion is but indirectly concerned. And it does not begin with the new creation, with the evangelical experience, the moral redemption, Eternal Life in Jesus Christ. It begins with the world and not with the Word, with thought and not faith, with love and not grace, with kindness and not holiness. It is cosmological, or it is psychological, being preoccupied with the structure and action of nature or of mind; whereas religion (and the Christian faith certainly) is teleological, being preoccupied with God's purpose and goal for things, and for history, and for the soul. The one makes a specification of life and knowledge, and requires any religion which tenders to comply. It thinks of man's rational structure more than his moral need, of his power to understand more than his weakness to trust and obey. The other lays hold of God's object with life, finding in Christ both the goal and its guarantee. The one gives no finality, because the schemes of life and drafts of the world are changing with progress; the other has finality or nothing, because it begins with God's chief end for history in its salvation in Jesus Christ. In Christ it finds in advance the eternal and final purpose of God. We see not yet all things – but we see Jesus. It is teleological and redemptive. In a word, if theology is to be modernized it must be by its own Gospel.

The two methods differ in their start, then. The one begins with man, the other with God, the one with science or sentiment, the other with the Gospel, the one with the healthy heart and its satisfaction, the other with the ruined conscience and its redemption. The one begins with the world (as I say), the other with the Word. But, in practice, we find this – that to begin with the world is to become dubious about the Word; whereas to begin with the Word is to become sure about the world. A philosophy can bring us to no security of a revelation; but a revelation develops a philosophy, or a view of the world; it is adjustable to many schemes of the world; and it is hospitable to many of the modern principles of interpreting the world. It is not the victim of modern theories like monism, but it has welcome for many modern principles like evolution. In the face of modern *theories* or dogmas the Word of revelation is autonomous. It has its own dogmas by an equal right. But in face of modern *principles* it discerns in them, and often through their means, the hidden treasures of its own wealth. But whether on suggestion from without, or on impulse from within, it develops its latent wealth by its own native genius and freedom. It reforms and rediscovers itself, as it did in the Reformation. The creeds are discoveries of the Church to itself by the heresies, which are therefore negative blessings. And these two things, the Church's recognition of modern principles and its rediscovery of its own, combine to modernize the theology it presents to intelligence. It is friendly and reasonable to theories like evolution, but it is commanded by the fact of redemption and its experience. It claims that its experience of God reconciling in Christ is as real and valid as any experience of the world. Its faith is an organ of real knowledge.[1] What science does for our knowledge of things and forces,

---

[1]   See, among many others, *Paulsen's Ethik*, passim.

faith does for our knowledge of persons, our knowledge, above all, of our personal God and His saving will.

*

I. And if I may first ask what are the positive doctrines which, amid all that is modernized in it, make Christianity still a Gospel of the Grace of God, the answer would in my judgment be this.[2] They are the Eternal Sonship, the Mediatorship, and the Resurrection of Jesus Christ.

1. *It is a Gospel of Jesus the Eternal Son of God.* It sets Christ's person in the centre of theology no less than of religion. If the nineteenth century had done no more than restore the person of Christ to the centre of theology, it would have done a very great theological work. The historic Jesus is personally identical with the Christian principle or with the Eternal Christ. He stood thus in a unique relation to Eternal God. It was a relation unique not only as being unattained so far by other men. For that is not denied by the liberalism of the hour as a mere historic verdict. But He was unique in a dogmatic sense, in a way unattainable not only by any man but by collective humanity. This unique relation to God constituted His person, and it was not simply an exercise of His person. It was not attained by Him, but He was constituted in it. He began by being the Son of God in eternal fact, though He ended by being the Son in historic power. The idea of a metaphysical sonship is not absurd, though our data make its express form tentative only. The metaphysical unity with God is postulated by the evangelical unity, however far it may be from being defined. It is a unity which is far more than harmony of will. It involves parity of being, which places the historic Jesus with the Creator, rather than the creature, and beside the Creator, rather than under Him. He was of Godhead. If we take in their full earnest the words that God was in Christ reconciling we have in this Christ the real presence and action of a forgiving God. The act of Christ was still more God's act, and not a mere reflection of it. His love was God's love, and not a

---

[2] See Theodore Kaftan, *Die neue Theologie des alten Glaubens.*

mere response to it. We have Christ doing what God alone could do – forgiving sin committed against God alone. None but the injured could either forgive or save. If God was not saving in Christ, if Christ was not God saving, He was saving from God. And we can do but lean justice to Christ's own description of His consciousness at the close of Matthew xi. if we do not set Him apart in kind as well as function from the rest of the race, and find just there the secret of His unique identification with the race. No one who was simply one of the race could contain and shelter the race as Christ felt He could when He said, 'Come unto Me, all ye that labour.' To come *unto* this Christ is to come *into* Him. No one who was simply of the race could identify himself so completely with the whole race as redemption demands. And it was as God that He was worshipped by the first Church. Be the story of His birth fact or symbol, at least it proves that. In Jesus, then, we do not hear of God, we meet Him. He does not simply reveal God; He is God in revelation, the gracious God revealed.

*

2. *It is a Gospel of Jesus the Mediator*. He mediates the holy grace of God, not as the preacher does, but in a way that the preacher has to preach. He is the Mediator and not the medium. He is the Redeemer, and not the champion, of mankind. He is the Revealer, and not the rival, of God. In His Cross He confessed and satisfied the holiness of God in a way so intimate, so absolute, that it was also the radical exposure of sin in all its sinfulness, and thus it became its destruction. If the sinless could not confess sin, He exposed it. He could, and did, confess the holiness which throws sin into complete exposure and ruin. The divine morality, established in the holiness of the Atoning Cross, is the true source of our modern ethicizing of theology and our future ethicizing of society. Christ's work was not to proclaim forgiveness in the loftiest, kindest, amplest way. Others did that. Israel did that – not indeed as a people, but in its elect and inner self as a Messiah people. But Christ brought forgiveness as the Son of God alone could, as God forgiving, as forgiveness incarnate, as one actually redeeming and not offering redemption, as the divine destroyer of

guilt, as the Eternal Salvation in God made historic and visible. Christianity is a mediatorial religion always. Always, through all Eternity, Jesus Christ is our Mediator with the Father. The mediation of Christ belongs to the perennial nature of communion with God, and not merely to a historic point of our religion. We are sons always only in Him Who was Son in none. We are the sons of God's Grace, He alone is the Son of His love. God's relation to him is not the matter of grace it must be for every one of us forgiven sinners. His place with God is by nature and absolute right. He was and ever *is* the Son that I must *become* through him. And His absolute Sonship became effective and historic in the consummation of the Cross.

When we say that the Cross is a Gospel of holy love, gracious to human sin, we mean that the first concern of Christ was with God and not with man. It was with God's holiness, and its accentuation of man's sin. He poured out His soul unto death, not to impress man but to confess God. Therefore He impresses man infinitely, inexhaustibly. There is nothing that makes sin so terrible as its full exhibition before God by God's own holiness, by His own Holy One; in whom the holiness goes out as love, suffers the judgment, and redeems as grace. Love is only divine because it is holy love. And only as holy does it elicit the faith that has all love latent in it. It is in this holiness of God that all our faith and all our theology begin. It is this that must perpetually exalt them, and correct them, and moralize them, and infuse them with passion, compassion, imagination and majesty. All the reconstruction of belief must begin with the holiness of God. All the recovery of faith from mere religion must be brought about by His holiness. And when we come to speak of God's love, and ask how it should differ from the benignities of ideal gods, or nature gods, how it should celestialize human love, the answer is the same. It is as holy love. It is as the love is in the Cross. The purity of the speculative idea falls short, in practical religion, of the holiness in the Cross. It is ethereal rather than divine, and sublimated more than sublime. Herein is love, not that we loved who easily forgo propitiation, but that He loved, Who so loved as to make His own unsparing propitiation under the conditions of judgment. Herein is love, not as we love, but as He loves who loves His holy name before all His children, His holy name before all His prodigals, and therefore spared not even His only Son. Herein is our salvation as sure and perennial as the holiness for which we are saved. And love is thus sure, because it is the holy foundation of the real, the moral world.

*

3. *Christianity is a Gospel of Christ's Resurrection.* The same Jesus who died also rose, and lives as the King of heavenly Glory and Lord of human destiny. The fact that *He* rose, and that He rose, is the main matter; it is not the manner of it, or its circumstances. The point is that the same continuous personality that mastered life during life, in death also triumphed over death, appeared to sundry in that victory, and lives in its full power and glory for us evermore. The Son of God, in heavenly power and glory now, was and is our dear, real, earthly Jesus. The physical conditions are subordinate. The empty tomb I would leave a question as open as the Virgin Birth.[3] I believe the tomb was emptied – else the body would have been produced to refute the apostles. But, even if it had not been, the crucified body was not the redeeming person. And God could prepare, and Christ could take, for His purposes a body as it pleased Him.

The mistake we make here, especially in preaching, is in treating the Resurrection of Christ as evidence to the world, as a proof, instead of an exercise, of His divine power. The evidential value of miracles is quite gone. As has been said, 'instead of the miracles helping faith it takes all our faith to help us to believe the miracles.' It is a misuse of miracle to make it evidentiary. None

---

[3] Nothing would more help us to find where we are, and to deal faithfully with our crypto-unitarianism, than to realize that our real difference with the Socinians is not as to the Virgin Birth (which is irrelevant to the Incarnation) but as to the Atonement. The locus of the issue is not the cradle but the cross. It is where it was with the first Socinianism – a question as to the standing need and conditions of forgiveness, whether forgiveness is the one gift, the one all-inclusive gift of God in Christ (Rom. viii. 32). The Unitarian issue is the Evangelical.

of Christ's miracles were so used by Him (in the Synoptics at least). Indeed, He did His best to hush them up. He always refused them as a sign. They were pure, almost irrepressible, acts of real pity and help. They were not advertisements; they were not credentials. They were not given to unfaith, but to faith. They were no mere exhibitions of power. Christ was not thaumaturgic. He was no impressionist. He would never coerce faith. The reaction against miracle is largely a protest against our un-Christlike abuse of it. We have given it a wrong place, a place which Christ would not allow it to have, even for His contemporaries. And we do not erase miracles, therefore, when we restore them to their true and blessed place for faith.

The resurrection of Christ is thus not evidential, but it is real. It is not the surest thing in scientific history, but it is an essential fact to Christian faith. It gave faith back its Lord. It roused faith to know itself and its Master. The apostles did not critically examine the evidence for the resurrection; they hailed the risen Lord. It was not a resurrection that impressed them, but a returned Saviour. The matter of moment is the reality of the risen Lord, the identity of the Christ now in heaven with the Jesus of the finished victory in the Cross. The great thing is the power given to believers to say and feel with real meaning that they are in Christ and Christ in them. It is to realize that the victorious Jesus was seen of many, and was in converse with them; that as Christ, He still rules the Kingdom He set up; and that (if He endure at all) He is not sitting apart, solemnly superannuate like a retired and cloistered emperor, and watching, with only a founder's interest, the progress of the realm which once He set going but which now runs of itself. Nay, but He watches the Kingdom as the King who ever rules. And the Kingdom will never be but what He is continually making it.

*

II.   But now what has a modernized theology to offer in the way of recognizing modern principles as well as in the way of preaching its own?[4]

---

[4]   I still make free use of Kaftan's essay.

1. Ever since the Reformation Protestantism has grown in the recognition of one modern principle which it did so much to create – *the freedom of the individual from external authority*. Whether that authority be Bible, Church, or Dogma, merely as such, faith renounces them all. The Bible is no code of either precept or belief. It is not a doctrinal protocol. The Word of God is in the Bible, as the soul is in the body. The one authority is the grace of the Bible speaking to the soul of man. That is to say, the one authority is the Gospel not only in the soul and speaking to the soul, but making the soul. It is a spiritual, practical, creative authority. It is not prescriptive. To be sure, it is an authority which acts under psychological conditions, which conditions alone psychology is competent to explore. But with the sanctions of that authority no science is competent to deal, either in challenge or support. The idea of authority is not destroyed because it ceases to be external. Because it ceases to be external it does not cease to be objective, to be presented to consciousness and not produced from it. The moral law which hounds the sinner is nothing external, but it is fearfully, inevitably, objective. And the Gospel that saves is no less objective and authoritative than the law that damns. Its voice may be inward and private. But these inner voices are what make the real authority; when the soul is spoken to by another who is its own other. There is no voice so poignant in condemnation as the voice that is dear. Remorse is more than half the grief of many a decent widower. There is no judgment so serious as that of our kin, the judgment of love. The most terrible accusers of the culprit's crime are the children it brands and who never upbraid. The law of Society bears so closely upon us because we ourselves are not insulated wills but products of the same society that made the law. And there is no authority so ubiquitous, and therefore so objective, as the Word of God that emerges in the colloquy or conflict of the soul God made.

It is quite true that a huge problem is set to the Gospel in the present moral anarchy of western civilization. We have not yet found for society the Word which the individual freely finds, the Word to replace for the public the external authority of the medieval Church. But so long as the individual is made to find

that Word for himself in the historic Gospel, there need be no fear
that Society will not find it in due course for purposes of public
control.

*

2. A second great modern idea is here suggested which profoundly affects the type of our Christian faith – the social idea.
We always have been greatly affected by the social idea in the
shape of the Church. Our Christian theology has been developed
as the intelligent expression on the face of a living Church. It has
been in vital connexion with the consciousness of a living society.
No church, no theology. But it is also becoming amenable to the
form and pressure of a society wider though not greater – civil
society; and especially in respect of its weak. The Brotherhood in
the deep Christian sense becomes much affected by the Brotherhood in the broad humane sense. In the past the *strength* of Society
has much moulded Christian thought and institutions. The Holy
Empire, the dynasties, the philosophies have all been shaping
powers. The ablest jurisprudence at one time much coloured the
theology of atonement, for instance. But now the *weakness* and
need of Society exert more and more the modifying pressure. The
appeal from the helpless, the passion of pity, affects the whole
frame of Christian method, institution, ethic, and even thought,
in a growing way. It bears home to us the fact that every single
soul is saved in an act which was the organic salvation, the
salvation into a kingdom, of the whole race. We are not really
saved if we are saved into neglect of a social salvation. The Gospel
preached to the soul must be a Gospel which leaves the saved soul
much more concerned than he used to be about the saving of
civilization, the salvation of the just as well as of the lost, and the
restoration of the poor as well as of the wicked. There are very
great social changes involved in the modernization of our theology which is now going on. Christian truth must be socialized by
the same power as socializes Christian wealth. And it ought in
fairness to be added that medieval theology was much more social
than Protestantism has been except on its Calvinistic side. It was
far more social than our debased and individualized Calvinism.
It is easy to see why Catholicism, Anglican or Roman, whose

golden age was the medieval, should be more socialist than current Protestantism.

*

3.   There is another point where the ethicizing of Christianity has been greatly affected by modern thought – *the rescue of personality from individualism, the socializing of its idea*. The influence is social, but it comes from the psychological side. It proceeds first from that growth of the principle of personality which has been mainly promoted by Christianity. Christ is certainly no less concerned than Nietzsche that the personality should receive the fullest development of which it is capable, and be more and more of a power. The difference between them lies in the moral method by which the personality is put into possession of itself and its resources – in the one case by asserting self, in the other by losing it; in the one case by self-pleasing, in the other by self-renunciation. Christianity is interested in the first degree in the modern emphasis on personality, because it is its chief creator. But the influence I allude to is more than that. It lies, secondly, in the conviction that the *strength* of personality, after an early stage, is damaged by the mere *force* of individualism, and is a social product. Personality does not come into the world with us ready made, but it has a history and a growth. Education is not merely its training, it is its creation. In all of us the personality is incomplete; and it misleads us in the most grave way when we use it as an analogy for the ever complete and holy personality of God. We are but persons in the making. Personality is created by social influences, and finds itself only in these. We complete our personality only as we fall into place and service in the vital movement of the society in which we live. Isolation means arrested development. The aggressive egotist is working his own moral destruction by stunting and shrinking his true personality. Social life, duty, and sympathy, are the only conditions under which a true personality can be shaped. And if it be asked how a society so crude, imperfect, unmoral, and even immoral as that in which we live is to mould a personality truly moral, it is here that Christ comes to the rescue with the gift to faith both of an active Spirit and of a society complete in Himself, which in Him is none of these evil

things, the society of the Kingdom of God, which plays a part so great in the modern construction of the Gospel. We are saved only in a salvation which set up a kingdom, and did not merely set it on foot. We have the Kingdom not with Christ but in Christ. Do not leave Christ out of the Kingdom, as if He were detachable from it like any common king. The individual is saved only in this social salvation. And the more you insist that a soul can only be saved, and a personality secured, by Christ's finished work, the more you must contend that the Kingdom of God is not merely coming but is come, and is active in the Spirit among us now. There is the closest connexion, if not identity, when you go deep enough, between the theology of salvation and the moral principles of social regeneration. The principle of our salvation is the principle of human ethic, not only of private, as has long been seen, but of public ethic, as we now come to see. A great economist has lately traced in an original and masterly way the vital connexion between the ethic of Calvinism and modern economics. To dismiss the moral necessity for God of Christ's Cross is, in the long run, to banish moral principles from public affairs; since the greatest public affair in history would then have in it no causation in the eternal and immutable morality of the universe.

*

4. With the modern stress laid by Christianity upon a kingdom, *we must recognize the distinction* so marked in recent thought ever since Kant *between theoretical and practical knowledge, and we must fall in with the modern stress on the latter*. Ethic is a far mightier matter than science, and Christian experience a far more precious thing than Christian correctitude. We move to a Gospel of act and experience, which in the long run is independent of either philosophy or criticism. The real Gospel of the Cross is beyond either. In the strict sense of the word theology, that too is immune. For it rests on the contact of indubitable history (viz. Christ's Person and Cross) with present experience. What is vulnerable is a theosophy, a secondary theology which has grown up round experimental theology, and is largely drawn from cosmic or juristic speculation. These speculations are, of course, bound to arise. For the more free we are in the practical experience

of our positive Gospel, the more freely we discuss and appropriate from the theoretic world. The more sure we are in our positive Gospel, the less we are tempted to try to control and manipulate philosophy so as to take the danger out of it. But it is by no philosophy or theosophy that we stand or fall. A man speculates with a free judgment if he is not speculating with the capital which means his livelihood. And so we have a new liberty for thought in the primacy of the moral, and the certainty of our moral redemption in experience.

And we are not only *free* to go on from that standpoint to be occupied with the interpretation of the world. We *must* so go on. The faith that makes us free is the faith of a universal, nay a cosmic, redemption. The truths and questions of science are not freaks or hobbies, arbitrary or gratuitous. They are necessary and inevitable. They rise from life, from actual contact with the world. They present real life to us in certain aspects. They represent not only the objective world, but the objective world as it emerges in human experience, in human consciousness and will. The philosophy which cannot license us yet does enrich us. It does not give us our grasp, but it enlarges it. It does not give us a footing, but it does give a horizon.

I venture to say, therefore, that that separation of the theoretical and the practical (with the stress on the latter) which has been so influential ever since Kant, and rises again with Neo-Kantianism, Pragmatism, and Activism like Eucken's, is a principle of great value both for the certainty and the freedom of our Christian faith in contact with the world. The more we are secured in our practical experience of the Gospel, the more we are free to listen to all representations from philosophy or science in shaping to a doctrine our capacious life with Christ in God.

All this means that our theology must be ethicized. It must be framed with more regard to the practical than to the speculative ideals of life and faith. To modernize theology it must be ethicized, but more from the revelation of God's holiness in the Cross than from the progress of natural or social ethic, however refined.

*

5. *Christianity in being ethicized, is popularized.* The classical and pagan view of the world was theoretic. It would solve the great riddle intellectually. But this was possible for the few alone. It was the work of experts. But when the problem is that of the conscience, it concerns us all. It is accessible to all, nay, it presses on all. The great issue is not being thought out, it is being lived out, loved out, worked out, and fought out. The power for life concerns all, the scheme of life but a few. The whole reality of life is on its moral side, and that is the side which the Gospel appeals to, and so it appeals to all. The last stand of the Gospel is in the whole reality of practical life, individual and social, in homes, marts, senates, and churches. It is not in the schools. It is only paganism (whether Haeckel's or Hegel's) that rests in the self-sufficiency of thought or the idea. The Gospel is the moral, the universal, the final interpretation of life. Christ came not with a reading of life but with its redemption; not with the answer to a riddle but with the solution of a practical problem. He did not come with a body of new truth, but with a power of new reality, not with the profoundest knowledge but with Eternal Life.

*

6. I need hardly include among the marks of a modern Christianity *the extent to which its whole outlook has been modified by the doctrine of evolution, and especially historic evolution.* This might almost go without saying. Even the Roman Church has recognized it, and the line of its apologetic has been profoundly changed by its doctrine of development as formulated by Möhler and Newman. First the blade, then the ear, then the full corn in the ear. Protestantism has recognized the principle more fully still. Dr. Adams Brown, in the most able outline of Theology which we now possess in English, has said that the three types of Christianity usually given – the Greek, Roman, and Protestant – should be extended by dividing the latter into two – the Reformation type and the modern type; because the difference between these two is as great as that between the Greek and the Roman type. And he notes as the distinctive feature of modern Protestantism the effect of this doctrine of evolution. (*Outlines of Theology, p. 62 n*). There are other features, as I venture to point out; and I

should myself lay more stress on the new ethical note. But the evolutionary idea is especially attractive to a scientific age. We have certainly no quarrel with that idea till it is lifted from being a method and elevated into a dogma – indeed *the* dogma; till it is treated as a *vera causa*, and made to explain not simply the mode of change but the principle of change, the germinating principle of the seed as well as the phases of its process. It is a philosophy which explains much, and makes us patient of much, and hopeful of more. But it cannot give us hope in the Christian and certain sense. Because it cannot give us the goal of its own movements any more than their real cause. And a religion has to do rather with the source and the goal than with the path, with the meaning rather than the method. We must welcome the new force given by this theory to many a word of Christ, and many a movement of the Spirit. It is really not evolution we have to watch, but the Monism which is so often supposed to be inseparable from it by those who have more science than philosophy, more imagination than either, little ethical insight, and theology least of all.

The whole attitude of the Church to its truth has been altered by the destruction through evolution of the idea of a final system of belief, or a monopolist form of polity. Its intellectual hospitality has been indefinitely extended. And it is free, with a large liberty, from a burden too great for even faith to bear. It can regard the new philosophies as helpers so long as they do not claim to be suzerains, so long as they do not aspire to prescribe belief but only to enrich it, to correct its statement, and to enhance its scope. They help to place us in a new relation of mastery and ease to the Bible and the stage which the Bible registers. And they give us a new grasp of the long action of the Spirit and its way with the Church and the world. The more subtle and plastic the Spirit, the mightier and more irresistible is its action. And the less monumental our Christ is, in a stiff Byzantine figure, the more pervasive He is as a constant and subduing power. When evolution escapes from the bondage of the physical sciences, and its *mésalliance* with monistic dogma, it is a distinguished badge and blessing of a modern Church. Only let it be taken as a supplement to creation, and not as a substitute for redemption, and it gives a wonderful flexibility and grace to much theological thought that once was formal and hard.

*

7. Nothing is more characteristic of the modern mind than its passion for reality. It is a passion that takes all sorts of extravagant, and some noxious, forms. But it is a worthy instinct. And it is a demand that elicits the moral realism, the unsparing spiritual thoroughness, of the Gospel. Hence the Gospel not only tolerates, it demands, science and criticism. If it can succumb to these it should. The criticism may be the moral caustic applied to Christian society by an Ibsen, or it may be the Higher Criticism of the Bible or the creeds by the schools. Our treasure in Bible or Church is in an earthen vessel which is fairly exposed to the critic. And especially historic criticism touches us, as we have the water only in the historic vessel. But every historic phenomenon, in so far as it is historic, must admit criticism, and stand the test of that reality. Be it book or creed, or even Christ Himself so far as He is a historic personality – we cannot seclude them from competent criticism. But then the historic Jesus is no mere historic figure. Even in so far as He is historic, as the object of our faith He is, though not immune from critical action, yet secure. For the living person of Christ stands, and its consummation on the Cross, and its continued life in our experience. And that is where our real faith is fixed – on the finished redeeming work of the Saviour on the Cross, sealed indeed in the Resurrection but finished on the Cross, published in the Resurrection but achieved on the Cross. That is faith's reality, the reality that faith knows. No criticism can shake that if it be thoroughly settled into our experience. From that vantage ground we recognize the rights of criticism because we are in a position to deny its rule. That Jesus we cannot criticize either historically or morally. For we cannot criticize our Judge and our Redeemer. We can criticize His knowledge about the Old Testament and the like, but we cannot criticize his ownership of our souls. He is for us the last reality, which enables us to criticize all else. His saints shall judge the world.

*

III. Thus it is not with a critical issue we have really to do, it is with a dogmatic. And this I ask your leave to explain.

The question of recent criticism and its effect on your Gospel will often arise in your mind, or it will be put to you by others. And unless you found on the true rock it may cost you much trouble and pain.

You will be wise if you keep it out of your preaching. That is to say, do not preach much about it. Preach as men who know about it. Preach habitually neither its methods nor its results, but preach a Gospel which has taken due account of both. The Christ we have to declare is neither a residuum which the critics are pleased to leave us, nor an asbestos quite unaffected by the fire. What criticism acts on is the Bible, the record. And, closely as Christ is bound up with the Bible, He is more closely bound up with the Gospel than with the Bible. When it becomes a religious question, that is, a question of the Gospel, criticism takes quite a secondary place, and, in cases, may even be irrelevant. The matter then ceasing to turn on facts, but turning on a living person, passes into the hands of the believer, and through him to the theologian. It is a dogmatic question.

*

Take the case of the Bible itself for instance. The momentous question does not concern its mode of origin, its *provenance*, its constituent parts, authors, dates. It does not concern the equal value for historic science of every portion, or for theological truth of every thought it contains. It is a question of a special and real revelation from God to the conscience. Have we here, on the whole, the effective history of redemption? It is not the history of Israel, or the biography of Christ, that the Bible exists to give. Its history is the history of grace, the exposition of a long action and a final act of grace. And, as I said at the outset, it is history not of a scientific but of a preached kind. It is a kind of history, and an amount of history, prescribed by the practical purpose of conveying the grace of God. It is sacramental history. It is broken bread – such portions of history as form sacramental elements, adequate for the spiritual purpose in hand. It does not exist primarily to instruct us about God, but to convey God to us. The New

Testament is not a mere monument of the first century. Nor, on the other hand, is it a mere book of devotion. Revelation is not there to convey theology, nor to elevate piety, but to convey God Himself. It is His self-revelation, which means His self-communication. It is not concerned with thought, nor with mere hints or indications of His action, 'making Him broken gleams in a stifled splendour and gloom.' These you find in other religions. In a looser sense they too convey revelations of God, self-intimations of God, indications of His presence, His thought, His movement, in some sort. They suggest principles which Christ realized in a person. But we want more than signs of God's presence and movement. We want action positive and final. What we want in revelation is God's total final will, His purpose, His heart, His central and final self, the whole counsel of God in a compendious sense. We want answer to the question, not, Is He here? Is He accessible? But, What is He going to do with us? What is He doing with us and for us? What must I do to be saved? And that is the question put and answered, once for all, in the Bible. The best that the religion of nature does for us is to wake us to a helpless sense of the contradiction and crisis in which we are, and make us feel that what we want is not knowledge but salvation. So that while in other religions the element uppermost is man seeking God, in Israel and in Christ the uppermost thing is God seeking man and finding him for good and all. But in all other religions God and man are seeking each other in the dark; in Christianity they find each other.

We need fear no criticism which leaves us with that. That is the marrow of all the impossible old theories of inspiration. Their object was, often in very unfortunate ways, to secure the uniqueness, the immediacy, the reality, and the finality of God's self-revelation in the Bible. Let us do them that justice, even against themselves. Let us try, in so far as they survive, to get their advocates to see that if they treat the Bible with respect, we, who sympathize with the critical method, do so out of a respect greater still. We let the Bible speak for itself. The great question, then, as to the Bible is not about the historic impregnability of certain detailed facts under the full fire of criticism. It is a question whether the record as a whole is effective and sacramental, whether we have the history of a special movement and action of God for our redemption, or whether we have but a wonderful exhalation of the religious instinct and faculty of man. It is really a dogmatic question. Ὁ Θεὸς Θεολογίζει.

*

So much for the Bible. Now it is so in a like manner with Jesus Christ. The great question is dogmatic. It is, Who is He? What did He do? What does He do? What is His present relation to us and to the future? Was He really the Son of God, or was He but the choice epitome of man? Have we in Him the final approach and self-bestowal of God, the sempiternal presence and final action of the divine reality; or have we a distillation, so to say, of all that is best in religious humanity? Was He an achievement of human nature to make us proud, or was He an achievement of God's nature on our race, called out by the race's deed and shame? His work was an act of sacrifice, of faith, of pity and of love – was it the act of God? Was it God in action? Was He, is He, the true Son of God, for ever Mediator and for ever Lord; or was He just the greatest of all the prophets, apostles, and martyrs of the spiritual life? Do we possess in Him God, or a messenger from God? You can see what a difference must be made in our preaching, according as we answer these alternatives.

Criticism may settle that Jesus loved, taught, blessed, and died. It may decide that to His contemporaries He did pass for one who performed miracles, and accepted that reputation; that He held Himself, rightly or wrongly, to be directly and uniquely from and with God, in the sense of Matthew xi. 25 ff.; and that the first church was only made possible, historically, by its belief that He really rose from the dead. But these are not the prime questions. If they were, our faith would be at the mercy of the critics. The great question is, Did He do the things the apostles believed? Was He really what He held Himself to be? These claims and beliefs were actual. They existed as claims and beliefs. The claims were made, the beliefs were held. Were they real and valid? Could He, can He, make them good? Have we in the Jesus who so lived, and so thought both of Himself and God – have we the living God?

And do we have Him to-day as living, immortal, royal, redeeming Lord God? Was He, is He, of Deity? May we worship Him? The New Testament Church did. They could not help it. The impression left on them was such that worship was a psychological necessity quite inevitable, quite intelligible, quite explicable, as the psychology of religion goes. But while thus inevitable was it really illicit? Was it an extravagance which our better knowledge of reality must correct and reduce? Must we beware of that tendency to worship Him, and arrest it? Must we hear His own voice arresting us, ever fainter and farther as time goes on, 'Why do you call Me so good? Little children, keep yourselves from idols.'

Now, the answer to these questions is not critical but dogmatic. No criticism can certify us of these things, and therefore no criticism can take certainty from us. The man, the Church, that is in living intercourse with the risen Christ is in possession of a fact of experience as real as any mere historic fact, or any experience of reality, that the critic has to found on and make a standard. And with that experience, a man is bound to approach the critical evidence of Christ's Resurrection in a different frame of mind from the merely scientific man who has no such experience. This makes a great difference for criticism between the Old Testament and the New Testament. In the Old Testament we have no historic character with whom we are in daily personal relation still, and who is the greatest contemporary of every age. The fact that the risen Christ appeared only to believers is of immense significance; as I have said, it impairs the value of the Resurrection as proof to the sceptical world, and defines its chief value as being for the Church, for the revival of faith, and not its creation. The external evidence for it, I have owned, is not scientifically complete, nor, suppose it were, is the bearing of the fact upon the rational world, but upon the believing Church. It did not found redemption. That was done and finished on the Cross. But it founded the Church as a historic company, by the resurrection of its faith from the dead. It did not found redemption, but it put God's seal on the completeness of redemption, and it launched the Church. 'If our knowledge of Christ closed with the grave, I fear no faith could have arisen in Christ's victory over death. It could not have been a postulate from the outcome of His early action. And if it had it would have been too weak to resist doubt.'[5]

The living Christ who died has destroyed my guilt, and brought me God. That is not the action of the Resurrection but of the Cross. I believe that the divine power in Him which wells up in my faith, rather than the irrepressible vitality of His divine 'nature,' is the power by which Christ rose. But it is still more the power by which He gained His finished victory on the Cross. Without the primary theology of the Cross the Resurrection of Christ would have no more value than a reanimation. The most present and real fact of our Christian faith is the fact accessible to faith alone. It is the fact that Christ has brought us God and destroyed our guilt. You do not yet know the inner Christ who are but His lovers or friends. You need to have been His patients and to owe Him your life. This is Christianity. A Church without that experience at its centre is not Christianity. What makes a Church Christian is not the historic fact of His death, but the theological, spiritual, experimental fact that His death meant that, and did that, and ever does it. Where there is no such experience it is hard, if not impossible, to convince anybody that His death was more than the close of His life, or the sealing of His witness with His martyr blood. But as a present fact that evangelical action of Christ's death is far more real, and therefore more effective, with us than the death of any Jewish martyr at Roman hands 2,000 years ago. Therefore dogmatic conviction of this kind may have a great effect on criticism, but criticism has only a minor effect upon it. We may be led to recast some of our ideas as to the historical conditions amid which the great life and death transpired. We may modify much in our views as to Christ's omniscience, and similar things affected by His emptying of Himself. He accepted some of the limitations of human ignorance. He consented not to know, with a nescience divinely wise. The story is all recorded in a book, and therefore literary criticism has its rights. Christ worked through history, and in the concretest

---

[5] Metzger quoted by Reischle Z. f. Th. and K. vii. 205.

relation to the history of His race and age; and, in so far as you have history, historic criticism has its rights. Christ lived a real, and therefore a growing, human life, as a historic personality. Therefore, being in psychological conditions, He is amenable so far to psychological criticism. But allowing for all such things, the question remains dogmatic, Was He, is He, what Christian faith essentially believes? Did these convictions, of His and of the Church, correspond to reality? Was He, is He, in God what He thought He was, and what He was held to be? When the first Church worshipped Him with God's name, and set Him on God's throne, were they a new race of idolaters? Was his influence so poor in quality that it could not protect them from that? He thought Himself Redeemer; did He really redeem? Did God redeem in Him? Was God the real actor in His saving action? These are the questions; and in all such questions, criticism is *ultra vires*. These things are settled in another and higher court, and criticism must work under that settlement. The soundest criticism is the criticism by a believing Church, daily living on the Grace of the Cross and the venture of faith.

It is quite true that these truths become dogmas which, in their statement, are fair matter for criticism. The theology of the Church is not a closed product of the Holy Spirit, any more than the Bible is a closed product of verbal inspiration. A process of criticism, adjustment, and correction has always been going on. Theology, on the whole, has been constantly modernized. But it all proceeds on the basis of a reality above logic and beyond criticism, the reality of experienced redemption in the Cross, of faith's knowledge, and the Church's communion with Christ. It is thus something within dogma itself that is the great corrective of dogma. Christian truth in a Church carries in itself the conditions, and the resources, of its own self-preservation through self-correction. The Church's dogmatic faith is the great corrective of the Church's dogmatic thought. The religious life in a risen and royal Redeemer is always ahead of the religious thought about the nature and method of Redemption. The old faith is always making theology new. The true critic of Christian history is its primary theology. You ex-pected me perhaps to say the true critic of a Christian theology is its history. But that is now a commonplace. I meant something less obvious. It is a theological Christ we have centrally to do with – an atoning Christ. And it is only a theological Christ that we need take immense pains to preserve for the future. It is that piece of experienced theology, an atoning, reconciling, redeeming Christ, that has made all the rest of theology. And it must therefore be its living test. With historical criticism, simply as a branch of exact science, pursued by the scholars, and taught in the schools, you have as preachers only a minor concern. You may take it up as you might any other science, only as your nearest pursuit. But you do not wait on it for your message. You must deliver that message while the critics are still at war. Christ is there and urgent, whatever is happening to the story of Christ. A knowledge of criticism may help you to disengage the kernel from the husk, to save the time so often lost in the defence of outposts, to discard obsolete weapons and superfluous baggage, and to concentrate on the things that really matter for eternal life and godliness – like the Reconciliation of the Cross. All true science teaches us also its own limits, and so destroys its own tyranny. But the real criticism with which we have to do, from which all our religion starts when we take the whole Christian field into account, is not our criticism of Christ, but Christ's criticism of us, His saving judgment of us. The higher criticism casts us on the highest. There is a secondary theology of corollaries from faith, and there is a primary of faith's essence. To handle this great and primary theology the first condition is the new man. Our most judicious thing is to treat Christ as our judge, to know Him as we are first known of Him, and to search Him as those who are searched to the marrow by His subtle Spirit.

*

Might I venture here to speak of myself, and of more than thirty years given to progressive thought in connexion, for the most part, with a pulpit and the care of souls? Will you forgive me? I am addressing young men who have the ministry before them, as most of mine is behind, strewn indeed with mistakes, yet led up of the Spirit.

There was a time when I was interested in the first degree with purely scientific criticism. Bred among academic scholarship of the classics and philosophy, I carried these habits to the Bible, and I found in the subject a new fascination, in proportion as the stakes were so much higher. But, fortunately for me, I was not condemned to the mere scholar's cloistered life. I could not treat the matter as an academic quest. I was kept close to practical conditions. I was in a relation of life, duty, and responsibility for others. I could not contemplate conclusions without asking how they would affect these people, and my word to them, in doubt, death, grief, or repentance. I could not call on them to accept my verdict on points that came so near their souls. That is not our conception of the ministry. And they were people in the press and care of life. They could not give their minds to such critical questions. If they had had the time, they had not the training. I saw amateurs making the attempt either in the pew or in the pulpit. And the result was a warning. Yet there were Christian matters which men must decide for themselves, trained or not. Therefore, these matters could not be the things which were at issue in historic criticism taken alone. Moreover, I looked beyond my immediate charge, and viewed the state of mind and faith in the Church at large – especially in those sections of it nearest myself. And I became convinced that they were in no spiritual condition to have forced on them those preaching questions on which scholars so delighted and differed. They were not entrenched in that reality of experience and that certainty of salvation which is the position of safety and command in all critical matters. It also pleased God by the revelation of His holiness and grace, which the great theologians taught me to find in the Bible, to bring home to me my sin in a way that submerged all the school questions in weight, urgency, and poignancy. I was turned from a Christian to a believer, from a lover of love to an object of grace. And so, whereas I first thought that what the Churches needed was enlightened instruction and liberal theology, I came to be sure that what they needed was evangelization, in something more than the conventional sense of that word. 'What we need is not the dechurching of Christianity, but the Christianizing of the Church.' For the sake of critical freedom, in the long run that is so. Religion without an experimental foundation in grace, readily feels panic in the presence of criticism, and is apt to do wild and unjust things in its terror. The Churches are not, in the main, in the spiritual condition of certainty which enables them to be composed and fair to critical methods. They either expect too much from them, and then round upon them in disappointed anger when it is not forthcoming. Or they expect so little from them that they despise them as only ignorance can. They run either to rationalism or to obscurantism. There was something to be done, I felt, before they could freely handle the work of the scholars on the central positions.

And that something was to revive the faith of the Churches in what made them Churches; to turn them from the ill-found sentiment which had sapped faith; to re-open their eyes to the meaning of their own salvation; to rectify their Christian charity by more concern for Christian truth; to banish the amiable religiosity which had taken possession of them in the name of Christian love; and to restore some sense not only of love's severity, but of the unsparing moral mordancy in the Cross and its judgment, which means salvation to the uttermost; to recreate an experience of redemption, both profound and poignant, which should enable them to deal reasonably, without extravagance and without panic, with the scholars' results as these came in. What was needed before we discussed the evidence for the resurrection, was a revival of the sense of God's judgment-grace in the Cross, a renewal of the sense of holiness, and so of sin, as the Cross set forth the one, and exposed the other in its light. We needed to restore their Christian footing to many in the Churches who were far within the zone which criticism occupies. In a word, it seemed to me that what the critical movement called for was not a mere palliation of orthodoxy, in the shape of liberal views, but a new positivity of Gospel. It was not a new comprehensiveness, but a new concentration, a new evangelization, that was demanded by the situation.

But the defective theological education of the ministry seemed to put a great obstacle in the way of such a revival as I have described. For, incredible as it may seem to many, and even alarming, theology was (for reasons on which it would be ungracious for me to enter) not only distrusted, but hated by many of the stewards of the Θεοῦ λόγος. And I have longed and prayed to see the man arise to alter all this, with an equal knowledge of his sin, his Saviour, and his subject, to do the work that had to be done in rearing men with a real, thorough, humble and joyous belief in their own message, and to do it on a scale to compel the attention, and even the concern, of our Churches.

Meantime my own course seemed prescribed. It was, in the space of life, strength, and work which was yet mine, to labour as one who waited for that messianic hope, and to try to persuade those who would hear to join me in preparation for so great a gift of God. I withdrew my prime attention from much of the scholar's work and gave it to those theological interests, imbibed first from Maurice, and then more mightily through Ritschl, which come nearer to life than science, sentiment, or ethic ever can do. I immersed myself in the Logic of Hegel,[6] and corrected it by the theology of Paul, and its continuity in the Reformation, because I was all the time being corrected and humiliated by the Holy Spirit. To me John Newton's hymn which I spoke of[7] is almost holy writ. My faith in critical methods is unchanged. My acceptance of many of the new results is as it was. This applies to the criticism of traditional dogma no less than of scripture. But the need of the hour, among the only circles I can reach, is not that. The time for it will come, but not yet. It is a slow matter. For what is needed is no mere change of view, but a change and a deepening in the type of personal religion, amounting in cases to a new conversion. There is that amiss with the Churches which free criticism can never cure, and no breadth or freshness of view amend. There is a lack of depth and height, an attenuation of experience, a slackness of grasp, a displacement of the centre, a false realism, a dislocation of perspective, amid which the things that make Christianity permanently Christian are in danger of fading from power, if not from view. In a word, I was driven to a change of front though not of footing – to the preacher's and the pastor's treatment of the situation, which is also the New Testament view, and which is very different from

---

[6] I desire to own here how very much I owe to Dr. Fairbairn.
[7] See Hymn, p. 237.

the scholar's. The savant may or must frame results and utter them regardless of their public effect, but the preacher may not. The order of truth he deals with has its own methods, his office has its own paedagogic, and his duty its own conscience. In most cases the best contribution the preacher can make at present to the new theology is to deepen and clear the old faith, and to rescue it from a kind of religion which is only religion and hardly Christian faith. What has often passed as the new theology is no more, sometimes, than a theology of fatigue, or a theology of the press, or a theology of views, or a theology of revolt. Or it is an accommodation theology, a theology accommodated only to the actual interests of the cultured hour.[8] The effort made is to substitute for the old faith something more human in its origin, more humane in its temper, and more halting in its creed, something more genial and more rational and more shallow. It is that rather than the effort to deepen the old theology by a sympathetic re-interpretation, which pierces farther into its content of revelation, and speaks the old faith in a new tongue. The tongue is new enough, but it is not certain that it speaks the old thing, or develops its position from a profounder acquaintance with the holiness of the love of God within the Cross. It analyses the Bible, but it does not reconstruct from the Bible, but from what is known as the Christian principle, which is mainly human nature re-edited and bowdlerised.

---

[8] While I was writing this I read the address of an estimable preacher of up-to-date theology who was demanding that the theologians should come down and accept a theology imposed by three things – physical science, historical study (especially as to the origin of the Bible), and comparative religion. Well, these results are pretty familiar to most of us by now, and very sterile. But you will hardly believe that there was not a word about the study of the Gospel, our application to the contents of Christ's revelation of God, the implicates of His idea of God, or the principles of His work. No, that would have put the preacher beside the theologians. He would have had to ask questions about what was meant by God's most holy love in Christ, questions which science of nature, history or religion can answer. Our spiritual shyness of God's holiness has more than something to do with the ordinary reaction against theology.

I am sure no new theology can really be theology, whatever novelty, unless it express and develop the old faith which made those theologies that are now old the mightiest things of the age when they were new. Well do I know how little a theology in itself can do, and how the mighty doer is the living faith. But I know well also that that faith is not the real thing unless it compels and loves an adequate theology; and if it cannot produce it, it dies. I know well also how seldom it is really objections to an outworn system that keep men from Christ, and retard the Gospel. I am sure that, if we had a theology brought entirely up to date in regard to current thought, we should not then have the great condition for the Kingdom of God. It is the wills of men, and not their views, that are the great obstacle to the Gospel, and the things most intractable. The power to deal with those wills is the power of the Gospel as the eternal act of the will and heart of God. And the power of the Gospel as a preached thing is shaped in a message which has had from the first a theological language of its own creation as its most adequate vehicle. To discard that language entirely is to maim the utterance of the Gospel. To substitute a vocabulary of mere humane sympathies or notions for the great phrases and thoughts which are theology compressed into diamonds is like the attempt to improve a great historic language, which is a nation's record, treasure and trust, by reducing it to Saxon monosyllables, and these to phonetics. I cannot conceive a Christianity to hold the future without words like grace, sin, judgment, repentance, incarnation, atonement, redemption, justification, sacrifice, faith and eternal life. No words of less volume than these can do justice to the meaning of God, however easy their access to the minds of modern men. It needs such words to act on the scale of God and of the race. And the preacher who sets out to discard them or, what is more common, to eviscerate them, is imperilling the great Church for a passing effect with the small. For a living and modern theology our chief need is a living and positive faith, moving in those great categories, and full of confident power to absorb and organize the sound thought of the time. To rouse and feed this faith is the great work of the preacher. And thus the service the preacher does to theology is at least no less than the service theology does to him. A mere theology may strain and stiffen the preacher. But the preacher who is a true steward of the Christian Word makes a living theology inevitable, which, because it lives, demands new form and fitness for each succeeding time.

In closing his recent admirable *History of New England Theology*, Dr. Frank Hugh Foster says: 'The questions of the present hour are more fundamental than those with which New England Theology, or its immediate successors, have had to concern themselves. A ringing call is sounding through the air to face the true issue – the reality of God's supernatural interference in the history of man *versus* the universal reign of unmodified law [or ideas and processes]. The question is not whether the old evangelical scheme needs some adjustments to adapt it to our present knowledge, but whether its most fundamental conception, the very idea of the Gospel, is true. Before this all the halfway compromises of the present day must be given up. Men must take sides. They must be for the Gospel or against it.'

And for or against a historic Gospel, is what Dr. Foster means.

Eight

The Preacher and Modern Ethic

The modern ethical note – An ethicized Christianity means a more positive doctrine of the Cross – The moral paradox of God's forgiveness – The primacy of the moral – The ethicizing of religion by the idea of the holy – The Cross as the consummation of holiness – Judgment as an essential factor in God's Holy Love – The analogy of Fatherhood and its danger – The Cross as the centre of the Kingdom – So Christianity, as supremely moral, appeals to a society intent on moral righteousness – But the preacher has his opportunity also in the moral weakness of society.

From the varied features of modern life that I have indicated I should like to select for further treatment the ethical interest and its development. There is no note in the modern mind more welcome or hopeful to us than this ethical note, the moralizing of society in its ideas, its conduct, its systems, and its institutions. In the case of institutions you may be more struck with the *humanizing* of them, as for instance, of war.[1] But the *moralizing* movement is much deeper, and much more permanent, and it carries the other, the humanizing element, with it.

It is most to our purpose to note the ethicizing of theology, among other legacies of the past. I must have already said that a modern theology is not simply theology *à la mode*. The main part of the modernizing of theology is the moralizing of it, – this much more than its rationalizing. But indeed this tendency is nothing

---

[1] In 1907.

new. It is but continuing a long process in the Christian Church. It was Christ's own action on Judaism. It was Paul's task with his Pharisaism. And a great step in this movement was taken in the Middle Ages, when the work of Christ ceased to be regarded as a traffic with Satan for His captives, and became for Anselm a satisfaction made by Christ to the wounded honour of God. It was another step when the principles of a great social discipline like jurisprudence were applied to explain the situation. It was a real advance when the Reformation introduced the idea of public justice, instead of wounded honour, as the object of satisfaction. The much decried forensic idea was ethically far ahead of the previous idea which recognized in Satan rights of property in souls, ahead also of the feudal idea of the honour of God. And still we move up the moral scale as we substitute for retributive justice with its individualism, universal righteousness and eternal holiness with the social note. So also when we discard the idea of equivalent penalty in favour of Christ's obedient sanctity as the satisfying thing before God. The whole great movement of thought on that question has been on an ascending moral scale. The more we modernize it the more we moralize it. And the modifications called for to-day are in the same direction. Our revisions but continue the long process of moral refinement in the Christian mind. And it appears *en route* that we cannot ethicize Christianity without pursuing a doctrine of Atonement ever more positive. The more ethical we become the more exigent is holiness; and therefore the more necessary is Atonement as the action of love and grace at the instance of holiness and in its interests.

Let us only flee the amateur notion that in the Cross there is no ultimate ethical issue involved, that it is a simple religious appeal to the heart. The pulpit is doomed to futility if it appeal to the heart in any sense that discredits the final appeal to the conscience. I mean it is doomed if it keep declaring that, with such a Father as Christ's, forgiveness is a matter of course; the only difficulty being to insert it into men's hearty belief. There is no doubt that is a very popular notion. 'How natural for God to forgive. It is just like Him.' Whereas the real truth is that it is only like the God familiar to us from the Cross, and not from our natural expectation. Real forgiveness is not natural. Nor is it natural and easy to consent to be forgiven. The more quick our moral sensibility is the more slow we are to accept our forgiveness. And that not through pride always, but often through the exact opposite – through shame, and the inability to forgive one's self. Is it Newman who says that the good man never forgives himself? I wish a great many more said it. We should then have a better hold of the forgiveness of God. We should realize how far from a matter of course forgiveness was for a holy, and justly angry, God, for all His love. A free forgiveness flows from moral strength, but an easy forgiveness only means moral weakness. How natural for God to forgive! Nay, if there be one thing in the world for ever supernatural it is real forgiveness – especially on the scale of redemption. It is natural only to the Supernatural. The natural man does not forgive. He resents and revenges. His wrath smoulders till it flash. And the man who forgives easily, jauntily, and thoughtlessly, when it is a real offence, is neither natural nor supernatural but subnatural. He is not only less than God, he is less than man.

*

Is not God's forgiveness the great moral paradox, the great incredibility of the moral life, needing all the miracle of Christ's person and action to make us realize it when we grasp the terms? A recent authority on preaching warns us that the effective preacher must not be afraid of paradox. For the politician, or the journalist, on the other hand, nothing is more fatal. But that is the region of the ordinary able man, for whom all things must be plain – with a tendency to be dull. In that world an epigram is a frivolity, an antithesis mere ingenuity, and a paradox is mere perversity.

Are there not two distinct classes of mind? The one finds in what is given him just what is given, and he is impatient of anything beyond. His world is as obvious as the primrose quotation from Wordsworth would here be. The other tends always to divine in the given the not yet given. The second truth, the rest of the truth, the hidden truth, the dark twin, is the weighty, fascinating pole of it. The idea latent, the subtle illusion, the mockery of the face-value, the slow result, the subversive effect, the irony of providence, the absurdities of God stronger than all the wisdom of men, the mighty futility of the Cross – these are the things that appeal to such a mind, rather than the obvious which smites you in the face. To have the palpable thrown in its face is what the public loves, and it turns the other cheek. And many are the professors of the obvious, and traffickers in the simple, and great is their reward in the heaven of their *clientèle*. But, for all that, when the soul, even of the public, is moved to its depths, it is beyond the reach of help or comfort from the obvious. The review satisfies not, the politician aids not, and the simple pulpit has no stay. Then do we lift our eyes to the hills, even to the twin peaks of Parnassus; and we flee for strength to the truths of paradox, and to the men who see all things double one against another. Then we find more sense in those who speak of 'dying to live' than in those who say 'all that a man hath will he give for his life.' There is more in those who bid us lose our soul if we would find our soul for us at a price current. There is a poverty that makes many rich. And Christian wealth consists in our ceasing to possess. And you will remember a whole series of these pregnant epigrams as the only expression of the Apostles' experience in 2 Cor. iv. 8–11.

Life from its beginning is a vast vital contradiction. It proceeds by the tension and balance of forces that destroy and forces that build. We are born with the death sentence in us. We die every hour we live. We live, spiritually, moreover, in a standing contradiction of liberty and dependence, freedom and grace, object and subject. Personality itself is – I will not say an illogical – but an alogical unity; else it could not be a power. All scientific experience is paradoxically against the personality whose unity and continuity alone make any experience possible. *Credo quia absurdum* is much less absurd than it looks. A dogma which contains a contradiction like that of the God-man may, for that very reason, be the only adequate expression for the experience of the soul and its last and greatest height.

However it may be with the writer, the preacher must not be afraid of paradox. It is his dread of paradox, his addiction to the obvious, that so often makes him a bore. His simplicity succeeds

only in being bald and passionless. Of course, a string of paradoxes may easily bore us, but not more than a string of common-
places. And a string of paradoxes, ingeniously invented, is one
thing. It is smart, metallic, offensive. But the great recurrent
paradox of the spiritual life, revealed or discovered, is another
thing. The haunting moral paradox of the Cross is another thing.
And if we shun that, and water that down, and extenuate that,
we have no Gospel to preach, or we preach what we have without
passion. Who has tasted the spiritual life that knows nothing of
the deep, eternal, commanding nonsense of 'rejoicing in tribulation' or being 'more than conquerors' as the 'slaves of Christ?'
Nonsense is just the word a cultivated Roman would have used
for such speech. The offence of the Cross, the scandal of it, the
blazing indiscretion and audacious paradox of it, has not ceased.
Nor has its appeal ceased to that region of us to which we come
when our plain palpable world startles and deceives us by smiting
us to the dust and rolling over us – as if a man should lean upon
a wall and a snake bit him, or went for a walk and a lion met
him. We do not touch the deep illogical things of God till we find
paradox their only expression. Life under God is one grand
paradox of dependence and liberty. These two logical incompat-
ibles are only solved in the living active unity of the moral person,
especially towards God. So with life and death. The tremendous
passion for life is God's paradoxical way of expressing the
intense significance of death as life's consummation and solution.
What we call the passion of Christ is the divine reflection of the
passion of human life. His awful death is but the obverse and not
the doom of His solemn and abounding life. And it not only
embodies life's intensity but interprets it. It is the whole passion
and power of life *sub specie œternitatis*. The passion of life with
which we shrink from death is the negative, but eloquent, expression of the intensity of life's Immortality. That massive and
peaceful lake has slumbering in it all the volume and power of
the roaring river of earthly life that fills it. Thoughts like these
serve to compose and dignify us, where the plain is but the trivial,
and the clear is but the thin.

Now holy forgiveness is the greatest moral paradox, the most exalting, pacifying paradox, the greatest practical paradox, in the world. Do not think that the word of your Gospel is not a moral paradox – law and love, the just and the justifier of the unjust, the holy and the sanctifier of the unholy, holy severity and loving mercy, yea, the Holy made sin. Of their union the Cross is not only the evidential fact but the effecting fact. It not only reveals it, it brings it about. That God might be just and also the justifier of the sinner meant all the moral mystery of the Cross, and all its offence to the natural moral man. The natural moral man either does not forgive – and there are none more unforgiving than some sticklers for morality; or else he forgives as he shaves – 'I suppose I ought to;' or as he dines – 'because I like to.' He believes in a God who either does not forgive, or who forgives of course – *c'est son métier.* But the true supernatural forgiveness is a revolution and not an evolution – yea, it means a solemn and ordered crisis within God Himself. But crisis is Greek for judgment. The forgiveness of the world can only be accomplished by the judgment of the world. That is the indispensable paradox whereby Christianity makes morality spiritual. And not to realize that means a step back and not forward in the great modernizing drift which moralizes spiritual things.

*

It is a poor error to think that the ethicizing of religion is its prompt application to present problems, or the reduction of religion to ethics, and faith to cold morality. Rather, by concentrating religion in a crisis between holiness and sin it gives to it a moral nature and a moral core, a moral focus and a moral soul. Sin, it has been said, is the one fact in which religion and morality are inseparably bound. It is still more true of Christ's conquest of sin. In particular, the ethicizing of the Cross means this. It does not mean simply treating the Cross as the apotheosis of that self-sacrifice which is the crown of humane ethic, or the epitome of that altruism which cements society. It does not mean that the Cross is viewed as the grand object lesson in ethics to men, and the great lever in the hand of a changeless God to lift them back to the rails they had left. It does not mean that the Cross must be construed wholly by the

moral category of fatherhood instead of the juristic category of
judgment. Those who so speak forget that there are other and
larger moral categories than the domestic relations, and a world
far vaster than the home. Christ's domestic life was a tragedy. His
family thought him mad. He has nothing to say of family feeling
or fireside joy. 'Who doeth the will of God is to me kith and kin.'
And Paul was of like mind. Those who would translate God's ways
wholly in homely categories forget that when we are dealing with
God we are dealing on the scale of all human society, dealing with
the social and not merely the affectional conscience, indeed with
the eternal moral order of existence. They forget that juristic
principles form one aspect of that social ethic which is such an
enthusiasm of the modern world. They forget that to moralize the
Cross means to explain it not simply by the enlargement of the best
private ethic but by the introduction of the largest public ethic of
the time. This was so when the jurists played such a part as
theologians, at the close of the middle age. And to-day the demand
for social righteousness rather than charity ('Curse your charity!
give us work!') when it is applied to the Cross as the centre of the
Kingdom of God, means the demand for its explanation in terms
of the holiness of God rather than His pitying love or altruism
alone. But to this I must recur later.

*

To ethicize religion, I say then, does not mean to reduce it to
pedestrian morality but to recognize in its heart the action of the
greatest influence in the higher movement of civilization – I mean
the primacy of the moral. To the preacher this is an observation
of the first importance, for it means the primacy and finality of
the holy in his construction of the Gospel. Faith is not ethic, but
it is nothing if it be not ethical. We could not have *faith* even in
infinite love were it not *holy* love. That is what makes the eternal
steadfastness on which faith rests. Faith acts on the heart but its
seat is in the conscience, and its reflection is found in the pure
bench of a great realm no less than in its kindly homes. The
rational, therefore, must take here a second place, and with it goes
the hegemony of the doctrinaire. With it goes the rule of intellectualism, whether as orthodoxy or heresy, and the reign of the

sentimental, which rationalism always brings as a sweet sauce to moisten its sapless drought.

In almost every department we are forced to recognize this ethicizing movement. I need not waste time in pointing out to you that it is identical with the purification of society, its reform, its rescue from politics and commerce, from the tyranny of monarchy, aristocracy, democracy, and plutocracy. I need not remind you how much more it means than philanthropy, how it means the salvation of philanthropy itself, and its provision with staying power. For we preachers have this great advantage in these days. The primacy of the moral, the leadership of the will among the faculties, is really the same as our cardinal principle of justification by faith alone. For faith is the greatest moral act a man can perform, as the grace it answers is the supreme moral possibility for God, the supreme triumph of His holiness. Faith is the moral act which covers, pervades, and assigns the whole man as a living person. Therefore this modern claim for the primacy of the moral is one which we preachers should welcome, for we have in our charge the supreme means of giving it effect. Much of this, however, may be among things obvious.

But it may be less obvious, and it may not be beyond our purpose, if I make special allusion to the spread of this movement in philosophy, and especially in psychology; to the defeat of rationalism, even of the nobler kind, with the retreat of Hegel; and to the triumph of voluntarism in a revised Kant, through men like Schopenhauer, Paulsen, Wundt, Eucken, and James. Even positivism worked up this direction of subduing intellectualism to the will of love. The reason is but the tool of the will. The will is real life. Reality is experience, and experience is the contact of personalities. It is a plexus of wills. Life is not a shadow, or a thing, but an energy, a will to live, as God Himself is not an infinite spiritual presence in repose, but an infinite spiritual power in essential action. Even for Aristotle God was an ἐνέργεια. The moral will is the will to live fully, the passionate self-asseveration of life, slowly shaped by relations social and divine, by humanity and God. Life rises from the unit, through the social stage, to eternal life. Action is good which promotes the life of the race in all its resources; and the life of the race is good when it fulfils and enriches the life of God in all its fulness. That is to say, man is good not in happiness but in perfection; that is in holiness. The good is what enhances true life, the bad is what cramps and kills it. Life, spirit, is the first thing and the last. Energy, vitality, fulness of experience takes the place of mechanism, constructions, and schemes. Action takes the place of vision; the redemption of the world takes the place of its interpretation. Science therefore retires to its due place. Our first need is to know the destiny of the world and not its scheme. It is not ability that has the secret of life but energy, moral power. Reality is life, and not mere truth, it is life as will, as power, as spirit. It is spiritual ethical, personal life, a world of moral values, becoming absolute and eternal in God's holiness. We need urgently that we get over the aesthetic idea of holiness, the idea of white and even burning purity as of Eternal light, and attain the active idea of Eternal *Life* and absolute moral and personal energy. God the holy is not like a snowy peak on the roof of the world wreathed with the incense of our contemplation; but rather is he a sun of power in our heaven and the source of all vital force. This will-life, personal, but more, is the prime and creative factor in the soul. Men must achieve themselves, and acquire their souls, rather than think correctly. The theologian, for instance, should first be not a philosopher but a saved man, with eternal life working in him. Christian theology is the theology not of illumination but of conversion. The supreme Christian gift is not eternal truth but eternal life, more life, fuller life, godlier life, holier life, a life inspired spiritually from the past but not ruled romantically by the past, ruled rather by perfection. Life, which began in spontaneity and not in thought, is raised by a faith passing logic to share in a spontaneity infinite and eternal in the Spirit. To the eye of spiritual reality we are outgrowing the age of science. We are outgrowing intellectual constructions of the world, whether they be those of modern physics, or of the ecclesiastical systems which represent the best science of centuries ago. Our chief business is not to portray the world we are in but to realize and effect it. We have to divine rather than define. We have to divine its meaning rather than make pictures and concepts of its state. We are in an actual situation and not in a painted scene. Our first concern is not a sketch, narrow or broad, but a purpose. It is not, How is our world built? but, What does it intend? We interpret not from a knowledge of the past but from a revelation of the perfect. There is no such thing as totally disinterested knowledge. It is all in the interest of life, all dominated by the will to live. There is no such thing as pure science, absolutely poised and impartial. There are no pure intelligences. They would be monsters. Intellect is a function of personality. Beliefs depend on the will to believe. The ideals we live by are not a product of the intellect, but of the will, of our life energy, of life's ideal, of life energizing at its future best. They are, so to say, the retroaction of our life's urgent future and fulness; or the beneficent pressure of posterity, which plays a part so much greater than heredity. An ideal is a value, not a mere vision; and a value is a judgment of the will. If you have no will you have no ideals; and no description of ideals by any preacher will move you. Knowledge always follows life-interest in the long run. We prosecute the knowledge of what we are interested in, of what appeals to life, feeling, force, concern. We hate and dread the ennui which is the absence of these things. Religion is so far superstition in that both represent the deep instinct of escape from the rational. We interpret men and movements diversely according to our supreme interest in life. No doubt sects and parties thus arise. But they are better than a unanimity of frozen thought like the Greek Church, or of imperious thought like the Roman. No scheme of the world can give us more than an orthodoxy or a heresy. It cannot give us the main thing, which is the meaning, the drift, the issue, the goal, the settlement of the world. That meaning resides in its action, its movement, its history, its destiny, its purpose. It resides, in a word, in its God, its immanent, transcendent, relative, absolute, and final God. It is only that sectarianism of thought which is called specialism that denies a theology. A theology is borne in upon us the more urgently the larger our purview of the world is.

This moral movement, therefore, so conspicuous in society and philosophy, affects theology no less. The burthen of a real theology is not a cosmology but a teleology. It reveals and assures the moral purpose of the world. It presents us with our future in advance. It builds on the supremacy and finality of intelligent action toward a moral purpose, toward a consummation of life, not of science, whether sacred or secular. A real theology is that which is framed under the primacy, not of the rational or scientific, but of the moral, that is, of the holy. Everything here turns on the hegemony of personality, on its central organ as conscience, on its central energy as will, on its central malady as sin, on its central destiny as redemption. The great object of things is not the self-expression of the Eternal in time but His self-effectuation as holy in a kingdom. The work of Christ was not simply the revelation of a new world but its achievement. The world is not God's expression, but His action, His conflict, His conquest. What theology has in charge is the message of a final and holy consummation, awaiting history, yet anticipated in history, in the consummate, victorious Christ. It is the prepayment of our divine destiny. We see not yet all things put under either God or man but we see Jesus, faith's source and consummator alike.[2]

*

I said the interpretation of history comes not from a scientific or inductive knowledge of the past but from the idea of life's perfection, i.e. the revelation, which is also the effectuation, of life's destined holiness. I am particular to say its destined holiness, and not its innate or essential, because it is not intrinsic to man but is the gift and revelation of God. Where then is that creative revelation? For the Christian it is given in history, but it is not an induction from history, nor an intuition of consciousness. It is given first in the inner history of a people with a moral destiny, a select people, Israel, issuing secondly in the life and action of an elect person, Christ. That gift is the great charter of the preacher. He has to do with a situation which is moral above all things, with men and interests that have their *raison d'être* there, whose bearing and action are on the will. He is also the steward of a historic act in Christ, whose perennial power over life is in striking contrast with our success as yet in giving any

---

[2] See for the continuation of this line of thought the Appendix to this lecture.

rational account of it. The Apostles were not made preachers by a theology but by a personal act and the experience of it, by a new life and not a new creed, a new power and not a new institution. There was, indeed, a new society but it was made by the new power. What roused the Apostles was Christ as the crown of a long revelation coming through historic action. And when they gave such supreme value to Christ's death, it was not simply the Judaic notion of symbolic sacrifice that moved them. Symbols make poets but not missionaries. The missionary needs a much more real and ethical inspiration. Symbols but reflect, they do not effect. And the effectual thing was the ethical action at the core of Israel's destiny, the long action of election, right-eousness, judgment, love; which had its consummation in Christ, and gave Christ His unique appeal as Captain of the elect to Israel's choicest sons. In the ethicizing of theology by the idea of the holy we but return to the fountain-head.

*

The trust of Israel and its gift to the world was not mere mono-theism. It was the ethical monotheism which could not rest till it rose to grasp the one God only as the holy God. The God of Israel was not a monopolist. He was not sole as ousting and consuming other deities by sheer push and power; but as the unity of righteousness and peace, of judgment and mercy, of unapproach-able sanctity and of approaching grace. The very history of the word holiness in the Old Testament displays the gradual transcen-dence of the idea of separation by that of sanctity. It traverses a path in which the quantitative idea of *tabu* changes to the quali-tative idea of active and absolute purity. The religious grows ethical, that it may become not only more religious but the one religion for the conscience and for the world. The one God can only be the holy God.

When Israel sank to Judaism the ethical element retired before official rule and imperial ambition – as to-day Curialism and Ultramontanism have submerged the ethical spirituality which made men like St. Bernard in the great medieval Church. When Christ came the ethical Israel was in the trough of a wave. Judaism had come to what some of our active and forward Churches have reached. It had lost the sense of sanctity in the pursuit of a righteousness based, now on equity, now on charity, but always disjoined from grace. For Judaism it was the formal righteousness of an ecclesiastical society, for us it is the distributive justice of an economic society. But, for both, righteousness and kindness submerge holiness and grace. We are far more kind to our neighbours than we feel God gracious to us. For many in our Churches a meal to poor children or cripples is associated with more stir of interest and sense of benefit than the Communion. There is more heart-certainty and satisfaction about it. If that spread it means that *philanthropia* is taking the place of *philadelphia*, the natural brotherhood of the supernatural, pity of faith, and man of Christ. The one is taking the place of the other, instead of growing out of it. The true Christian love of man is that which blossoms on a far deeper and more lively faith in Christ. Let us not linger to lament this state of things but let us interrogate it and understand it. It means inordinate affection which is idolatry. It means the loss of the insight of holiness. We may be getting ready, when the critical time comes, for a blunder as stupendous as that which Judaism made. For does it matter at last what amount of well-doing mark a Church; will that keep it a Church? If it has lost the sense of holiness and what is due to it, if it has lost that worship and culture of holiness which centres about a real Atonement, is it not deserted by the Holy Spirit? And unless He return it may be any kind of admirable society for the promotion of goodness and mercy, but it ceases to be a Church. It may contribute much to civilization, culture, and charity, as Judaism does to this day, but it ceases to be the unearthly organ of the holy Kingdom of God.

When this dullness of spiritual ethic rejected Christ, Judaism kept the monotheism but lost the holiness whose consummation Christ was. And hence Judaism ever since, while it has produced plenty of geniuses in many kinds, and plenty of mystics, has not produced moral leaders for the world. If it has produced saints they are not such as have by their sanctity impressed the world. It is too tribal for the last universality, too narrow, however fine, in its practical ethic. The finer and wider ethic of Judaism is no more to-day than Hillel was in Pharisaism, or Stoicism in Greece and Rome. It cannot save the situation. Only when ethic rises to holiness can it become really universal; and only when holiness gets effect in an Atonement real and not symbolic. The Atonement to God's holiness is the focus of Christian (that is, of all) ethic, the one meeting-point of religion and morals, of grace and conscience, and therefore it is the real secret of Christ's universalism. It was the atoning Cross that made Christ absolutely human.

Is it not so? Is not the great universality that of the conscience; and the final universality – is it not God's conscience, that is, God's holiness, of which the Cross is the supreme energy? It was in Christ and, within Christ, in His Cross (as Paul was crushed to discover) that the ethical soul of the Hebrew God broke into white flame. The true Israelites always found in Israel's God no mere autocrat, whose doings were limited only by logical possibility, but a moral Jehovah, whose power was governed by the absolute holiness of His own nature, and even limited into history in order to achieve the purpose of that holiness. He led His people in the paths of righteousness for His own name's sake. A God of mercy, truly, but also a God of right; a God, therefore, whose passion of mercy could act only by way of historic redemption into righteousness. He was a God of grace, but of grace that could never sacrifice His moral nature, or simply waive His moral order. He must honour it. And He could not simply honour it in secret, bear the cost and say nothing about it. That would not be to the ethical point. For it would not be honouring holiness where it was defied, or establishing it in the presence of its enemies. The judge of all the earth must do public right. And, besides, He was a God of revelation, of self-bestowal. He must be shown as honouring His own holiness in the motive and act of the revelation itself. He must not be revealed simply as one who incidentally held His holiness in respect. But the act of revelation must be the act of respect, the self-respect of the holy. He must be revealed in the act of honouring it, honouring it by the very act that gave and saved. He must pity in a way to set up for ever the public right and glory of His holiness. That is to say, He was a God whose great act of grace was also, because he was holy, a great act of judgment. For to Israel the Messianic time was always a great day of judgment –

terrible, but still more glorious than terrible, a time of hope more than fear. Such, then, was the Hebrew idea of God. Such was God's revelation of Himself to Israel. It was a revelation, and a God, supremely ethical, as being supremely holy – so supremely holy that, from the Cross onwards, holiness ceased to be an attribute of God, and became, in the Holy Spirit, a constituent father and active subject in the Godhead itself.

This is the God that was in Christ reconciling, redeeming the world. The more we grasp this function of the Cross the more we ethicize it. And it is the only radical way of ethicizing it. To moralize Christianity anew we must replace the idea of judgment among all the gains we have won for the other and sympathetic side of faith. The consummation of this historic union of grace and judgment was in the death of Christ. And as the grace of God was on Christ, and not only through Christ on us, so also the judgment of God was on Christ and not only through Christ on us. That is the serious solemn point, disputed by many, and to be pressed only with a grave sense that it alone meets the moral demand of holiness and completes it. Christ not only exercises the judgment of God on us; He absorbs it, so that we are judged not only by Him but in Him. And so in Him we are judged unto salvation. 'The chastisement of our peace was on Him.'

In the Cross, then, we have the ethical consummation, perfect and prolific, of the old paradox of grace and judgment. During His life Christ was at one time pitiful, at another severe. He was merciful to one class, and stern to another. But in the Cross this separation of grace and judgment disappears, as the distinction of all times and classes disappears in the one issue of the universal conscience. And the goodness and the severity of God are perfectly one, as God is one in His passion of movement toward the sinner and reaction from his sin, of grace to the one and wrath to the other.

It is not wonderful that the Disciples with their national past should find in Christ's death something else than the priestly idea of sacrifice symbolized in their ritual. They found in Him a living epistle *to* the Hebrews, and not merely *from* the Hebrews. He was as much a manifesto to Israel from God as from Israel to the world. They found in Christ the priest no less than the sacrifice. They found also this prophetic note of blended grace and judgment, which made them preachers of a Gospel in His death rather than narrators of His memorable life. Even in Paul there was more Hebraism than Judaism, far more prophet than priest. The great prophetic note finds itself at last in the apostolic. Prophetism by its very failure was itself a prophecy. Its holy ideal strained on and up into the Holy One, His doom, and His work, wherein history changed key into eternity. The Apostles found in the Cross that involution of mercy and sanctity, of grace and righteousness, that revelation of sin as well as love, which met at once the greatest intuitions of their religious history, and the deepest needs of their shamed conscience. The Cross, which was the chief shame of their soul, personal or national, became their sure moral triumph. In it the national past found itself in historic effect, and their personal past found itself in a regenerate life. Some of them had denied it, one had betrayed, and one had persecuted it; but they all came to find in it a moral power from which they never went back. It was final for them and their hereditary ideals, because it was the last judgment and the last mercy in a nation whose history and whose song had all along been of mercy and judgment. The justified had the last judgment behind them. The holy morality, eternal in the heavens, became actual on earth. It was the Holy made Sin, the absolute moral miracle – or else the merest ingenuity of nonsense.

*

A gospel which is not final is a mere programme of reform, and there is no finality in any Gospel which ignores the moral element of judgment in God's revelation of love. And therefore there is in such a Gospel no indefectible power. Yet that element is widely ignored in the popular Gospel of sympathy which has replaced the once popular Gospel of orthodoxy. The primacy usurped by the intellect has been taken by the humane affections instead of the evangelical conscience. Judgment has ceased to be preached as an essential factor in a revelation of holy love. Where it is preached it is often in crude forms, without insight, and with non-moral associations which rob it of its practical power. It is preached as 'the last day' or the 'great assize' or the 'quenchless fire.' But it is useless to put judgment at the close of history if it have not a decisive place at the centre of history. Indeed it is impossible. The judgment day of the great future assize draws its true solemnity of meaning from the judgment day in Pilate's hall. To repudiate as mere theology this element of judgment in the Cross, to eliminate the awe of it from our practical habit of piety, is to subside in due course into a non-ethical religion, which finally becomes but a sweetened paganism. For it is in the moral element in the Cross that the real *differentia* of Christianity comes to light. It is the Cross, and it is this in the Cross, that makes Christ more than man. The Incarnation as an article of our faith rests on our experience of the Atonement alone, on our ethical experience there, on the treatment of our sin there, on what God found precious and divine there. Christ must be chiefly for us what He is chiefly to God. We press to a historic view of Christ and we do well; but we must do better, and press still more to the theological view of Him, which sets out what He is to God. We must learn to regard Him as God does. And that is as the consort of His throne, in whose Cross and its judgment the Eternal holiness found itself for the universe again. To minimize the judgment really effected on evil in the Cross once for all is to subside into a humane paganism, in which, after due and usual course, the paganism will submerge the humanity. Our gentler, sweeter, more sympathetic piety will show itself, as it often does show itself, unable to bear up our public life against the moral declensions, seductions, vulgarities, and crimes of a too rich, prosperous and miserable world. Some sweet and facile evangelicals have had a bad business name. You might thus find a charming and pious home, where yet the business activity of its head could best be described as preying on the public. People object to the pagan suggestions of a word like expiation. But it is the want of the thing, truly and ethically understood, that is the real pagan danger, the absence of any satisfaction in holiness to the grieved holiness of God. It is a satisfaction which man, as he came to his senses, would insist on making, even if God did not insist on providing it. For this lack the conscience of the Church comes short at its creative centre – just as it came short when to expiation was given but the pagan and unmoral sense of mollification. The conscience of the Church loses its moral source and bracing school. And Christianity falls victim to fanciful subjectivity, bustling energies, religious romancers, or the fireside pieties.

These things are attractive enough to a humanist age and to half-culture. And they take often far nobler and graver forms than would be suggested by the words I have just used to describe their effect in many. But they are ineffectual for the great public purposes of the Kingdom. They are ineffectual against the pagan ethic of the natural man, or a society full of moral failures and moral vulgarities. If the death of Christ be preached only for the *pathos* of its effect on us and not for the *ethos* of its effect on God, we lack that prime hallowing of His name which exercises on us the profoundest moral effect of all, and which bases our ethic on holiness immutable and eternal. For, as I have already said, the spectacle of Christ dealing with God for us and our sin moves us more deeply than the spectacle of Christ dealing with us for God. As our priest and victim he is far more subduing than as a prophet of the Lord. Yet each without the other is false. It is a redemption by revealed grace through effective judgment that is the moral principle of social regeneration. Whether the public take or refuse the dogmas of theologians as such is a light matter. But it is a great matter if the dogmas of the theologians cover living powers and moral energies, by which society stands or falls. And that is the aspect of theology by which theology and society will stand or fall – the aspect of it which equips the preacher to be not only a voice but an authority to his time. Public freedom at last depends on spiritual freedom, and spiritual freedom is not in human nature but in its redemption. And the first principle of the Christian redemption is the holy recognition of God's wounded holiness, its holy satisfaction in Christ's holy obedience amid the last conditions of human wickedness. The moral perfection of our race is to offer that obedience in sequel and in detail. Man's chief end is not to make the most of himself, but to glorify a holy God by the holiness which alone can satisfy holiness. And that is what sinful man can do only in the power of the atoning holiness of Christ.

*

I know there are those whom we have great reason to honour, who press duly into the heart of the Atonement with the lamp of modern ethic, but who light their lamp at the social and moral relation of fatherhood. That, they say, is the one key put into our hands, by the very constitution of society, for the moral world. The true authentic word of the conscience is the word of father and son. The pillar and ground of social ethic is the family. It was this Word that Christ took up and clothed with eternal validity. It was the Father He preached, and for the Father He died. It was in the name of a disowned Father that He dealt with the conscience. It was to a holy Father that He offered His own conscience. And He retrieved our case by His perfect sympathetic unity with His Father on the one hand, and with His brethren on the other. Accordingly, this theory is offered as a real and near point of attachment for the preacher who has to address people that care more for their families than anything else – Bible, Church or Gospel.

But do they who speak thus go to the bottom of their own plea that it was to a Holy Father that Christ offered His own conscience? Do they grasp the fact that it was not in the Fatherhood but in the holiness of it that Christ's originality lay? Do they realize the immense difference it makes when we extend the fatherhood which we learn in the small kind of family sympathy, to a universal fatherhood – a fatherhood which is the guardian of the whole moral order, amidst warring interests, and of the absolute holiness of the Eternal against those who hate the holy for its holiness? Are the paternal affections the only, or the chief interest of history? Is the Father of our Lord Jesus Christ the crucified simply a magnified and supernatural sire? Had Jesus much of the family feeling? was His family experience quite happy? Was Joseph a type that he had simply to enlarge to find God? Where do we find the authority for erecting the house-father, at his spiritual best, into God? The reply is of course that the authority is Christ. Well, we all admit that Christ is our authority. The question only begins after that. What aspect or action of Christ is selected as the vehicle of the supreme revelation? Where in Christ is the oracle of the Father's will? Where is the Father's authentic Word? Where is *the* revelation of the Father? Surely in the act into which was put the whole life and personality of the Son. Surely in the redeeming act, if the main work of a Father or a Son, in a case like ours, be redemption. Surely in the Cross. Everything turns on the interpretation of the Cross. And what is to interpret it? Must it not interpret itself, and all else, if it be the focus of revelation? Must not the redemption it brings to pass create in us the power to interpret it? Must it not be interpreted by its effect rather than by its antecedents? Antecedents may account for it, explain it, but not interpret it. All great interpretation is teleological. The supreme spiritual events have their meaning either in themselves, or in their outcome, rather than in their *provenance*. That is the Christian way of treating evolution. The interpretation of the series is at its summit. It is man that interprets the world, and not the world man. And, by the same principle, as it is Christ that interprets Israel, so it is the Cross that interprets Christ. It is not the teaching of Jesus that interprets the Cross; it is the Cross that interprets the teaching of Jesus. It may have been so even to Himself. On that I cannot enter here. I will only express my conviction that, unless Christ was principally a teacher aiming at a right interpretation of God, rather than a Redeemer effecting the righteous action of God in the reconstruction of man, it is to the Cross we must look for the true interpretation of Fatherhood in Him. The Cross interprets the Father, not the Father the Cross. And that interpretation was seized and given by John, when the Cross had had more of its perfect work – in John with his manifold insistence upon the *Holy* Father. The nature of the Cross is more revealed in the adjective than in the noun. It is the adjective there that represents the Cross's own interpretation of itself. We thus understand the insight of Luther when he found the true commentary on Christ in the Epistles rather than the Gospels.

I am afraid the thinkers whom I regret here to oppose use an analogy as a revelation. They overlook the fact that the seat of revelation must be sought in the centre of redemption; that it lies not in our experience, paternal or filial, but in our faith of salvation; and that all Christ ever said about God has its true gloss only in what He did about God, and still in our conscience does.

And through the effect of the Cross upon the whole conscience, and especially upon the sinful saved conscience, we are driven to think of its prime action as being objective upon God, or upon the evil power, or both. It is there that we have the chief source even of its effect on us. The chief value of the Cross is its value for God, rather than for man.

If that be so we must not allow ourselves to be led by either our affections, or even the seeming words of Christ, to interpret the Fatherhood of God as the apotheosis of the natural heart and of the sympathetic, endlessly patient and hospitable sire. If the Cross and not paternity is the supreme locus of the conscience of the race, if, that is, it be a historic locus and not a sociological, then our effort to ethicize faith must begin with the ethic of the Cross. We must not start to ethicize the Cross at a standard of fatherhood brought from elsewhere, whether that elsewhere be in social psychology, in the voice of our affections, or even in the words of Christ Himself. My case would be that the highest ethic is the ethic of holiness; and that we cannot bring that ethic to the Cross to explain it, but we must draw it from the supreme assertion of holiness, from the Cross and its revelation in the conscience it redeems. I hope it may not be thought an unfair thing to say that, as the great jubilants of the Cross have been the great sinners it saved, so its great interpreters are men who, *ceteris paribus*, have that scorching of hell upon them, even in heaven, which so many who are interested in theology seem to lack. And because of the lack, when they seek to ethicize they but humanize. They have more humane sympathy than evangelical experience. But the Cross comes with its own ethic in broken and contrite men. All that is provided by the new ethical or paternal interest in modern society is a congenial *nidus* for Christian ethic; it does not provide the illuminative principle. The Cross is really luminous only where it is active. It is its own energy that makes its own light. And its truest interpreters, *ceteris paribus*, are the sinners it has plucked from the gates of death and the mouth of hell. The greatest apostolate is made out of deserters or persecutors, of prodigals more than model sons.

*

The Church has very properly returned to a scriptural interest in *the Kingdom of God*. Her theologians, like Ritschl, have led the way, and her preachers press the new ideal. But it does not seem to meet from the mass of Christians a response which corresponds to the enthusiasm for it of the pulpit. It falls on many as a somewhat archaic conception, too small and primitive for the compass of a modern and complex society. And why? For one reason because its advocates so often forget that it was only the Cross that founded it, it was universalized by the Cross, the apostolic Cross first gave it range and currency. When Christ had overcome the sharpness of death He opened the Kingdom of Heaven to all believers. People plant themselves too exclusively on Christ's teaching of the Kingdom – often expressed in forms more germane to the first century than the twentieth, and to the East rather than to the West. The Saviour is really a more modern idea in these democratic days than the King; and the Cross has an ethical significance more immortal than the kingdom. In construing the social relations by Christianity, therefore, our first duty is not to analyse the metaphor of the Kingdom. Christ has given us the thing. Christ Himself translated the metaphor into reality for us by His death. He was condemned because of His claim to be a king, and 'He did not die for a metaphor.' It was there that He really founded the revelation, not in His parables, prophecies, or precepts. These were addressed to Jews. And some of them are heavily coated with the apocalyptic colour of the time. Our first charge in the ethic and service of the Kingdom is to accept and apply love as we find it in Christ crucified, as saving holy grace. All the Kingdom is latent in that Cross. All its ethic has its creative centre there. Christian ethic consists in living out the life of the Cross freely in the Spirit, rather than in obeying all the precepts of the Sermon on the Mount as precepts, which but leads to the attractive crudities of Tolstoi. The true nature and universality of the Kingdom broke out in the Cross. It was Christ's first and final appeal to the world as distinct from Israel. There, for instance, the true charter of missions lies, not in certain injunctions, or 'marching orders,' which are at the mercy of criticism. Accordingly the doctrine of Christianity as an ellipse, with its two centres of the Kingdom and the Cross, will not hold good. If we speak of two centres they must represent the two great categories for interpreting the Cross – Reconciliation and Redemption, which pass but do not fade into each other. We have but the one centre of the Cross for the Kingdom, for the new humanity, and for its ethic. Even in the Lord's Prayer we have the Cross before the Kingdom. The hallowing of God's name is a prior interest to the coming of the Kingdom. It is the action in the heavens which is the constant prelude of the doing of God's will on earth. The Eternal Spirit of Christ's self-oblation to God is the inspiration of the new world. There we find the resources of the Kingdom in one fontal act where that eternal sacrifice looks forth. And it is there that we find it in the ethical form native to the inner Israel, and equally relevant to every age. There we have the focus of that moral eternity of action, that spiritual universe of energy, which is the contemporary of every age, and therefore is always modern. Christian ethic in Christian society is the mutual relation of sons, not under a loving father, but under a certain kind of loving father – under the Father revealed by a Cross whose first concern was holiness and the dues of holiness. See what manner of love the Father hath bestowed on us. God so loved that He gave His Son to be a propitiation and to hallow His name. It was not enough that evil should be mastered; holiness had to be set up and secured in history. And the continuous agent of that holiness is the conscience in us which was first created on the Cross by the offering of holiness to the Holy One. The prime vocation of the society of the Cross is holiness unto the Lord. And as human society grows more Christian this must become its waxing note. It sounds the dominant over all – even over love. It is the power, the life, which all love serves. If we are to fill life full, and spread the reign of love, let us preach the holy God, and the Cross where He is at His fullest and Holiest of all. Our Gospel is not simply God is love, but God's love is holy, for the Holy One is love.

What is this final appeal even of love to holiness but asserting for God what everything that is best in modern life tends to assert for man – the primacy of the moral, the supremacy of life and will to thought or truth? What is it but the ethicizing of religion?

For God the moral and the supreme is His holy will of love. You cannot ethicize either religion or life without adjusting it to the holiness of God. And that practical adjustment, objective and subjective, was Christ's work in the atoning Cross. Pardon is the perpetual demand of our actual moral situation. And pardon is only pardon, not when it wipes the slate, but as it is the supreme expression and establishment of moral reality. Its conditions are those required by moral reality on an eternal scale – that is, by the holy.

*

What an advantage, then, the preacher of holiness as it is in the Cross has in addressing the society of these days, set upon moral righteousness as it never was before. For both the Cross and the public the moral is the first thing. I do not mean that the preacher should preach the moral philosophy of the Cross, or confine himself to Christian ethics, but he has to preach a Gospel which has supreme in its heart this moral note of holy grace and judgment love; and he preaches it to a public in which the moral passion is rising steadily. The modern appeal to the will is the native note of the Christian apostle, the appeal to the moral will, to the conscience.

There is nothing you will oftener hear from pulpits that strive to be abreast of things than this: 'Christianity is not a creed; it is a life.' What is meant by it? Not surely that Christianity is but a certain course or manner of living. That drops all to mere moralism. Not that it is a way of feeling, a certain sympathetic strain. That makes it a sentimentalism. Not that it is simply the copying of a heroic example. That makes it a depressing legalism, or a no less depressing idealism. If it mean anything it surely means that Christianity is a solution of the problem of life, which is a moral problem. And Christianity means still more, giving us the moral solution of life as a present. Here is another paradox – the gift of a moral achievement, moral victory, as a present. You can compare it with that parallel audacity 'The Father hath *given* the Son to have life *in Himself*.' Such is the secret of Christianity and such its gift – the gift of a life that masters the supreme moral condition of holiness – eternal life, as it was achieved in the Cross, in the holy satisfaction of the Cross. Such is the paradox of the cross, its alogical nature, its defiance of a perfectly consistent theology, its ethical offence to monism, its inner contradiction as the only adequate harmony of religious experience, its dualism as the only condition of the moral and holy life.

*

This Gospel appeals not only to the strength of modern society – its interest in righteousness, and in a social righteousness – but also to its weakness. Because the weakness of the hour (for all our ethical progress) is a moral weakness. In every other respect society is stronger than it ever was before. Never was man's mastery of the world so complete. Never had he such resources in dealing with it, and compelling it to his purpose. Yes, but it is the matter of his purpose that is the weak place. What is his purpose when he has one? What is to repair his lack of one? Our trouble is the paganism of the age, with its moral hollowness and its shell of self-confidence. On the one side you have the weakness of over-energy – men engrossed with practical activity, like old Rome, till they have neither leisure nor power to note the crumbling of their moral interior. That you may have in a young country. And, on the other hand, you have what you find in the old and decadent lands – the weakness of no-energy, the hebetude of the outworn, the failure of will, the lack of moral interest. You have the conscience narcotised by civilization, by science, by culture, by religion, by morality itself. All these things conspire to stifle in the conscience the deepest issues which drive us to the Cross. Even religion in this respect can be very mischievous to Christianity, on the principle that the good is the enemy of the best. And at the extreme end you have the moral paralytics, who find life no longer worth living except in moments of some kind of intoxication; you have the moral degenerates or cretins, the victims of the age's overfed individualism and its moral fatigue, who live in a perpetual depression because they have no motives; and you have the moral melancholics and irresolutes, who, by the very wealth of their ideas, have so many motives that they are unable to choose any one of them. I am thinking on the one hand of the famous Melancholia of Dürer, limp and listless in the midst

of all the resources of science and art. I think on the other hand
of a victim of 'psychological rumination' so noble yet so over-in-
terested as Amiel. And between these two extremes you have a
varied gamut of people whose trouble is moral marasmus, and
who so often leap at the manifold quackeries of volitional religion,
or self-salvation, or will-idolatry. They all betray a narcotised
conscience, a light sense and a light healing of our mortal wounds.
Nothing reveals the incompetency of much popular religion more
than its inability to gauge the poignancy of the moral situation on
the one hand, or the true depth of the moral resources of Christianity on the other.

*

In those circumstances let the preacher who is sure be of new
cheer. It is the prophet's opportunity. The conscience of society is
awake but it is not illuminated; and where illuminated it has not
power. It is awake enough to cry for a redemption, but not enough
to take the Christian redemption home, far less to bring it to pass
around. It is power for the conscience the preacher brings. His
great object is not to produce either loving affections or correct
views of Christian truth, whether broad or narrow, neither sympathies, liberalisms, nor orthodoxies, but the moral power of the
Christian Gospel. The correct science of our faith is all very well,
but, whether old or new, it is not faith. And the ethics of love,
gathering about the dear person of Christ, is very well, but it is
only a partial solution of the problem offered us by the world.
That is a moral, a practical problem, a problem not of the
sympathies, but of the will and conscience. The ethic of love has
more effect on those who are in the Church than on the world. It
moves chiefly the already well disposed. It is a Gospel for the
sensitive. And it lacks the note of authority which is the modern
world's chief need, and which is heard in its power, not in the
heart but the conscience. Authority's seat and source is not God's
love, but God's holiness. Have I not said that the love in God must
itself rest on the holiness of God, that we can trust love with real
faith only if it show itself absolutely holy? That is to say, the
Church's Word, the preacher's Word, must issue from a Gospel
not of love alone but of holy love. It sounds from a Cross which

does not merely show love but honours holiness. It flows from a grace which does not merely display compassion, but effects judgment, achieves redemption, does the one deed demanded in the real moral situation by the holy authority of God. The Word of grace is a deed of God. And the answer of faith must be a deed no less. Faith is not a sympathy but an act. It is the moral victory that overcomes the active world by an act greater still, inspired from a world more active still. The faith that the preacher would stir is the greatest of moral deeds. It searches the deep and devious recesses of the conscience upon the scale of the whole world – yea of the holy world unseen. And it breeds that new mystic life which is the only condition of a new heaven and a new earth wherein dwells holiness. 'This is *the* work of God, that they should believe in Him whom He hath sent to be a propitiation for us.'

May I resume? The history of the world morally viewed is a tragedy. All the great tragedy of the world turns upon its guilt. Aeschylus, Shakespeare, Goethe, Ibsen, all tell it you. The solution of the world, therefore, is what destroys its guilt. And nothing can destroy guilt but the very holiness that makes guilt guilt. And that destruction is the work of Christ upon His Cross, the Word of Life Eternal in your hands and in your souls. The relevancy of His Cross is not to a church, or a sect, or a creed, but to the total moral world in its actual radical case. The moral world, I say, is the real world, the ever modern world. And the supreme problem of the moral world is sin. Its one need is to be forgiven. And nothing but holiness can forgive. Love cannot. We are both forgiven and redeemed in Jesus Christ and in Him as crucified unto the world for the holiness of God and the sin of men.

Appendix

There is one qualification which has to be made, however, when we use the Pragmatism or Voluntarism of recent philosophy as a calculus for the specific action of Christianity. Action is indeed the material of truth (*Wesen – Actus*) – the organ, too, by which we reach it as well as spread it, and become true as well as see true. But we have to do with something more than the action either of nature, of men, or of mankind. To fall back thus on the will, energy, or resource of man is to make religion in the end impossible, except by a kind of moral positivism which leaves humanity to worship but itself and its deed. What we have to realize is a spiritual world not simply in man but in which man is, a world that has to temper him and master him, that has to prevent him from taking his needs, passions and energies for charter or standard, a world that has to stand over him, test him, sift him, lift him, and end by setting him on a totally different base from the egotism in which he began. That is, we have to do, above all, not simply with an ideal world of process, but with a spiritual world of value.

And this spiritual world is not quiescent but active. It does not simply envelop us, it acts on us, and we react on it; and in that reaction we find ourselves, and we grow into spiritual persons with which we never set out. It does not swathe us and erase us, it besets us, it applies itself to us. It does not simply stand at the door, or pass and suck us into its wake; it knocks, enters, finds, and saves us – all in the way of creating our moral personality and giving us to ourselves by rescuing us from ourselves. It is an active not a static world. It moves, it works, it creates.

Its movement is not process, as so many to-day are seduced to construe it, in the wake of the great cosmic processionalist and marshal, Hegel, with his staff of subordinate evolutionists. This of Hegel's, indeed, is a conception which lifts us over much of the triviality and slavery of life; but only to substitute for petty bondage a vast tyranny, and to replace a prison by a despotism, with a first show of freedom but a final atmosphere of death. And especially it leaves us with a loss of moral liberty, and ethical dignity, and spiritual initiative and personal consummation. The actual course of history is not a process. And it is not through yielding to a process that history is created by its great actors. There are stagnations, too, degenerations, enmities which forbid us to call life a process, at the same time as they prevent us from treating its movement as our being rolled over and ground up in a greater process. Mere process ends in mechanism, coarse or fine, and extinguishes a soul. Behind everything that seems process on any large scale our active moral soul insists on placing an act, and an act from a new world – something ethical and personal in its kind.

If this spiritual world, so active, be one; if we are to escape pluralism, as well as monism; if we are not to escape being rolled over by a vast process only to be crushed by the active but awful collision of more spiritual worlds than one; then its action must be one infinite and unitary *concursus*, one compendious personal act, the *actus purus* of an infinite personality who is not only ethical but self-sufficient in his ethic. But what is an infinite moral self-sufficiency, an active, changeless, self-completeness, but *holiness?* The total action of the spiritual world both in us and around is holiness. We find ourselves before and within a holy God, a spiritually moral personality, self-determined and self-complete.

But no less, if this spiritual world and power be universal, it must assert itself supremely in the region of *history*. If its inmost nature be action we cannot think of it as secluded from that one region where action has real meaning and effect for man. It must assert, express, reveal and effect itself in history for the holy and mastering power it is.

Yet such a power cannot adequately reveal itself *dispersed through* history, or merely parallel with it, nor even in 'mutual involution.' For such a diffused revelation would not represent, and might even belie, a spiritual power whose nature was not only action but action of the sole kind which possesses moral unity, namely, the action of a moral person. If it reveal itself – I do not merely mean assert itself – in history it must surely do so in an act corresponding to its own total ethical nature in the spiritual world, in an act which gathers and commands cosmic history, as its nature is to focus and utter all spiritual being. A world of spiritual action with moral coherency can only be revealed in history by a supreme spiritual act, the supreme act of a person who both gathers up and controls human existence, and delivers it from that submersion in self and the world which in the long run is fatal to man's action as man. If spiritual existence be an infinite and eternal act, such must also be its revelation.

And this is the act of Christ in the *Cross*, the act of the Gospel. It is the act of God's grace, met by the act of our faith – an act into which a whole divine life was put, and one that issues in a whole life on our part. This act is the gift of God; whose freedom we attain by no mere development of our own liberty, but by a free act which renounces our liberty for His, breaks with what is behind and beneath us, breaks with the old self, and, by accepting a new creation, exchanges an assertive individualism for a redeemed personality. The energy of such a spiritual world as we postulate in God can only act on us in the way of redemption and not more evolution from the world of our first stage. We cease to be self-made men, and we are men who let God make us, and make us by His grace and not His evolution. We achieve by this grace a personality we had not at the first. As we reach our freedom we acquire and attain ourselves; and we reach our freedom by surrendering it to God's. The best use we can make of our freedom is to forgo it, and to sign it away to one whose work and joy it is to create in us a freedom we can never acquire. We are but persons in the making, and we are not made till grace make us and faith is made. Our supreme ethical act is the faith that gives us at once our Saviour and ourselves. We exhaust our own exertions, and we deliver ourselves to a faithful Creator. And our perfecting God is a God of grace, not only because He finishes us, but finishes us as alone we can be perfected – by redemption, by a change of base, centre, and affection. He is a gracious God and not simply a benevolent God, because He lets us exhaust, and even wreck, our private powers, instead of only guiding their education, so that with His free and creative act He may make of us what all our native force could never do.

Nine

The Moral Poignancy of the Cross

The inadequacy of the common view of God's benignant Fatherhood – Popularity not the test of the Gospel – The complexity of the soul's situation – Sin as enmity to God – God's love brought home not by a spectacle but by a finished universal act – An ethicized Theology must emphasize holiness – Christ as God forgiving – The need of moral mordancy, of iron in our blood – The Cross not a martyrdom but God's decisive and creative act – Christ not only redeemed, He atoned – The element of judgment, the wrath of God – The Atonement to God – This aspect of propitiation essential to the final prospects of Christianity – Conclusion.

The leading doctrine of much modern theology is the Fatherhood of God in a sense I have already indicated. It offers us a God genial, benignant, patient, and too great in His love to make so much as Paulinism does of the sin of a mere child like man. Now, how does such a conception really affect modern preaching? It is another form of the question if we ask how it affects the Church whose voice preaching is. No such vast doctrine can be tested by either the feeling or the character of an individual, even if he be a most successful preacher. There are plenty of individuals, and indeed one whole sex, to whom a religion of naïve fatherly love is perfectly satisfactory – so much so that they can not only think of nothing beyond, but they grow impatient when anything more is pressed, as if it were a sophistication, an impertinence, or a foray of dogma. But the real question is not about individuals, but it is this – Is that the faith once committed to the Church? Is it the faith that has formed the real *continuum* of the Church, its distinctive note and staying power in history? And what would the moral and religious result be if the whole Church accepted that position, and lived on that level and climate of faith? What would be the result then to the preacher's message, and to his ultimate moral effect on life or society?

It is easy, of course, to say that above all things we need a simple religion, and that this gospel of fatherly love is of the simplest; that it speaks the language of the heart, and the piety of our mother's knee; and that it is the order of faith that befits an age of democracy, when Christianity is straining every nerve to get at the untaught mass.

*

Now, on this there are several remarks. First, Is the test of a Gospel the welcome it receives, the rapidity of its success? Is the distinctive note of the Church's Gospel that which immediately appeals to the democracy or the minor? Is Christianity to stand or fall by its direct effect on the workman or the youth? Is it great, universal, and final as a religion because it is within the effortless comprehension of the ignorant or the weak? It shall, indeed, be for these. The wayfaring man, though a fool, need not err therein. But is he the criterion of the religion? Is everything to be sacrificed from Bible, Church, or Creed which does not attract or hold the masses of the natural man? Is it the case that what we now find most valuable in Christianity has arrested and commanded the prompt welcome of men in its course through history? These are questions which it is not superfluous to discuss in the connexion.

*

Second, the situation of the soul is not a simple one. The moral difficulty of society is not that we are strayed children, great babes in a wood. It is that we are sinful men in a sinful race. We are mutinous. It is not a pathetic situation that the preacher confronts so much as a tragic. The first question for a Redeemer is still the old one, *quanti ponderis sit peccatum*. The forgiveness of sin is the foundation and genesis of Christianity; it is not an incident in it, nor in the Christian life. Not to know sin is not to know Christ.

That is true for the race if not for every soul in it. No one can describe the situation as simple who has earned the right to an opinion by gauging that fundamental question, or by knowledge of the moral world round him. Let us not go to war without counting the cost. A remedy for such a situation which is merely simple is a pill for an earthquake, or a poultice for a cancer. The disease is mortal. And, moreover, what is in question is a diseased world. It is a society that is sick to death, and not a stray soul. We have to deal with a radical evil in human nature, and spiritual wickedness in deep places. We have not only to restore the prodigal but to reorganize the household of the elder brother. In life's daily affairs it may be wisdom not to take things tragically. But they have to be taken tragically somewhere if we are to have moral realism at all. And the men of power and thoroughness do so take it, whether Kant or Ibsen. The world as a world has to be tragically taken, and converted to a *divina commedia*. If it is our wisdom not to be tragic it is only the wisdom of faith, which does not ignore the tragedy, but is able to cast it on One who did take things tragically, and who underwent and overcame at the moral centre of men and things.

*

And, thirdly, we may ask how far this view does justice to the revelation which is the κήρυγμα of the Church, and the preacher's capital in the Bible. The Church has not only to read the present situation; she has to read her own Gospel before that; which is what multitudes of people, and even preachers, are not doing. How far does this view do justice to the revelation 'God is love,' in the face of such a world of muddle, misery and anomaly, of guilt, grief, and devilry? The preacher's business is to make that principle of love real and effective in a world of extreme wickedness, a world with Goneril in it, and Regan, and Iago, and Mephistopheles, with the Inquisition in it, and the Russian bureaucracy. It is not Hamlet that is the real trouble, though he most arrests the attention of today. And the preacher's first inquiry is, How is that revelation 'God is love' made effective by God? How does God Himself face the world's worst in the Gospel which is put into the preacher's hands? It is not the unwieldy mass of a gross average world that makes the problem of the Cross, but the world's wickedness, condensed, organized pointed, deliberate, and Satanic, not missing or losing God but challenging Him. It is not a misunderstanding but war *a l'outrance*. It is sin's death or God's. For we must keep urging that what is given the preacher is not a truth but a Gospel; nor is it an offer of God at the mercy of human experience, but an objective finished deed. What is this deed? How does God reveal Himself as love? I should like to devote this lecture to an answer to that question more explicit than my previous references, because all these references have been accumulating such a necessity for me; and because it is the question which goes to the root of the preacher's power; meaning thereby chiefly the Church's message as the preacher to the world. For it is easy (I said) to be misled by the effect of idiosyncrasy in individual preachers, or by their effect on individual cases. An invalid might be greatly consoled by a kindly preacher whose net public effect was to undermine the Christian Gospel.

*

We are all agreed that the Gospel is the revelation of God's love to the sinful world. My points are, first, that no revelation of divine love to such a world is possible unless the revelation is an act of redemption. Men had to be delivered into the very power to see a revelation; so that mere manifestation is but one factor in revelation. And my second point is that the redemption of man is inseparable from the satisfaction of God in an Atonement.

*

1. On the first head, I would begin by recalling the educational principle, that as no lesson is really taught till it is learned, so revelation is not revelation till it get home, till it return to God in faith. And we have to be saved into faith before we are saved by it. The power of sin is such that we cannot believe to saving purpose except we are redeemed into that power. We cannot believe even when we wish to. The voice of our distress is,

> *Hilf, Vater mein,*
> *Dem Knechte dein,*
> *Ich glaub' und kann nicht glauben.*

Faith itself, we say, is the work of the Spirit. And the Spirit itself proceeds from the Cross, and is the Spirit of our redemption. And just as a great and original artist like Turner, or a similar poet like Browning, had first to create the very taste that understands them, so it is with the tremendous and creative revelation of God in Christ. It had to recreate man, and redeem him into the very power of realizing it. The difficulty in believing in an Atonement is in great measure due to the fact that the belief needs self-surrender. The real necessity of an Atonement only comes home where it has done its work – only to the conscience redeemed. You cannot prove it to the world, or force it on the natural man. If a man say 'I do not see the need of it' you can go little farther with him, beyond a caution that he shall not make his myopia the standard of vision.

We may, and we must, modernize our theories of Atonement, but for preaching, in such a world as this, the Church must have the thing, the deed. It cannot act effectively in a world where evil is so able, so practical, so passionate, so sordid, and so established, with a mere exhibition of fatherhood; nor can it treat the history of sonship as man's natural evolution under Christ's benignant sunshine up to a spiritual plane.

How then are we to do justice to God's holy love? Well, how did He? He might conceivably have done it through a sage that taught this love. But this is too futile, and He did not act so. He might have done it through a prophet, inspired by his own experience of such righteous love, and aglow with its passion. But prophetism, with all its moral fervour, was a failure for the saving either of Israel or the world. Yea, as a prophet only, Jesus Himself was a failure both with the people and His disciples. Or He might have done it by a sinless but statuesque personality, who embodied His love, and visualized it to us as its living image and our perfect example or type. But even that is more of a spectacle than a salvation; it is something more aesthetic for our spiritual contemplation than dynamic for our moral redemption. So to view Christ is no doubt a great matter. But it is the nature of a *tableau vivant*. It leaves Him still a somewhat inert personality, a spiritual figure finished all but the arms. He cannot take hold of the world and wrestle with it. He is not among the mighty doers of the race. He remains but a gracious influence. We meet in Him with that nearness of the divine presence which marks an early stage of religion, but not with His searching divine act which makes God the last moral reality. The last moral reality is a person not in repose but in action with the world. The real God is present in the soul, active in history, and master of the world. Now the pure and sinless personality of Christ leaves us indeed with a divine presence in whom our selfhood may be lost, but not with the divine act of new creation in which we are given our true moral place in a saved world. It leaves us with a religion of worship but not with a religion of power, with a message which exhibits rather than achieves, and says rather than does.

And, therefore, God's way of carrying home His love to the world was by a person who was realized in one act corresponding to the unity of the person and the scale of the world; a person whose consummation of Himself was in the great man's way of crucial action; an action giving effect to His whole universal personality and therefore having effect on the whole of man's relation to God. God in Christ's Cross not only manifests His love but gives effect to it in human history. He enters that stream, and rides on its rage, and rules its flood, and bends its course. He reseats His love in command upon the active centre of human reality. He does the thing which is crucial for human destiny. Christ effected God's purpose with the race, He did not merely contribute the chief condition to that end. The Cross *effects* the reconciliation of man and God; it does not simply announce it, or simply *prepare* it. It does not simply provide either a preliminary which God needs in a propitiation, or the stimulus man needs in a spiritual hero, or a moving martyr. The propitiation is the redemption. The only satisfaction to a holy God is the absolute establishment of holiness, as Christ did it in all but the empirical way. The Cross is the redemption in principle and effect. It does not avert the great last judgment, it is the action of that judgment. Do not persist in thinking of the last judgment as mainly dreadful and damnatory. In the Bible and especially in the Old Testament, I have already said, the day of the Lord is an awful joy, as the final vindication of goodness, the final establishment of righteousness. Judgment is the grand justification, not prepared by the Cross, but effected and completed on the Cross and the justification there. The justified have the last judgment behind them. There the eschatological becomes ethical, the remote near, the last first. The justification in the Cross does not produce the salvation; it is the salvation. In Christ we have no mere preface or auxiliary to the supreme crisis of humanity. We have that crisis. The day of the Lord is here. We are in its midst. Only as the race is living out Christ's death, for weal or woe, can we truly say *Die Welt-geschichte ist das Weltgericht*. The work was finished there as well as begun. But it was finished more than begun. It began its career as a finished work. But to this point I must return later.

*

Christ does not come to us merely announcing His view of God. Nor does He come afire with the ardour of holiness. Nor does He come to present to the world a perfect but lapidary sanctity. What He carries home to us is not the existence of God but the grace of God. He comes to be the standing, saving action of a holy God in and on the world. He is in it as one who is in perpetual conquest over it. He is in it sacramentally, not as immanent but as incarnate, not as its substance but as its purpose, not as filling it but as effectuating it, not pervading it but subduing and reclaiming it, not as its ground but as its King.

In Christ God does not simply announce Himself, and He cannot be preached by a mere announcement. He gives no mere revelation about Himself. The revelation *about* God is the bane common both to orthodoxy and to rationalism. Both are the victims of that intellectualism. What we need, what God has given, what preaching has to convey, is Himself. It is sacramental work. His revelation is His actual coming and doing. He is there *in* Christ, not *through* Christ. Revelation is self-communication; and it is self-communication which is not the mere offer of Himself but the actual bestowal of Himself, His effectual occupation of Man-soul and not His mere claim of it, not the soul's opportunity but the soul's seizure by an act of conquest. God is the matter of His own revelation; and, therefore, He only succeeds if he win, not the soul's assent, but the soul itself. If it was Himself He gave, it is man's self He must have. And He is not really revealed to man, for all His outgoing, till He receive that answer, till He redeem, and return upon Himself with man's soul for a prey. Revelation must take effect in restored communion. God is not really opened to me till He opens me to Him.

All this is only possible if revelation and preaching be much more than declaration. Revelation must be an act. Reality is action. *Im Anfang war die That.* Christ spoke far less of love than he practised it. He did not publish a new idea of the Father – rather He was the first true Son. Christ as God's revelation is God's act; and our conveyance of Christ in preaching is Christ's act. Otherwise, God's love would be a mere lenient word, or a mere affection on His part, lacking in moral energy and in power to give effect to itself. God then would not fully identify Himself with the human case. He feels for men, and speaks to them, but He does nothing. He sends, but He does not come. This sending, no doubt, is a great thing, but it is not a Gospel that inspires preaching in the high and powerful sense, in a sense commensurate either with tragic humanity or a triumphant Church. And the philanthropy based on this, prolific as it may be for a time, has not a future, for lack of staying power. The divinest love which could not put its whole self into a saving act might but wring its hands on the shore, or wade a little in, as many do, who mean the very best, but who can only tickle the evil of a world with which they cannot grapple. When we preachers ask about the revelation of God's love what we ask for is its deed.

Remember above all things that the love we have to do with is holy love. And holiness is the eternal moral power which must do, and do, till it see itself everywhere. That is its only satisfaction and atonement, not the pound of flesh but entire absolute response in its own active kind. And that is what we have in Christ as our head.

*

The modernizing of theology (I have urged) means above all things its ethicizing. And its ethicizing can only mean its control at all points by the supreme ethical power. But that must mean not its reformation from without but its self reformation from within. For the supreme ethical idea is one which the Gospel itself provides, which the Gospel alone provides, and, still more, puts in action and makes effective. It is not an idea imported from culture as a corrective to faith. It is given in faith as the idea and the power which necessitated the Cross of Christ and made it mighty, the idea and power of God's holiness, its word and deed.

And what does that holiness mean and demand if we become more explicit?

Turn to man himself. Begin with him as a moral personality. Man finds the moral order of the world uttered for him in his conscience. In that conscience he even finds the voice of God. He carries back the moral order, whether in himself or without, to God. God as holy is its absolute ground.

For that conscience is not a voice from a corner of man's being. It is the verdict of his whole moral self. It is himself, as a complete moral personality, pronouncing on himself as something else, either short of that, or hostile to it. It is the expression of his own moral autonomy. In so far as it is a law to him it is the law of his full free moral self.

But it has power over him not only as being his, but as taking the same supreme place for every moral being. It has this supreme place therefore for humanity. The sanctity of man is the sanctity of man's full, free, and collective moral self.

But that very complete fulness must go back on a divine ground of it all, the ground of our very autonomy. We are again confronted with the paradox of dependence and freedom 'He hath *given* the Son to have life *in Himself*.' 'Work, for it is God working.' We go back to secure our autonomy on an autonomy which has its ground in itself, that is to say, to God. Without this divine autonomy, underlying and guaranteeing all ours, we have no principle that gives the moral law a supreme sanction, and raises it above all our wilful doubt or passion.

Now this principle is the holiness of God. Or rather it is God the holy. It is God as self-complete and absolute moral personality, the universal and eternal holy God whose sufficiency is of Himself, the self-contained, and self-determined moral reality of

the universe, for which all things work together in a supreme
concursus, which must endure if all else fail, and must be secured
at any cost beside. Better it were that man should wreck than that
God's holiness be defiled and defied. 'The dignity of man himself
is better secured if it break in the maintenance of God's holiness
than if that holiness suffer defeat for man's mere existence.' It is
a holiness whose claim must be not only made, but made good,
and given unmistakable effect. (I beg you to bear with my phra-
seology often. For we are here almost beyond the limits of human
speech and caught up to the verge of realities which it is not given
to man to utter.)

It is not enough, therefore, to emphasize the person of Christ,
to set it again in the centre as modern theology was bound to do,
and has done ever since Schleiermacher, in order to repair much
historic neglect. We may dwell on the person of Christ and mean
no more than a perfectly saintly soul reposing in God. But this is
a conception too sabbatic for a universe which is an act, and
whose energy runs up into human history. Christ's person has its
reality in its active relation to other persons – God or men. We
must find the key to it in something Christ did with His entirety,
and did in relation to that holiness of God which means so much
more than all Humanity is worth.

The true key to Christ's person is in His work. It lies not in a
miraculous manner of birth, nor in a metaphysical manner of two
co-existent natures, but in a moral way of atoning experience. It
lies in His personal action, and in our experience of saving benefits
from Him. It lies not in His constitution but in His blessings. His
love to us is not the image, the reflexion, or even the result of
God's love, it is a part of it, the very present action of it. We feel
this particularly when we are forgiven. It is only the holy love we
have so wronged that has the right to forgive. And the forgiveness
we take from Christ is taken directly from the hand and heart of
God, immediately though not unmediated. Christ is God forgiving. He does not help us to God, He brings God. In Him God
comes. He is not the agent of God but the Son of God; He is God
the Son. As we must preach Christ and not merely about Christ,
so Christ does not merely bring access to God, He brings God.

God is Love only if Jesus is God. Otherwise Jesus would become our real God.

God's love then is love in holy action, in forgiveness, in redemption. It is the love for sinners of a God above all things *holy*, whose holiness makes sin damnable as sin and love active as grace. It can only act in a way that shall do justice to holiness, and restore it. Short of that, love does no more than pass a lenient sentence on sin. It meets the strain of the situation by reducing the severity of the demand. It empties of meaning the wrath of God. And it reduces the holy law of His nature to a by-law He can suspend, or a habit He can break.

*

Any conception of God which exalts His Fatherhood at the cost of His holiness, or to its neglect, unsettles the moral throne of the universe. Any reaction of ours from a too exacting God which leaves us with but a kindly God, a patient and a pitiful, is a reaction which sends us over the edge of the moral world. And it robs us of moral energy. The fatherly God of recent religious liberalism is indeed a conception for which we have to bless Him when we look back on much that went before. But the gain brings loss. It is a conception which by itself tends to do less than justice even to God's love. It tends to take the authority out of the Gospel, the sinew out of preaching, the insight out of faith, the stamina out of character, and discipline out of the home. Such a view of God is not in sufficient moral earnest – though nothing could exceed the moral eagerness of many who hold it. It does not pierce and destroy our self-satisfaction. It has not spiritual depth, real and sincere as the piety is of many of its advocates. It has not what I have already called adequate moral mordancy. The question at last is not of its particular advocates but of the result that would follow if this become the view of the whole church. 'As is Thy majesty so is Thy mercy,' says the sage. But what I describe is a view of mercy which does justice neither to the majesty of God, nor to the greatness of man. It has certainly no due sense of the human tragedy, the moral tragedy of the race. And, accordingly, it takes from preaching the element of imaginative greatness and moral poignancy. It lacks the note of doom and the searching realism of the greatest moral seers. It is no more true to Shakespeare than to the Bible, to Dante than to Paul. It robs faith of its energy, its virility, its command, its compass, and its solemnity. The temperature of religion falls. The horizon of the soul contacts. Piety becomes prosaic, action conventional, goodness domestic, and mercy but kind. We have churches of the nicest, kindest people, who have nothing apostolic or missionary, who never knew the soul's despair or its breathless gratitude. God becomes either a spectacular and inert God, or a God who acts amiably; with the strictness of affection at best, and not the judgment of sanctity; without the consuming fire, and the great white throne. He is not dramatic in the great sense of the word. He is not adequate to history. He is not on the scale of the race. He is the centre of a religious scene instead of the protagonist in the moral drama of Man and Time. The whole relation between God and man is reduced to attitude and not action – to a pose, at last. It is more sympathetic than searching. The Cross becomes a *parergon*. We tend then to a Christianity without force, passion, or effect; a suburban piety, homely and kindly but unfit to cope with the actual moral case of the world, its giant souls and hearty sinners. We cannot deal to any purpose with the great sins or the great fearless transgressors, the exceeding sinfulness and deep damnation of the race. Our word is as a very lovely song of one that has a pleasant voice and can play well on an instrument. And the people hear, but do not. They hear, but do not fear. They are enchanted, but unchanged. Moral taste takes the place of moral insight. Religious sensibility stands where evangelical faith should be. Education takes the place of conversion, a happy nature of the new nature. Love takes the place of faith, uneasiness of concern, regret of repentance, and criticism of judgment. Sin becomes a thing of short weight. It was largely our ignorance; and when we thought of God's anger we were misreading Him by reading into Him our choleric selves. Our salvation becomes a somewhat common thing, and glorious heavens or fiery hells die into the light of drab and drowsy day. Much is done by enlightened views in the way of correcting our conception of God, to fit it into its place in the rest of knowledge, and to lift it to a higher stage in the long religious evolution. But it is all apologetic, all theosophic. It aims at adjusting the grace of God to the natural realm rather than interpreting it by our moral soul and our moral coil. It is not theology; it is not religion, it is not vital godliness. It does not do much in the way of effectively restoring the actual living relation between God and the soul. I am compelled to recognize often that the most deeply and practically pious people in the Church are among those whose orthodox theology I do not share. I even distrust it for the Church's future. But they have the pearl of price.

*

To lay the stress of Christ's revelation elsewhere than on the atoning Cross is to make Him no more than a martyr, whose testimony was not given by His death, but only sealed by it. His message must then be sought in His words; and His death only certifies the strength of conviction behind them. Or it may be sought in the spell of His character to which His death but gives the impressive close.

But His message was of Himself, even through His words and deeds. 'Come unto Me,' 'Confess Me if in the judgment you would have Me confess you.' The cup of cold water was blessed like the cup of the supper – for His sake. I need not add to these passages. If, then, He was a martyr, He was a martyr to Himself. But a man who is a martyr to himself on this scale is either a megalomaniac egotist, or he is a redeeming God. But Christ's long moral majesty and influence with man forbid the former alternative, unless the whole race is a moral lunatic and history a freak. He was God, therefore, and His death was God in action. He was not simply the witness of God's grace, He was its fact, its incarnation. His death was not merely a seal to His work; it was His consummate work. It gathered up His whole person. It was more than a confirmatory pledge, it was the effective sacrament of the gracious God, with His real presence at its core. Something was done there once for all, and the subject doer of it was God. The real acting person in the Cross was God. Christ's death was not the sealing of a preacher's testimony; it altered from God's part the whole relation between God and man for ever. It did not declare something, or prove something, it achieved something decisive for history, nay for eternity.

If it be otherwise, does it not but add another to our moral problems, and the greatest of them all? If the holiest of men but suffered here the last calamity, and if it was not the Holy God gaining the last victory, then we have but another, and the greatest, of the many problems that haunt us about God's justice or love in history. The imaginative greatness of the problem is no sufficient answer to it. How could we read God's love in the sinless Christ if His death was but another case of fate submerging love? Even His resurrection would be no proof of love's final victory had that victory not been essentially won in His death. Resurrection might then be no more than a personal reward for extreme but futile fidelity. It would not seal love's final victory for the race, it would not confirm redemption on the world scale. The Cross would simply be the last and worst case of the stoning of love's prophets. And we should be presented with the alternatives, either that the supreme power was ignorant of it, or indifferent; or, if not indifferent, he was an angry spectator; and, in His anger, either helpless, or accumulating a wrath which would break, one day, upon us in avenging judgment and nothing more. This is a dilemma which we escape only if we can regard Christ, not as the witness, nor even as the mere aesthetic incarnation of God's holy love, but as that love itself in its crucial moral act of eternal judgment and grace.

*

If sin be man's fatal act the Cross is God's vital act. But it is action we have to do with. It is will meeting will, yet not in transaction but interaction. It is redemption mastering perdition. What slew Christ was an act of man, but it was for Him much more than an infliction and a fate of which He was the passive martyr. It was much more than man's act and Christ's fate. It was an act on His side much more even than on theirs; and an act, not of resignation but of conquest absolute over both His own fate and ours. He was more active in His death than was the world, the fate, the sin, which inflicted it. Rather, when we view things on the largest scale, we must reverse the positions. It was not His fate and the world's act, it was His act and the world's fate. The world's condemnation of Him was His condemnation of the world – but a condemnation unto forgiveness and salvation. In the Cross the world was doomed to – salvation. All were shut up unto sin, that there might be mercy on all. The world's one sin was made by grace the world's one hope.

It was the world's one sin; and it was so because it was committed against the one central visitation of man by God. The crucifying of Christ was the greatest crime of history, not in itself, but because it was inflicted on the Holiest. It is not the travesty of justice that is so unique, it is not the crime against humanity. Against humanity alone other crimes may have been as great or greater – political, papal, dynastic, Napoleonic, Russian crimes. But this was the crime against the unique action of the Holy God, the sin against the Holy Ghost. And therefore to Israel as a national unity it is unforgiven. It was man's sin indeed, but it was through Israel. And for the salvation of the whole the offending member was cut off. Israel died as the body, that its spirit, as Christ, might conquer mankind.

As, therefore, the one sin was consummate in the act of man the one salvation can be nothing less than the act of God. The death of Christ completes by action God's love embodied in His person. It is the one thing that gives His person its full scope and effect. And it does so as a decisive creative act, an act of God and not merely a martyr act. It copes with man's act, it does not but endure it meekly. It was not merely the evidence of a divine love, sensitive yet unpierced at the centre by sin. It was the deed of a love stung to the core, stung to act for its life, to act once for all and make an end.

*

II. But in His death Christ not only acted and redeemed, He suffered and atoned.[1] He acted as only a divine sufferer could. His act of sacrifice became an endurance of judgment. Nothing else

---

[1] I do not say much in these lectures about the reconciling effect of His work upon men. That may not be understood as it should, but it is better understood to-day than the other aspects of his work.

than atonement could do full justice to Love. Love might do much, but if it did not suffer, and suffer not only pain but judgment, it could not do its divine utmost. That is to say, it might have contact with us, and blessed contact, but it would be short of identification with us. It could not enter into our self-condemnation. But surely love divine could not stop short of such an identification with our suffering as made Christ's suffering judicial. Must a divine love not go so far with us and for us as to enter the wrath of holiness? Even that was not beyond Christ's love. He was made sin. God did not punish Christ, but Christ entered the dark shadow of God's penalty on sin. We must press the results of God's holy love in completely identifying Himself with us. Holiness is not holiness till it go out in love, seek the sinner in grace, and react on his sin by judging it. But love is not divine identification with us till it become sacrifice. Nor is the identification with us complete till the sacrifice become judgment, till our Saviour share our self condemnation, our fatal judgment of ourselves in God's name. The priest, in his grace, becomes the victim, and completes his confession of God's holiness by meeting its action as judgment. To forgive sin he must bear sin.

As He took the suffering He took and bore the sin that caused it – the sin and not its consequences only. If he could not confess sin, He could and did confess, in experience and act, the holiness of God in its reaction on sin. He confessed the holiness, but the guilt He could not confess in the same sense. He could but realize it, bear it, as only the holy could, and so expose it in all its sinfulness. The revelation of love is a revelation no less of sin, because the love is holy love. That holy confession in act of the injured holiness, amid the conditions of sin and judgment, was the satisfaction He made to God. And the necessity for it lay in God's holy name. It was thus that He offered to God, and acted on God. He not only acted from God on man, but from man on God. I do not mean that He changed God's *feeling* to the race. That was grace always, the grace that sent Him. But He did change the *relation* between God and man. The reconciliation of one always means a great change for both parties. He made communion possible again on both sides. To do this He had to bear the

wrath, the judgment, the privation of God. He could not otherwise enact and reveal love, and do the revelation justice. The more
love there is in a holy God, the more wrath. Sin, in the sinner He
loves, against the law of His own nature, which He loves better
still, could not leave Him either indifferent, or merely pitiful. For
Love would then desert its own holiness. And being holy, God's
concern with sin is more than pity, and more than pain. It is
holiness in earnest reaction. It is wrath unto judgment. That wrath
Christ felt, not indeed as personal resentment, but as the dark
valley, as the horror of thick darkness. And He felt, moreover,
that it was God's will for Him, not indeed inflicted, so far as His
conscience was concerned, but still laid on Him by God through
His sympathy with us. It was not merely a darkening of His vision
of the Father; it was desertion by the Father in sympathy with the
complete fulfilment of their common task. As one might in certain
circumstances say 'I love you, but I must leave you,' 'I love you,
but for the sake of all that is at issue I may not show it.'? And it
was by recognizing, honouring, this very desertion as the wise,
righteous, loving will of God, that Christ converted it for us all
into a new and deeper communion. It was thus He approved His
Godhead, and achieved the Redemption. The real Incarnation lay
not in Christ's being made flesh for us, but in His being made sin.
And the dereliction was the real descent into hell, the bottoming
of salvation. Here beneath the depth of sin is the deeper depth of
God. 'If I make My bed in hell, Thou art there.'

Love, then, must go to entire identification (short of absorption). And Christ, in identifying Himself divinely with sinful man,
had to take the sin's consequence, and especially its judgment, else
the identification would not be complete, and the love would come
short. He must somehow identify Himself in a sympathetic way,
even *with man's self-condemnation which is the reflection of his
judgment by God*. I need hardly allude to the familiar illustrations
in the shame which innocent people feel through the crime of a
kinsman. If the chief function of Christ's love was to represent man
in a solidary way, a priestly way, He must make offering to God;
He must offer to God's holiness by a holy obedience, and not
merely to God's love by loving response. He could not experience

sin, for then He would be short of holy identification with God; yet He must experience and endure God's wrath against sin, else His love would be short of sympathetic identification with us. And unless he felt God's holy wrath and reaction against sin, He could not show forgiving love in full. No one can forgive in full who does not feel the fullness of the offence. To feel the fullness of the offence as the Holiest must, is also to feel the wrath the Holiest feels. But for one in perfect sympathy with man to feel what the Holiest feels is to feel the divine wrath, not as its holy subject only, but as its human object. Christ could not show the power of forgiving love in full unless He felt the weight of God's wrath in full, i.e. not God's temper but God's judgment; which for Him was God's withdrawal, the experience of God's total negation of the sin He was made. Grace could only be perfectly revealed in an act of judgment – though inflicted on Himself by the Judge. Atonement to God must be made, and it was only possible from God.

No one can feel more than I do that if all this be not absolute truth it is sheer nonsense. So it sifts men.

*

This aspect of the matter is not indeed vital to personal Christianity, but it is to the Church's total message and to the final prospects of Christianity. It presents the last issue in the moral war of God and man. It is essential to a full interpretation of God's love. God so loved the world, not quantitatively but qualitatively, not only so intensely, but in such a unique manner, that He gave His Son to be a propitiation. It is the provision of a propitiation that is the distinctive mark of God's love as transcending humane pity or affection in holy grace. Surely it must be so. The greater the love the closer it must come to life, and to the interior of life. It can the less ignore the realities of life. It does not leave us to ourselves, in a careless affection; it enters our ways, and sounds our depths, and measures all our tragic case. It has a comprehending, and not merely a kindly pity. It does not merely feel for our case, it assumes it wholly. Therefore, it must regard the last reality of sin, and deal with it according to *all* the circumstances – especially those visible to holiness alone, and to us in proportion as we are redeemed into holiness. So dealing with sin it forgives it; and forgives it effectually – not by way of amnesty, not by mere pardon, not by way of mere mercy upon our repentance, but by the radical way of redemption; not by indulgence, not by treating it as a matter of ignorance, weakness, misfortune, but as the crime of our freedom, grave in proportion to our freedom, most heinous in the face of the grace that gives our freedom. And as grace is far more than indulgence, so sin is far more than indifference. It is the nature of indifference to go on to become hate, if it be given time and occasion. The mercy, therefore, comes as no matter of paternal course, as no calm act of a parent too great and wise to be wounded by a child's ways. God is fundamentally affected by sin. He is stung and to the core. It does not simply try Him. It challenges His whole place in the moral world. It puts Him on His trial as God. It is, in its nature, an assault on His life. Its total object is to unseat Him. It has no part whatever in His purpose. It hates and kills Him. It is His total negation and death. It is not His other but An other. It is the one thing in the world that lies outside reconciliation, whether you mean by that the process or the act. It cannot be taken up into the supreme unity. It can only be destroyed. It drives Him not merely to action but to a passion of action, to action for His life, to action in suffering unto death. And what makes Him suffer most is not its results but its guilt. It has a guilt in proportion to the holy love it scorns. The greater the love the greater the guilt. And the closer the love the greater the reaction against the sin, the greater the wrath. Hence the problem of reconciliation – both of God and man – a problem so integral to Christianity, and so foreign to even the finest kinds of theism. It is not the reconciliation of man with his world, the establishment of his moral personality against nature. That were mere apologetic. But it is the reconciliation of man within himself and God. The channel of holy love must be the bearer, the victim of holy wrath. To bear holy love to us He must bear holy wrath for us. The forgiver of sin must realize inwardly the whole moral quality of the guilt – as Christ did in His dereliction in the Cross. Inwardly he must realize it, experimentally, not intellectually. No otherwise could a God, a love, be revealed, which would not let us go, yet was in absolute moral earnest about the holy.

It may freely be granted also that the reconciliation of God (by Himself in Christ) is not very explicit in the New Testament – for the same reasons which forbid the missionary preaching to his heathen on such a theme. The New Testament represents but the missionary stage of Christian thought and action. But the idea is not therefore untrue. If not explicit in the New Testament, it is integral to the Gospel. It is involved in the moral quality of holy forgiveness and in its divine psychology. In this respect it is like the full doctrine of the Trinity, and many another. The holiness of God, moreover, does not explicitly occupy the same supreme position in the New Testament as it does in the Old. Yet it is the very Godhead of God. It is the essence of Christ's idea of God. And (I think I have said) it really receives in the New Testament a position above any it had in the Old Testament. For it forms much more than an attribute of God. In the Holy Spirit it becomes a constituent element in the Godhead, on its way to become at last a coequal person in the Trinity.

*

To handle this matter means at the last a treatise. I have no such purpose. I wish but to point out that the expiatory idea of Christianity which is concerned with the notion of satisfaction is quite necessary to do justice to the conception of God as love, and to the closeness of His identification with us. It is not an outgrown notion, a relic of moral immaturity, like the patristic idea of Christ cheating Satan by His death, or even the Anselmic satisfaction of God's honour. I have sought to construe the satisfaction to a holy God as consisting only in a counterpart and equal holiness rendered under the conditions of sin and judgment. And especially I have wished to indicate that an expiatory atonement gives expression, by its searching moral realism, and its grasp both of holiness and sin, to an element in Christianity which has a crucial effect on the depth, wealth, and moral penetration of the preaching of the Gospel. The matter is, of course, a doctrine of the Church, and not a test of personal Christianity. It is not a *Quicunque vult*. I will only venture to say I never knew my sin so long as I but saw Christ suffering for me – never until I saw Him under its judgment and realized that the chastisement of my peace was upon Him.

There is something lacking to our preaching, by general consent. It lacks the note, the energy of spiritual profundity and poignancy as distinct from spiritual sympathy, and of moral majesty as distinct from ethical interest. And I am convinced that this is ultimately due to the loss of conviction as to a real, objective, and finished redemption, and to the disappearance from current faith of a real relation to the holiness and the wrath of God. The note of judgment has gone out of common piety. It is not here a question of either denouncing or unchurching those who cannot recognize an expiatory element in our Salvation. I would simply express the conviction that their interpretation of the Cross does less than justice to the Gospel, and cannot continue to carry the full $K\acute{\eta}\rho\upsilon\gamma\mu\alpha$ of the Church. It has not the promise of the moral future of the world. It is not sufficiently charged with repentance and remission. It does not break men to Christ, but only train them, or at most bend them. And it does not embody that break with the world which, after all, has been a leading note in all the great victories of the Cross.

Epilogue

Certain things, I trust, will have appeared among others, in the course of our journey.

1. Preaching to the Church must recognize more fully the element of judgment, and preaching to the world the element of love. Judgment must begin at the house of God. We must preach more severely to the Church, and more pitifully to the world. We must make the demand on the Church heavier than the demand on the world.

2. There is nothing the Church needs more profoundly, though there are many things it needs more loudly, than an ethical conversion in regard to its great doctrines. These early went astray in a metaphysical direction. Metaphysic we must have, but even to this day the whole ethic of the Churches suffers incalculably from the long prepossession by metaphysical instead of moral interests, by pursuing the notion of substance instead of subject, by intellect cultivated at the cost of conscience. This appears in the interminable, and often barren, strifes about the nature of Christ in the Church's early stage, and of the sacrament in the later. And in inverse proportion to the engrossment of ability with these insoluble problems (or rather with their pursuit on insoluble lines) has been the moral insight and energy of the Church, especially on the public scale. So that its idea of justice has become a by-word. Ecclesiastical justice is sport for the Philistines. The justice of a church court or of ecclesiastical politicians is a matter of mockery. In the great churches – the Catholic, Orthodox, or

Established – men of personal honour and uprightness lose the sense of social justice as soon as a question arises which threatens the interest of their Church. They are perfectly sincere, and equally incapable of grasping the just thing. It is a hereditary or 'miasmatic' paralysis, and not a personal vice. Something is very wrong in some vital place. And the deep root of it all lies in the Church's long moral neglect of the great justification by God. The mighty moral meaning there, original to itself and imperial for all else, has been submerged, where it should have been elucidated, by the maxims of human instincts, utilities, and codes. The intellectualism of the Church, and the counter-intellectualism of its critics, have sucked the sap and vigour from its ethic. Its conscience has not been educated at its Cross. Its eye, from peering into inaccessible heavens, has seen the moral values upon earth only through great flakes of darkness. Holiness has become mere sanctity, and righteousness but justice which is less equity than legality.

So that the very institution which was founded upon God's supreme act of public justice – the Church – has become the dullest to public justice of any institution, and as selfish as any association for the defence of a trade, a monopoly, or an ascendancy. From the point of view of Christian ethic there is no word more base-born than that word ascendancy.

3. The more ethically we construe the Gospel the more are we driven upon the holiness of God. And the deeper we enter that sacred ground the more we are seized by the necessity (for the very maintenance of our spiritual life) of a real and objective atonement offered to a holy God by the equal and satisfying holiness of Christ under the conditions of sin and judgment.

4. We must be critically liberal without ceasing to be theological. We must be free in our treatment of history, whether as doctrine or as Bible. But we must be firm on our faith's base in history. However we treat the Bible we must be positive in our treatment of the Bible's Gospel. We must reduce demand as to the Bible, and press it as to the Gospel. That way lies the future. That method meets the actual present situation. A mere abstract liberalism without content or responsibility, liberty to go anywhere

and believe anything, is pseudoliberalism. What makes us free at the last? For what are we made free? Not for certain views broad or narrow. But for the faith of a positive Gospel, understood as I have defined it, modified, perhaps, but certainly unchanged. Liberty of view is now assured. What is not secure is liberty of soul. And the only thing that can secure it is the faith of a positive Gospel. Liberty of view is a matter of mere science. It is religious liberty that concerns the public most. And that is only the fruit of the Gospel.

Nothing in the world is so precious as faith, hope and love. But the preacher of the Gospel must be sure on what abysses these rest and abide.

nobody gets left behind.

Letting go of his gun, he reached out and let his fingers close slowly over the cool metal tube. A glimmer of satisfaction passed through Quadesh's eyes as he stepped backward.

"Thank you, Colonel." He bowed, hands pressed over his heart. "The people of Kinahhi thank you."

Jack said nothing; he hadn't done it for the people of Kinahhi and he didn't deserve their thanks. "I need a way out," he said by way of a reply. "Not the stairs."

Quadesh nodded and pointed a slender finger towards a thick pillar standing at the far end of the chamber. "In there is a conveyor. It will take you to the surface."

Jack gave a curt nod. "I take it we won't be discussing this again?"

"We will not," Quadesh agreed. "I just pray that I was not seen leaving the city." Then, with a short, nervous nod he turned and hurried into the shadows. Jack watched as he touched something on the mosaic surface of a pillar and a door slid silently open. Quadesh looked back once and gave a half-hearted gesture of farewell before he stepped inside and disappeared.

In the silence that followed, Jack hefted the slim tube in his hand. It was light, weighed almost nothing. And yet it was heavy with danger, possibility and risk.

Coming Soon!
Available from www.stargatenovels.com
Register at the website for email
updates and special offers